17th August 1992 .

With love

The Hillier Guide to
Connoisseur's Plants

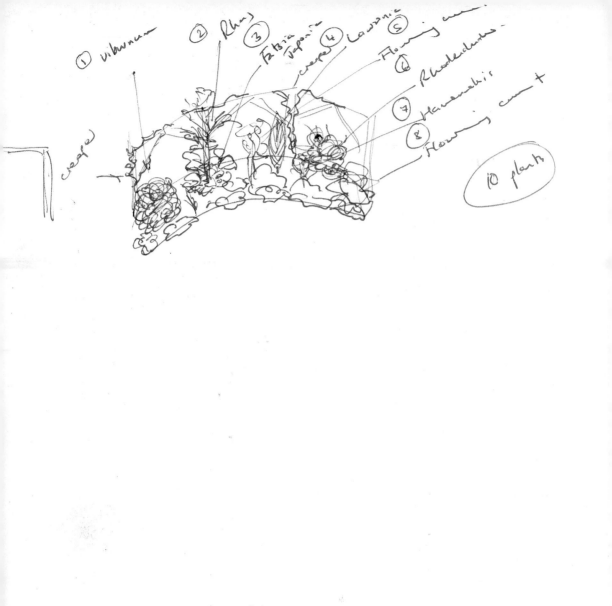

① viburnum

② Rhus

③ Fatzia Japonica

Crepe Lavania ④

⑤ Flowering cur...

Rhododendron ⑥

⑦ Hamamelis

Flowering cur t ⑧

Crepe

10 plants

EST
1864

The Hillier Guide to
Connoisseur's Plants

ALAN TOOGOOD

Photography by
John Glover

DAVID & CHARLES

British Library Cataloguing in Publication Data
Toogood, Alan
   The Hillier guide to connoisseur's plants
   I. Title
  635.9

   ISBN 0-7153-9859-8

Typeset by Ace Filmsetting Ltd, Frome
and printed in Hong Kong by Wing King Tong Co Ltd
for David & Charles plc
Brunel House, Newton Abbot, Devon

CONTENTS

INTRODUCTION

Firstly, we had better explain the meaning of the word connoisseur. Dictionary definitions include 'a judge in matters of taste' and 'an expert critic' (*Longman Modern English Dictionary*), and 'one skilled in judging of the fine arts' (*Cassell's Concise English Dictionary*). Applied to *The Hillier Guide to Connoisseur's Plants* it means choosing good and desirable plants. These are mainly for the garden but also for cool conservatories.

The guide is aimed at enthusiastic amateur gardeners who are true plant lovers and want a garden primarily for the enjoyment of plants – but only the best available and with a good selection that are not seen in every garden centre and consequently in everybody else's garden. We have included a good sprinkling of unusual plants, and a few rarities, but the majority are reasonably or very well known and certainly all are available.

The guide will, we hope, help gardeners to choose the best plants for their gardens and conservatories from the huge numbers offered today. The sheer quantity of plants available is utterly confusing to many people, who are in desperate need of guidance on selection.

Our choice of plants will provide year-round colour and interest in gardens and cool conservatories, and indeed we have invariably described plants under seasons of interest. Many ordinary private gardens are devoid of colour and interest in autumn and winter, so we emphasise these seasons in our choice of plants. Some readers may be surprised at the number of plants capable of providing colour and interest in the colder months.

There is increasing interest among amateur gardeners in grouping plants effectively, so we have given many examples of plant associations to provide contrast in colour, shape and texture. These include suggestions for groups to provide colour and interest during each season. Further advice on planting for best effect includes, where appropriate, bold or mass planting of subjects, as many plants look best when grown in bold groups or drifts rather than as individual specimens, which often creates an uncomfortable 'spotty' effect in beds and borders. On the other hand, many plants can be used singly, and this includes not only large specimen shrubs and trees but also plants with particularly distinctive characteristics that can be used as focal points in the garden.

We give advice on planning a garden for plants, but the 'hard landscaping' side of

Garden visiting is an excellent way of discovering
how to use plants effectively. In this lime-free
terrace garden azaleas feature in the spring
(*Hafod Garregog, Gwynedd*)

INTRODUCTION

gardening has been very much played down as we feel that the plant lover will require the minimum of artificial features. However, we have included construction of special features for displaying plants, such as rock gardens, scree gardens and peat gardens.

It is important to care for plants to the best of one's ability, so we have indicated not only the conditions (soils and aspect) required by all the plants described, but also topics such as soil cultivation, pruning, feeding and the like.

The guide embraces the following groups of plants: trees, which help to form the 'framework' of gardens; shrubs, which do the same; shrub roses, especially those with a long flowering period; conifers, for framework, specimen and background planting, plus dwarf and ground-cover kinds; climbers and wall shrubs, to make the most of vertical space; perennials and bulbs which are so useful for combining with shrubs; ferns and grasses (including bamboos), whose advantages are as for perennials; alpines and peat-garden plants; permanent plants like shrubs and climbers for cool conservatories; and plants suitable for patios and ornamental containers. Select lists of plants, and at-a-glance mini-features on planting schemes, extracted from the main text, have been provided for quick and easy reference. See also *The Hillier Book of Garden Planning and Planting*.

It is estimated that at least 1,500 different plants (species, varieties and cultivars) have been described in this guide. This sounds a lot, but in reality is only a fraction of the garden and conservatory plants available today. But as you will have realised by now, we have opted for quality rather than quantity. The superb photographs, which illustrate some two hundred of the plants described and show some stunning plant combinations, were specially taken by photographer John Glover, liaising closely with writer Alan Toogood.

POINTS TO NOTE WHEN USING THE GUIDE

Plant heights

Small tree	4.5–9m (15–30ft) at maturity
Medium tree	10–18m (33–60ft) at maturity
Large tree	over 18m (60ft) at maturity
Prostrate shrub	has a ground-hugging, creeping habit
Dwarf shrub	30–60cm (1–2ft)
Small shrub	90cm–1.5m (3–5ft)
Medium shrub	1.5–3m (5–10ft)
Large shrub	more than 3m (10ft)

Evergreen or deciduous

Please note that trees, shrubs, climbers, etc, are deciduous (drop their leaves for the winter) unless otherwise stated.

Aspect

Assume that, unless otherwise stated, plants are best grown in sunny positions (see section, Normal conditions, in Chapter 2 for explanation of sunny positions).

CHAPTER 1

DISCOVERING PLANTS

The connoisseur of garden plants is constantly on the lookout for good species, varieties and cultivars. Those chosen are judged to be worth growing. But what should we be looking for in plants? And what constitutes a good garden plant?

Unfortunately, many people wrongly think that all rare plants are desirable and worthy of garden space – but rarity does not necessarily mean a good plant. A garden containing nothing but rare plants could well be a dull place indeed. We should ask ourselves, why is a plant classed as rare? Perhaps it is because the plant is not particularly attractive and has therefore been shunned by gardeners. What, then, is the point of including it in your garden? Often, though, plants are rare because they are difficult or slow to propagate and therefore nurserymen are unable to produce them in large quantities. Also, growers and customers only have limited patience! We have included a few of these in this book.

It will not have gone unnoticed by keen gardeners that 'unusual plants' are in vogue. But what constitutes an unusual plant? They are simply plants that for various reasons have not become as well known as many others. The vast majority are certainly worth growing in gardens, otherwise nurserymen would not be producing them for sale to the gardening public. They are unusual, perhaps, because they have not received much publicity from the media, or they are overshadowed by the vast numbers of new cultivars that appear each year and which receive a lot of publicity, or because they were once almost lost to cultivation due to changing fashions.

If there is no public demand for a particular plant few nurserymen will bother to grow it. On the other hand, there are some who are pushing hard the lesser-known, good garden plants in an effort to make the gardening public aware of them. Many of the plants in the following chapters are still not widely known but certainly deserve to be.

Some people rule out plants which flower for a few weeks and then have no further attraction for the remainder of the year. As far as shrubs are concerned, this eliminates many good plants so we have not adopted this criterion in this book. Rather, we aim to make the best use of such shrubs while they are in flower by grouping them attractively with other shrubs, perennials, bulbs and the like, and then using other plants to ensure continued interest. For instance, what garden would be complete without a forsythia to herald the spring? Yet for about eleven months of the year it is decidedly dull. This can be avoided if a restrained climbing plant is grown through it, such as a clematis for summer or autumn flowers.

Some people say that hardy herbaceous perennials do not warrant garden space, for they spend five or six months in a dormant state, with nothing more than growth buds at ground level. But a garden without them is unthinkable, and indeed they are currently enjoying great popularity: never before has there been such a large and diverse range of perennials available. They are invaluable when mixed with other plants, some of which will continue to provide colour and interest when the perennials have died down for the winter. The same applies to many bulbs, of course.

Certainly, plants which have a long season of interest are worthy of garden space and should be sought out, together with those which perform over at least two seasons, like amelanchier, for instance, a shrub with flowers and attractive young foliage in spring and glorious leaf colour in autumn. But such plants are in the minority rather than the majority and few gardens are stocked completely with them.

Of course evergreens, especially if they have coloured or otherwise attractive foliage, will provide interest all year round and a garden should have a good selection. However, do not be tempted to overplant evergreens or the garden could take on a 'heavy', sombre atmosphere reminiscent of Victorian gardens, which often

Below:
Good garden plants should have at least one distinctive characteristic, but of course they can be combined to create pleasing contrasts in colour, shape and texture (*Vale End, Surrey*)

Right:
Every garden should have a good selection of evergreens, including conifers such as junipers, as they provide interest all the year round (*Hafod Garregog, Gwynedd*)

contained many of these shrubs. Instead, aim for a pleasantly contrasting combination of deciduous and evergreen plants which will then reflect the changing seasons. A balance that we find works well consists of two-third deciduous plants to one-third evergreens.

In so many books the authors fight shy of large plants and rampant, spreading kinds. Again, this dismisses with a few strokes of the pen many excellent garden plants. We can see the logic of this attitude when one is recommending plants for small gardens, but even here a few larger plants are useful to create a variation in height and form. A tall grass, for instance, might create the right effect in a small courtyard garden. Some larger or vigorously spreading plants could be grown in ornamental containers to keep them in check, so that they can be accommodated in the small garden, perhaps on a patio. For instance, try a fig (**Ficus carica**) or the bold foliage shrub, **Fatsia japonica**, in a tub. The bamboos also tend to spread into large clumps, but not if grown in containers.

Owners of large gardens are often neglected today by gardening writers, but not so here. We freely recommend many large plants, and also occasionally very vigorous or rampant kinds. Very often the owners of large gardens need to fill large areas quickly with plants, and it actually *helps* if they have a vigorous, spreading habit of growth.

In trying to give a complete answer to the question 'What constitutes a good garden plant?' (if, indeed, it is possible to answer this question fully) we must add, finally, that the plant should have at least one distinctive or desirable characteristic, such as a spectacular display of flowers (not necessarily an extremely long display, although this is also desirable); attractive foliage; handsome bark; a conspicuous crop of berries or fruits; or distinctive overall shape, such as weeping, conical, fastigiate, and so on.

HOW TO FIND PLANTS

The connoisseur of garden plants will often be out and about visiting gardens and flower shows in a continuous search for good subjects.

Garden visiting has never been more popular than it is today and this is an excellent way of discovering plants unknown to you. What is more, you can see them growing in their most suitable habitats. And, just as important, you will glean many ideas for companion plants. One of the skills of gardening is grouping plants effectively so that they contrast or harmonise in colour, shape and texture. Equally important, of course, is that all the plants in any one planting scheme should need the same soil and aspect. All this information is readily available to the keen observer equipped with a notebook and pen.

Privately owned gardens and those of horticultural societies are extremely rich in plants and are a good source of planting ideas, and botanic gardens should certainly not be neglected. In the latter plants are grouped into collections, so it is easy

Many gardens feature alpines and can provide numerous ideas on how to display them effectively. Here sink gardens are a feature, an excellent idea for small gardens (*Private garden, Surrey*)

Gardens of horticultural societies are extremely rich in plants and are a good source of planting and display ideas. For instance, various gardens feature alpine houses, to which many amateurs make pilgrimages if they become really enthusiastic about these plants (*Royal Horticultural Society's Garden, Wisley, Surrey*)

to compare the various species and cultivars within a genus. Botanic gardens also are good places to see greenhouse and conservatory plants.

Arboreta are well worth visiting to see trees and shrubs. The Hillier Gardens and Arboretum at Ampfield, near Romsey, Hampshire, UK, of which Hampshire County Council are trustees, contains a unique collection of plants assembled by the late Sir Harold Hillier CBE, VMH, FLS, and is open to the public throughout the year. New plantings and expansions continue to enhance this internationally important collection of woody plants.

It is well worth visiting the many flower shows which are held up and down the country throughout most of the year, in order to get to know good plants.

The highlight of the show year in the UK is the annual Chelsea Flower Show, held in London during May. A wealth of plants is to be found in the great marquee,

DISCOVERING PLANTS

Above:
Arboreta are well worth visiting to see trees and shrubs. The Hillier Arboretum at Ampfield, Hampshire, contains a unique collection of plants. In the autumn the pond effectively reflects autumn colour

Right:
The Hillier Arboretum in spring, when a superb collection of rhododendrons really comes into its own, set off by deciduous trees and shrubs

Left:
Arboreta are also the best places to see trees and shrubs which are noted for autumn leaf colour. Here Japanese maples are making a brilliant display; they are among the best subjects for this purpose (*Westonbirt Arboretum, Gloucestershire*)

DISCOVERING PLANTS

Above:
Specialist societies' shows, such as those of the
Alpine Garden Society, enable you to see a
comprehensive collection of one type of plant.
Here some superbly grown dionysias are featured

Right:
Camellias constitute a spring feature of the Hillier
Arboretum, Ampfield, Hampshire, seen here to
good effect with a background of **Acer negundo**
'Violaceum'

not just those of spring, but of most other seasons as well, including tender and
tropical kinds suitable for conservatories. Outside there are many gardens, some
suitable for those who are not necessarily keen gardeners but who want a well-
designed and planted garden. However, the trend in recent years has been towards
plantsmen's gardens, densely packed with good garden plants and with little or no
hard landscaping. Again, these gardens give visitors many ideas for plant associations.

The shows of specialist societies are also well worth visiting to see such plants as
alpines, roses, delphiniums and irises in large masses.

But, above all, we hope that the photographs and descriptions of hundreds of
good garden plants in this book will help you vastly to extend your knowledge of
plants, and that the many ideas on plant associations and features will result in you
creating an attractive and distinctive garden.

CHAPTER 2

PLANNING FOR PLANTS

A garden intended primarily for plants must be carefully planned so that it provides as many different habitats as possible. In this respect the owner of an old-established garden has a good lead over the owner of a brand-new plot devoid of plants. Then one should carefully choose plants to suit these habitats. But before planting, the soil must be well prepared and, if necessary, improved according to the types of plants that one desires to grow.

PLANT HABITATS

There are five basic habitats that can be provided in gardens (apart from those found under glass – see Chapter 13) so let us look at each in turn.

HOT AND DRY

One commonly encountered habitat is the hot, dry area. This receives a great deal of sun, perhaps all day long, and has extremely well-drained soil which frequently becomes dry. There are lots of plants that revel in these conditions. If the area is also well sheltered from winds one has a very favourable micro-climate in which less hardy plants may thrive, especially if one lives in a part of the country which is not prone to severe winters.

There are several interesting ways to treat a hot, dry area. Firstly, it would be ideal for a patio. Suitable plants could then be grown in containers, beds and borders in and around the paved area (see Chapter 14).

It would also make a good site for a gravel area. Here one plants a collection of bold dramatic specimens such as phormiums, yuccas, kniphofias, ornamental grasses and eryngiums. Such an area is very labour-saving, as few weeds grow through the gravel provided the soil has been rendered weed-free before planting. After planting, the soil surface (including any well-firmed soil intended to be used for pathways) is covered with a 2.5–5cm (1–2in) deep layer of pea shingle.

A hot, dry, well-sheltered area in a region not prone to harsh winters is ideal for turning into a garden for plants enjoying a Mediterranean climate. Not all the plants need be of Mediterranean origin by any means – for instance, dwarf ceanothus from

A hot, arid area would make a good site for a collection of bold dramatic plants such as yuccas, phormiums, cordylines and ornamental grasses. The area could be covered with gravel if desired (*Architectural Plants, Sussex*)

California could be grown there, as could various Australian and New Zealand shrubs. But do have a collection of cistus, which originate from the Mediterranean area, as their foliage gives off an aromatic fragrance in hot weather which helps to create an authentic Mediterranean atmosphere. If you want some trees, then hardy eucalyptus would be a good choice.

Another idea is to construct a rock or scree garden in this area, in which to grow alpines and other dwarf plants (see Chapter 12).

SUN AND MOISTURE

Another habitat is one which receives plenty of sun for much of the day, but at the same time has very moist soil. This set of conditions is mainly found at the side of a pool, lake or stream, where one can grow a wide range of moisture-loving plants such as waterside irises like **I. laevigata** and **I. sibirica**, dierama (wand flower), coloured-stemmed dogwoods (cornus) and **Gunnera manicata**.

Below:
A hot dry area is also an ideal place to construct a rock or scree garden in which to grow alpines and other dwarf plants, most of which like impeccable drainage and plenty of sun (*Private garden, Surrey*)

Right:
An area which receives plenty of sun but at the same time has very moist soil enables one to grow a wide range of moisture-loving plants, such as yellow and red-stemmed dogwoods or cornus, and coloured-stemmed willows or salix. The garden shown here has been designed specifically for winter interest (*Cambridge Botanic Garden, Cambridgeshire*)

MOIST SHADE

This is a most desirable habitat – partial shade with moist soil. Ideally it is provided by light woodland, the trees creating dappled shade which allows a reasonable amount of sun through. Here one can indulge in the vast array of woodland plants which range from shrubs like rhododendrons, camellias and pieris (if the soil is acid), to perennials like dicentras, meconopsis (blue poppies), hostas, polygonatum (Solomon's seal) and digitalis (foxgloves), and bulbs, including lilies.

Lucky indeed is the person who has established woodland for turning into a woodland garden. Do make sure to thin the trees if necessary, as the conditions must not be dark and gloomy or few plants will thrive. Large old trees may need to have their crowns thinned out to ensure the desired dappled shade. This must be undertaken only by qualified tree surgeons.

One can, of course, create woodland from scratch (see Woodland gardens in Chapter 4). A woodland garden is easily created by forming meandering paths through the area, which divide it into informal beds for planting. The paths are formed simply by consolidating the soil thoroughly. Ensure that you have some glades or open spaces where more sun penetrates, thus providing conditions for plants which need more sunshine, like lilies.

Moist shade can also be found in the vicinity of large buildings, although soil immediately in front of a wall can be dry. The area may receive sun for a small part of the day and shade for the greater part. Provided it is not subjected to the hottest sun of the day one could also grow woodland plants here, including ferns and other shade lovers.

Moist shade is also the ideal place to create a peat garden (see Chapter 12).

DRY SHADE

Partial shade with dry soil, as found under large trees or hedges which extract a lot of moisture from the soil, often poses a problem for many people. This is not surprising, for the range of plants that can be grown successfully in these conditions is limited. However, there are some remarkably tolerant plants around, including hollies (ilex), aucubas, ivies (hedera), ruscus, skimmias and perennials like bergenias, pachysandra and hardy geraniums.

Left:
A very desirable habitat is partial shade with moist soil, ideally provided by light woodland whose trees create dappled shade. Here one can indulge in the vast range of woodland plants (*Cobblers, East Sussex*)

Below:
Acer Palmatum and cultivars are highly recommended for providing autumn colour in a sheltered, woodland garden which has dappled shade with moist soil (*Hillier Arboretum, Ampfield, Hampshire*)

Rhododendrons and hostas or plantain lilies, a classic combination for a woodland garden with partial shade and moist, lime-free soil (*Savill Gardens, The Great Park, Windsor, Berkshire*)

Above:
Places with normal conditions, or open parts of the garden which receive full sun for at least half of the day and which have ordinary well-drained soil, are ideal for creating mixed or herbaceous borders (the latter is shown here) (*Jenkyn Place, Hampshire*)

Right:
You are lucky indeed if you take over an old, well-established garden, as it may be blessed with many plant habitats and divided into different areas well sheltered from cold winds (*East Lambrook Manor, Somerset*)

NORMAL CONDITIONS

What we have been considering so far are extreme conditions, most of them, however, providing ideal habitats for many plants.

What we term 'normal' conditions are open parts of the garden which receive full sun for a good part, say at least half, of the day (these would be sunny positions, see Introduction) and which have ordinary well – but not excessively – drained soil. This is the ideal place for creating mixed borders and beds in which a very wide variety of plants can be grown.

TAKING ON A GARDEN

Taking on a garden is always exciting, but exactly what plant habitats you will have immediately may depend on the garden itself. You will possibly have much more scope straightaway if your acquisition is an old, well-established garden, as opposed to a brand-new plot, when you will have to start from scratch.

AN OLD, WELL-ESTABLISHED GARDEN

This type of garden may be blessed with many or all of the plant habitats already described. Also, you may be fortunate enough to have a property divided into different areas or 'secret gardens' by screens of shrubs, hedges and the like, so that one is not able to see the entire plot in one glance. These areas may be well sheltered from cold winds, thereby extending the range of plants that can be grown. Many ideas will be found in our earlier book *The Sheltered Garden* (David & Charles, 1989).

The first piece of advice we would give to someone taking over an old, well-established garden, is to leave it alone for the first year to see exactly what plants it contains. See whether shrubs, perennials and other plants make a good show when they come into flower, and wait for any bulbs to appear before you start cultivating the soil or clearing whole areas.

Any plants which do not appeal to you should be grubbed up and disposed of. If you want a garden of desirable plants you have to be ruthless – you cannot afford to be sentimental. With any very old plants you will have to make a decision as to whether to scrap or try to rejuvenate them. For instance some shrubs, including rhododendrons, roses, amelanchier, laurels and many others, can be cut down to

Left:
This delightful, well-established old garden has a
wealth of interesting plants. The best advice when
taking over such a garden is to leave it alone for a
year, to see exactly what plants it contains (*Old
Rectory Cottage, Tidmarsh, Berkshire*)

Above:
Some old gardens already have interesting
features, such as the laburnum arch shown here.
It is underplanted with an ornamental onion,
Allium giganteum (*Barnsley House,
Gloucestershire*)

within a couple of feet of the ground and then they will produce a crop of new shoots
from the old wood. Again, the outer zone of old clumps of hardy perennials can be
split into small portions which will be young and vigorous, the old worn-out central
part being discarded.

If the garden is badly neglected and overgrown you may virtually have to start
again. Aim to keep as many large plants as acceptable, to help retain a sense of
maturity (if you wish, these can always be disposed of in later years when new
plants have become established), then kill off the jungle of weeds and worthless

plants with Tumbleweed (glyphosate) weedkiller. If the undergrowth is mainly tough and woody, like brambles and thickets of tree seedlings, then it may be better to spray it with a bushwood killer. Use these weedkillers strictly according to the manufacturer's instructions.

THE BRAND-NEW PLOT

With a brand-new plot you can, of course, easily design a garden for plants, embracing all the habitats that you need in order to grow the plants well. Possibly the first priority will be establishing areas of shade because it is likely that, without any established plants, much of the garden will be in full sun for a large part of the day, thus restricting the range of plants that can be grown.

This means planting some trees and/or groups of medium to large shrubs to create dappled shade. A pergola will provide an ideal home for climbers and will also cast shade once these plants are established. The initial planting should also, if desired, divide the garden into a number of different areas – 'secret gardens', as we mentioned earlier. This can be achieved with groups of large shrubs to act as screens, or with hedges, which are less interesting to the plantsman. Make sure

With a brand new plot you can, of course, easily design a garden for plants, embracing all the habitats that you need in order to grow them really well. Possibly the first priority will be providing shelter and areas of shade (*Hockley Cottages, Hampshire*)

that each 'secret garden' has a vista or long view to some other part of the garden to encourage one to explore. There should be a focal point at the end of each vista to catch the eye, such as a particularly distinctive shrub – say a weeping or fastigiate specimen, or one with coloured foliage.

At a very early stage the boundaries will need planting to disguise them (so aking the garden look larger than it really is), to hide fences or walls and to blot out any ugly views. Groups of large shrubs may be the answer, and certainly climbers and wall shrubs should be used to clothe any walls and fences.

Fortunately, a garden for plants needs little in the way of hard landscaping (paved areas, walls, etc) purely for the sake of it. You may well need paths linking the house with various parts of the garden, but these can be informal and meander through the plantings. Stepping-stones seem to fit the bill in the plantsman's garden. They can be paving slabs or, even better, natural stone or sections of treetrunk (first remove the bark, then treat with a horticultural wood preservative).

Whether or not you have a lawn is up to you, but many plantsmen find an area of grass uninteresting, and definitely boring when it comes to maintenance. However, you will need an open area for sitting and to create a sense of space in the garden, so why not consider a gravel area (see Plant habitats, Hot and dry, this chapter)? You will then be able to grow some interesting plants in it, as you could in an area laid with random natural paving stone (crazy paving), with soil joints. This could be an ideal home for carpeting, prostrate and dwarf, hummock-forming plants.

THE PLANTING PLAN

Overall, a garden for plants is generally informal and has a country-garden atmosphere about it. It will be packed with good garden plants of all kinds, contrasting beautifully in shape, colour and texture.

The main, permanent framework of many planting schemes (especially mixed borders, woodland gardens and the like) will consist of medium to large shrubs, with perhaps a few trees, and within this framework will be grown other plants like hardy perennials, smaller shrubs and bulbs.

Planting schemes should be planned for year-round colour and interest. This should be easy using this book, for we have grouped most plants under seasons in their chapters.

SOIL IMPROVEMENT

It pays to improve the soil as much as possible before planting anything. Firstly, all weeds, especially perennial kinds, should be eradicated. This can be achieved by spraying them when in full growth with Tumbleweed (glyphosate) weedkiller. Perennial weed grasses like couch can, alternatively, be killed with a weedkiller containing alloxydim sodium.

Once the ground has been cleared of weeds, other operations can be carried out.

PLANNING FOR PLANTS

If drainage is very poor you may need to consider installing drains. This is easy today, with the aid of a proprietary system of narrow 'pipes' which can be set in slit trenches. The manufacturer can advise on installation. The drainage system, in herringbone formation, slopes gently to a soakaway at the lowest part of the garden – a hole at least 1.8m (6ft) deep and 1.2m (4ft) wide, filled with rubble.

The soil should be dug thoroughly, ideally to two depths of the spade; this is known as double digging. This helps to improve drainage further by breaking up any hard layers of soil lower down, and encourages plants to root deeply. It also provides the opportunity to incorporate soil improvers.

The most commonly used soil improver is bulky organic matter such as well-rotted garden compost, thoroughly decomposed farmyard manure, composted pulverised bark, leafmould, spent hops, mushroom compost (not recommended for acid soils as it contains chalk) or one of the new coconut-fibre products. If you are creating an area for woodland plants then pulverised bark, leafmould or a coconut-fibre product can be recommended.

Bulky organic matter helps soils to retain moisture, so it is particularly advantageous when preparing hot dry areas and areas with dry shade. However, it should be used on all soils.

If you need to open up the soil (such as a heavy clay) to improve drainage and aeration, then include grit too. Bulky organic matter will also help in this respect. These materials should be worked into the bottom of each trench while double digging, and also into the top layer of soil.

pH AND FERTILISERS

The pH (acidity or alkalinity) of the soil must be ascertained before planting. This is easily achieved by testing samples from various parts of the garden with an inexpensive soil-testing outfit. The pH is a logarithmic scale, with 7.0 being the neutral point. Figures below 7.0 indicate increasing acidity, while figures above indicate increasing alkalinity. If the soil is acid, you are indeed fortunate as you will be able to grow not only calcifuge plants (those that will not tolerate alkaline soils, such as rhododendrons) but also many others, including those that thrive in neutral or alkaline conditions. Our advice is, never try to raise the pH of the soil (so that it becomes alkaline).

Even if the soil is alkaline (limey or chalky) you will still be able to grow a very wide range of plants indeed, besides calcicole plants (those that enjoy this type of chalky soil).

Throughout the book we have indicated those plants which definitely must have acid soils. The others are not fussy about soil pH.

Seven to ten days before planting it is the usual practice to apply a base dressing of fertiliser, which is worked into the top few inches of the soil surface. Make sure it contains nitrogen, phosphorus and potash; apart from this it can be organic or inorganic, depending on your preference.

CHAPTER 3

GROWING PLANTS WELL

It is essential to provide the right conditions for plants if they are to thrive in our gardens. In Chapter 2 we discussed the importance of ensuring the correct habitat for each plant, and throughout the plant chapters we have indicated the soils and aspect needed by the plants.

But that is not the end of the story. Plants must be planted correctly and at the right time. If they are to thrive they need regular care, such as feeding, mulching, watering, pruning, dead-heading, supporting and protection from pests, diseases and weeds. Some need lifting and dividing regularly. All of these tasks are described here.

PLANTING TIPS

Deciduous open-ground trees, shrubs, roses and climbers are planted while dormant between late autumn and early spring, provided the ground is not wet or frozen. Autumn is a good time, while the soil is still warm and contains moisture.

We all now know that peat bogs are a non-renewable resource. As gardeners become more aware of conservation issues, they are seeking alternatives to the use of peat – such as this attractive mulch of cocoa shells

Mulching prevents the germination of weed seeds and prevents rapid evaporation of soil moisture during warm dry weather. Here pulverised bark has been used

However, many plants are bought in containers today and these can be planted at any time of year if the soil is in a suitable state. However, we prefer to plant evergreen shrubs and trees (including conifers) and climbers in mid to late spring or in early to mid-autumn, as they then establish quickly.

Hardy perennials (including ferns and grasses) and alpines can be planted in early spring, but also in autumn if the soil is very well drained. Spring bulbs are planted in early to mid-autumn; autumn-flowering bulbs in summer.

The soil ball must be moist at planting time as it is very difficult to moisten it after planting, especially if the compost is peat based. Always plant to the same depth that the plant was growing in the nursery, indicated by a soil mark at the base of the stem with open-ground trees and shrubs. Provide a stout stake for trees for the first year or two, inserting it in the planting hole. With hardy perennials the crown of the plant, where the buds are situated, should be at soil level and not covered.

With shrubs and other plants supplied with a ball of soil around the roots, and container-grown plants, it is important to avoid disturbing the soilball when planting. The top of the ball should be just below the soil surface when the plant is in place. If planting in grass, leave a 90cm (3ft) diameter circle of bare soil around the plant as grass right up to the stem can result in retarded growth.

Evergreens planted in positions exposed to cold drying winds should be protected on the windward side until well established, using a screen of windbreak netting. If the weather is dry, evergreens can be sprayed overhead each evening with plain water for the first few weeks after planting, to help prevent desiccation.

FEEDING PLANTS

Plants should be fed on a regular basis to ensure they grow steadily, although the permanent plants that form the subject of this book do not need as much feeding as temporary, fast-growing ones like summer bedding and vegetables.

Generally an annual feed in the spring is sufficient, using a compound general-purpose fertiliser (containing nitrogen, phosphorus and potash) as a topdressing. If you are growing lime-hating plants, you must make sure the fertiliser is not alkaline. If desired, roses and other flowering shrubs can be fed with a special rose fertiliser. Provided you are not growing lime-hating plants you could use the organic blood, fish and bone fertiliser which also contains the three major plant foods. Always use fertilisers according to the maker's instructions and lightly hoe or fork the topdressing into the soil surface.

Pea shingle is widely used for mulching soil between plants, especially alpines, and is also used to create gravel areas, which are currently very popular garden features (*Coke's Barn, Sussex*)

MULCHING

This is the technique of spreading a layer of coarse organic matter or other materials over the soil surface around plants. The purpose is to prevent the germination of weed seeds, so cutting out the need for hoeing or other forms of weed control. Also it prevents the rapid evaporation of soil moisture during warm dry weather.

In most parts of the garden plants can be mulched with attractive-looking bulky organic matter. In our opinion the best is pulverised or chipped bark; this has a long life and can be spread 5–8cm (2–3in) deep. A deeper mulch would also protect the roots of any tender plants from frost.

Alpines on rock gardens are mulched with a thin layer of stone chippings or pea shingle; the latter is also used in gravel areas to cover the soil between plants.

A mulch should be applied only to weed-free, moist soil and topped up as necessary.

WATERING

All newly-planted subjects should be watered regularly if the soil starts drying out, until they are well established. It is essential that the soil ball is kept moist (see also Planting tips, this chapter). With trees, shrubs and climbers this may well be for the whole of the first growing season after planting. Plants which need moist soil conditions must not be allowed to dry out and therefore should be watered as necessary during dry periods.

Many people make the mistake of applying too little water, so that it does not penetrate the soil sufficiently deeply. Try to keep the top 15cm (6in) moist, which means watering when the top 2.5cm (1in) starts to dry out. To ensure water penetrates at least 15cm (6in), apply the equivalent of 2.5cm (1in) of rain. This represents a lot of water – 27 litres per square metre (4¾gal per square yard), in fact. You will need a sprinkler to provide this amount, which can be measured by standing some empty tin cans in the area being watered: when they have collected 2.5cm (1in) of water you can move the sprinkler to another area.

PRUNING

Pruning is a very comprehensive subject, so all we can do here is to outline some basic techniques. Anyone who really wants to study pruning in depth should consult a good book on the subject; however, be consoled by the fact that the majority of

Smooth pebbles make an attractive soil covering
or mulch in a modern setting, and are widely used
by garden designers today (*Private garden,
London*)

shrubs, trees, climbers, etc, need no regular pruning, just the removal of any dead or dying wood.

DECIDUOUS SHRUBS

A number of deciduous shrubs need regular pruning to ensure optimum flowering and production of young growth. Some that bloom in spring and early summer on shoots which grew during the previous season, particularly forysthia, **Kerria japonica**, deutzias, philadelphus, **Ribes sanguineum**, spiraeas such as **S. 'Arguta'** and **S. thunbergii**, and weigela, are pruned immediately after flowering. Cut back stems which carried flowers to young shoots which are growing lower down – these will carry next year's flowers. Also, remove entirely approximately a quarter of the very oldest stems.

Some shrubs which bloom on stems produced during the current year need pruning hard during late winter or early spring: vigorous new shoots are then produced from or near ground level and these flower during summer or early autumn. Cut down to ground level all the shoots of hardy fuchsias; with all buddlejas, except **B. alternifolia** and cultivars, allow a permanent framework of old stems to build up and prune back shoots produced from this to within one or two buds of their bases. The framework can be 60–90cm (2–3ft) in height. Deciduous ceanothus can be pruned back to good buds by just cutting out winter dieback.

The buddleja technique is also used for deciduous shrubs which are grown for their coloured bark, like **Cornus alba** and its cultivars, **Cornus stolonifera** 'Flaviramea', **Salix alba** 'Chermesina' and **Salix alba** 'Vitellina'. Prune these in early spring.

CLIMBERS

Some climbers need regular pruning either to promote flowering or to prevent congested growth.

Clematis head the list, and pruning varies according to their habit of growth and flowering. For hybrid clematis and species which flower during the late summer and autumn on stems formed in the current year (these include **C. tibetana vernayi (C. orientalis), C. tangutica** and **C. viticella**), prune down virtually to ground level in late winter, cutting to just above strong-looking growth buds.

Very vigorous species which bloom in early spring on short shoots that formed on last summer's stems, such as **C. macropetala** and **C. alpina**, can have all flowered shoots cut out to within a few centimetres of the main stems as soon as flowering is over, sometime in spring or early summer. However, the vigorous **C. montana** is best left unpruned – provide it with sufficient room to grow.

The large-flowered hybrids whose blooming period is from late spring to midsummer produce their blooms on last year's shoots. Well-known examples are 'Countess of Lovelace' and 'Henryi'. There are two ways to prune these. The first option: do not prune, or only prune lightly, but when the plants grow too large or become straggly cut them down to 90cm (3ft) in late winter. The second option: prune almost to ground level in late winter, cutting back to strong growth buds. The plants will not then flower until late summer.

With most other climbers, simply thin out congested or weak stems during late winter or early spring and ensure the main stems are tied in securely to their supports. However, some climbers need regular attention. Ivies (hedera), for instance, can become very heavy and may fall away from walls or fences. To prevent this, prune back all side shoots almost to the main stems in early spring. The plants will at first look rather bald but will soon produce fresh new foliage.

Best pruned annually, as soon as flowering is over, is **Jasminum nudiflorum** (winter jasmine). Side shoots which have flowered are pruned back almost to the main stems. The summer jasmine, **Jasminum officinale**, is best pruned regularly too, but this time by removing some of the older stems in late winter to prevent congestion. Also at that time you may need to prune honeysuckles (lonicera) by cutting back some older stems by half or two-thirds, again to prevent congested growth.

Wisteria forms long new shoots which can rapidly develop into a tangled mass if not pruned annually. Firstly, in midsummer prune back all new side shoots to within 15cm (6in) of the main stems. Then cut them back to two buds in late winter or early spring.

ROSES

The majority of roses described in Chapter 7 are shrubs and therefore do not need regular pruning. All you have to do is to remove as necessary any dead or very old, deteriorating stems. Climbing and rambler roses, however, need regular pruning. Climbing roses produce lateral shoots on the main stems and in early spring these should be cut back to leave from one to three growth buds. Rambler roses form new stems near to the ground and these produce flowers in the following year. As soon as flowering is over, the old stems which carried blooms are completely removed. The new stems are then spaced out and tied in to their supports.

DEAD-HEADING

Basically this is the removal of dead flowers immediately after flowering. It is beneficial to some shrubs, perennials and bulbs, the idea being to prevent them from expending much of their energy on seed production. If dead-headed they use this to produce strong vegetative growth instead.

Cytisus (brooms) form quantities of seed pods which should be removed by cutting out the tops of the stems, but do not cut into old wood. Hebes should have their seed pods cut off with secateurs. Trim heaths and heathers (calluna and erica) lightly with garden shears, but again do not prune into old stems. Lavender (lavandula) can be trimmed in the same way, just removing the dead flowers and their stalks.

Lilac (syringa) should have the clusters of seed pods cut off with secateurs, but be careful to avoid damaging the new growth buds below. This comment also applies to rhododendrons, which benefit greatly from having their seed heads twisted off. Unless hips are a feature, cut off the dead blooms of roses with secateurs.

Shrubby potentillas can be lightly trimmed with shears after flowering. This also ensures compact, bushy growth.

Unless you want them to self-sow, or you wish to save the seeds, it is also a good idea to remove the seed pods of bulbs, after which they would benefit from a feed with a liquid fertiliser to help them to build up. Remember you should not remove the leaves of bulbs until they are completely dead.

Hardy perennials should have their dead flowers removed, unless you want them to self-sow or wish to save the seeds. Sometimes dead-heading encourages more blooms to follow.

CUTTING DOWN PERENNIALS

The dead stems of herbaceous perennials can be cut down to the crown of the plant in the autumn. However, be selective, for the dead stems of some can be quite attractive over winter, for example those of some ornamental grasses.

Some people prefer to leave the dead stems of all herbaceous perennials until the early spring before cutting them down. Evergreen perennials do not need much attention apart from the removal of dead leaves as necessary.

LIFTING AND DIVIDING

To keep them young and vigorous most hardy perennials need to be lifted and divided regularly, certainly every three or four years.

However, this does not apply to all subjects as there are some, such as kniphofias and paeonias, which do not take too kindly to disturbance and are therefore best left alone unless you want to propagate the plants by division. Conversely a few others, especially aster (including Michaelmas daisies), benefit from annual division.

There is controversy regarding the best time of year to lift and divide perennials. Some people recommend autumn division while others prefer to undertake the task in early spring. As a simple rule of thumb, if you have extremely well-drained, light soil, then you can safely undertake autumn division. If the soil is heavy and inclined to lie wet and cold over winter, then early spring division is recommended. It is never a good idea to plant into cold, wet soil as the roots of plants are then liable to rot.

Plants which flower in early or midspring are best divided immediately after flowering, unless you decide to undertake autumn division. If you grow bearded irises (also known as German or flag irises), which flower in early summer, the best time to divide these is immediately after flowering.

To divide an established clump, first lift it and then shake as much soil as possible from the roots. Some perennials are easily split by pulling them apart. Others are very tough, and with these a good technique is to thrust two garden forks back to back through the centre of a clump and then pull the handles apart, repeating as many times as necessary. Reduce clumps to portions about 10–15cm (4–6in) in diameter. The centre part of a clump should then be thrown away as it will be declining in vigour. Save the outer parts for replanting.

Now for a few variations. With bearded irises each division should consist of a portion of rhizome complete with roots, plus a fan of leaves. After planting, the top of the rhizome should be above soil level. Asters can, if desired, be reduced to single shoots with roots attached which are then planted 5cm (2in) apart in bold groups.

Before replanting divisions, the soil can be dug over and improved if necessary as outlined in Chapter 2. This will give the plant a good start in its new position. When planting, remember to ensure the crown of each plant is at soil level – the growth buds must not be covered.

Many perennial alpine plants will need dividing, which again can be done in spring or early autumn. They are easily pulled apart.

When groups of bulbs and corms start to become congested they should be lifted when dormant, divided and replanted, but separate out the small bulblets/cormlets and plant them in a nursery bed to grow on to flowering size. Clumps of snowdrops (galanthus) and snowflakes (leucojum) are best lifted and separated immediately after flowering, while the leaves are still green.

PLANT SUPPORTS

Some tall, thin-stemmed hardy perennials may need supports to prevent them being flattened by wind and rain. A traditional and very effective method is to insert twiggy sticks around and between the clumps just after the plants have started into growth, when the new shoots are only 5–8cm (2–3in) high. Then the stems will grow up through the sticks and eventually hide them. The sticks should be 15–30cm (6–12in) lower than the ultimate flowering height of the plants, as one does not want to see them rising above the blooms: it is a case of knowing the ultimate height of the plants you want to support.

Delphiniums, with their comparatively few tall, thick stems, are supported differently. Each stem should ideally be provided with a stout bamboo cane at an early stage. Then, as the stems grow they are tied to the canes with soft garden string. So that eventually the canes are completely hidden, place them at the 'back' of the stems. Of course, the tops of the canes must be lower than the ultimate height of the delphiniums.

There are proprietary metal plant supports for perennials. They consist of rings supported on legs (available in various heights) and completely surround the plant's stems, so preventing them from flopping over. The supports are supplied in sections, these being linked together to provide various sizes.

Some young shrubs may need supports until they become established, especially tall specimens which are likely to be whipped around by the wind and loosened in the soil, particularly at the collar, such as **Genista aetnensis**. Simply use your judgement: if you feel that a newly planted specimen would benefit from support for the first year or so, then provide it. For the above types of plants a single stout bamboo cane will be sufficient, tying in the stem with soft garden string. Other tall plants, like cytisus, can be cut back at planting time.

WEED CONTROL

Weeds must be controlled, as dense growth between and around young plants can seriously retard their growth (as will grass right up to the trunk of a young tree). If all perennial weeds were eradicated during the preparation of beds and borders you will be well on the way to solving the weed problem. Weed seeds can be prevented from germinating by laying a permanent mulch between plants. A few weeds will come up through this or grow in it, but they are easily taken care of. If they are perennial weeds they can be spot-treated with Tumbleweed, a weedkiller containing glyphosate (make sure this does not come into contact with cultivated plants); annuals can be pulled out by hand.

If the soil is not mulched you will certainly be troubled by crops of annual weeds, at least in new plantings before the soil is well covered by cultivated plants. Among plant connoisseurs there is some controversy over how best to control them. It is quite likely that many people will be reluctant to use any method that eradicates everything growing between cultivated plants, because many of their self-sown seedlings will be destroyed. Hoeing, while certainly very effective at controlling annual weeds, if carried out on a warm, dry, breezy day when the weeds are in the seedling stage, will obliterate everything. So will 'blanket' spraying of weeds between shrubs and trees with paraquat weedkiller. Simazine weedkiller, applied to completely weed-free soil between shrubs and trees, will prevent the germination of weed seeds for almost a year if the soil is left undisturbed. Paraquat weedkiller must not come into contact with cultivated plants. However, both will create a barren look which is anathema to plant lovers.

Much better would be to hand-weed between plants. This can be most rewarding. You will get to know your plants better if you get down among them, and it is always exciting to come across self-sown seedlings of cultivated plants. These can

Pulverised or chipped bark is now widely used for mulching as it is one of the most effective and attractive-looking materials for this purpose (*Daily Express Garden, 1990 Chelsea Flower Show*)

be lifted and grown on elsewhere, say in a nursery bed.

However, we still have not given the best answer to weed control, and that is to completely cover the ground with cultivated plants so that there is little or no room for weeds to grow. You will find this is a theme, throughout this book, and it will certainly be the aim of the connoisseur.

Around larger plants such as shrubs can be mass-planted other smaller subjects, including hardy perennials, bulbs and shrubs of a ground-covering nature. However, as mentioned earlier, do not allow dense growth right up to the stems of shrubs etc, at least while they are young, as this can retard their growth. With such dense planting hand-weeding will be the norm, if indeed it is needed at all.

PESTS AND DISEASES

With a comprehensive mixture of plants in a garden, it is inevitable that pests and diseases will be something of an ongoing problem. We find it quite incredible how they manage to find some plants; let us give a couple of instances. One of the authors planted some Solomon's seal (polygonatum) and lilies in the woodland part in his recently renovated garden. To his knowledge these had not been grown before in the garden, which had in any event been neglected for years. But as soon as the Solomon's seal had attained flowering height it was invaded by the grey caterpillars of the Solomon's seal sawfly, which then proceeded to skeletonise the foliage. As soon as the lilies had produced stems and foliage they were visited by lily beetles (very attractive small cardinal-red beetles with black legs, which feed on the leaves).

These types of attacks are, in fact, easily controlled by hand-picking the pests. Indeed, we only use pesticides when an attack is really severe and hand-picking is out of the question. It really is not necessary to have an armoury of pesticides – try, wherever possible, to let nature take its course (biological control).

But a severe attack of, say, aphids, can seriously damage some plants. The most efficient method of control is to spray the affected plants with a systemic insecticide, which is absorbed by the plants and has a long-lasting effect. Pests which suck the sap or chew the leaves will be killed. Similarly, if a plant is badly attacked by a disease, then if possible spray it with a systemic fungicide, by far the most efficient method. One containing benomyl, for instance, will control a wide range of diseases such as the ubiquitous powdery mildew which has such crippling effects on some plants.

Slugs and snails are a great problem in the connoisseur's garden. They devour young shoots of many plants and ruin the appearance of hostas (plantain lilies) and some other large-leaved subjects. The answer is to sprinkle slug pellets containing methiocarb around susceptible plants as soon as, or just before, they start into growth, repeating as necessary thereafter. But do bear in mind that these can constitute a danger to pets and wildlife.

CHAPTER 4

TREES

Trees help to form the permanent framework of a garden, around and under which other plants are grown. They also ensure additional height in planting schemes – far more than most shrubs can provide.

Trees also help to provide shade, not only for the gardener but, perhaps more importantly, for shade-loving plants. With trees it is possible to choose the degree of shade required: for instance, dappled shade as provided by trees with a light canopy of foliage, such as the birches, or deeper, unbroken shade, resulting from trees with a large canopy of dense foliage, such as oaks.

Dappled shade, in other words a pattern of darkness and sunlight, is by far the best type for the majority of shade-loving plants; the deeper the shade, the fewer the plants that will thrive in it. Trees with large dense canopies of foliage can, in fact, be made to produce dappled shade by judicious thinning of the crown. However, this is a highly skilled operation and should only be undertaken by a tree surgeon.

If possible, every garden should have both shady and sunny areas as these not only allow a very wide range of plants to be grown, but also ensure a varied atmosphere, from hot and 'restless' to cool and 'tranquil'.

Trees have many other uses, of which more in a moment, but first perhaps we should dispel the myth that trees are suitable only for large gardens. This belief is quite possibly one of the reasons why comparatively few trees are planted by amateur gardeners.

TREES FOR ALL GARDENS

There are trees suitable for every size of garden, from the pocket-handkerchief plot to the large estate. For tiny gardens there are even several very narrow trees whose branches grow perfectly upright. These are known as fastigiate trees, and they take up no more lateral space than, say, a small, bushy shrub.

For little gardens there are many small trees with a compact head of branches, while for the largest gardens and estates there are plenty of medium and large trees from which to choose.

Bear in mind when choosing trees, especially for use as isolated specimens, that some are very slow growing and may be supplied as small plants: a good example is **Quercus ilex**. Such trees take many years to start creating an impression. One can, however, buy large and even semi-mature specimens of some trees; the alternative is to buy faster growers, like the prunus species.

WHERE TO PLANT TREES

Trees can be planted in various parts of a garden, but possibly the most popular areas are lawns, planting either isolated specimens or groups.

Trees are often used to create focal points – that is, they are used to draw the eye to particular parts of the garden and thus encourage one to explore. Here again they may be planted in a lawn – say at the far end or in a corner. Trees for focal points may also be planted wherever a path changes direction, or in the corners of a garden.

Trees to be used for specimen planting in lawns, and especially when used as

Betula utilis 'Jermyns' resplendent in autumn leaf colour. Birches are especially recommended for creating light woodland conditions, but they are thirsty trees (*Coates Manor, Sussex*)

focal points, must, of course, be of pleasing habit. There are some very distinctive trees available, such as weeping and fastigiate kinds, and these are especially recommended as focal points.

Trees may also be planted in mixed borders and beds, which are important features of today's gardens. Below them shade-loving shrubs, perennials, bulbs and other plants may be established.

Woodland gardens are, of course, created with trees. This type of gardening is becoming increasingly popular, not only with country but also with town gardeners. One does not necessarily have to possess several acres to create a woodland garden. A mini woodland garden formed by a group of a few small trees could be accommodated in gardens of, say, a quarter of an acre. Very often a woodland area is most conveniently sited at the end of a garden.

Never plant trees too near the house, because not only can they make the rooms dark but they could also damage foundations, drains, sewers and water supplies. Poplars are among the worst offenders as they have such an extensive root spread, so they should never be planted closer to a house than 18m (60ft). However, small trees, especially fastigiate kinds, could safely be planted about 6m (20ft) from the house. Do not plant trees where they will ultimately overhang neighbours' gardens, or the highway, or where the branches will eventually grow through overhead cables.

YEAR-ROUND INTEREST

Trees are capable of providing year-round interest and colour in gardens. One immediately thinks of autumn leaf colour but foliage can provide colour in spring and summer, too. For instance, some deciduous trees have gold, purple, grey or silver foliage, and others are variegated, for example with green and white leaves.

Numerous trees have what is best described as bold foliage. Here the leaves are large but they may be of various shapes, such as palmate or hand-shaped, or pinnate where the leaf is formed of a number of leaflets. These trees create an exotic atmosphere.

Many trees are noted for their flower displays. There are plenty which will provide spring and summer colour, and a few which produce their blossoms in the autumn or winter.

Several genera are notable for colourful fruits, and there are a few decorative trees which even produce edible fruits.

Bark is neglected by far too many gardeners, yet several trees are worth growing for this alone. Generally speaking, trees with ornamental bark come into their own in the winter, when they are likely to be more readily noticed as they have less competition from other plants.

The selection of trees in this chapter covers all these uses and characteristics, so let us now take a detailed look at them.

TREES WHICH MAKE GOOD FOCAL POINTS

We have already seen that a focal point can be created in a garden with a single tree of distinctive habit. Malus or flowering crabs are not generally thought of as being outstandingly distinctive in habit, but an exception is **Malus** 'Royal Beauty', a small weeping tree bearing large red flowers during mid to late spring, followed by red fruits in autumn. **M. trilobata**, on the other hand, is a medium-sized tree and ideal where space is limited. It has erect branches which carry white blossoms during mid to late spring, rarely followed by yellowish berries. The three-lobed maple-like leaves colour well in autumn. Crabs flourish in sun and any fertile soil.

A small fastigiate tree is the Japanese cherry, **Prunus** 'Amanogawa' (syn. **P. serrulata erecta**) which is wreathed in clusters of palest pink, semi-double fragrant flowers during midspring. The leaves open greenish-bronze. An ideal tree for the smallest garden.

Prunus 'Spire' is a small conical tree with a basal width of about 3m (10ft), raised on the Hillier Nurseries and which is covered with soft pink blossoms in midspring. The foliage assumes rich tints in the autumn. Prunus require an open sunny position and thrive in any ordinary soil, especially if it contains lime or chalk.

An excellent focal point for the larger garden is the columnar form of the Norway maple, **Acer platanoides** 'Columnare', a large tree with lobed leaves which turn clear bright yellow, or sometimes red, in autumn. Easily grown in any soil.

Fagus sylvatica 'Cockleshell', a cultivar of the common beech, is a medium-size columnar tree raised on the Hillier Nurseries, and producing small rounded leaves. It is a sport of **F. s.** 'Rotundifolia'.

The Dawyck beech, **F. s.** 'Dawyck', is a large slender upright tree but perhaps more attractive are 'Dawyck Gold' with golden foliage and the purple-leaved 'Dawyck Purple', both medium trees introduced by Hilliers and more compact than the type. The beeches thrive in extremely alkaline or acid soils, provided they are well drained and not clayey.

The columnar variety of the chestnut-leaved oak, **Quercus castaneifolia** 'Green Spire', raised on the Hillier Nurseries, is a medium-size tree of vigorous habit with dark green tooth-edged leaves. Another columnar oak is **Q. robur** 'Fastigiata', popularly known as the cypress oak, a large tree rather like a Lombardy poplar in shape. These oaks prefer deep fertile soils, including alkaline types if not shallow.

Weeping trees are ideal for creating focal points. For large gardens there are several weeping cultivars of the common beech, **Fagus sylvatica. F. s.** 'Aurea Pendula' is a small tree with golden-yellow foliage, best grown in partial shade. The weeping purple beech, **F. s.** 'Purpurea Pendula', is a small mushroom-headed tree with deep purple leaves.

Provided it is kept well away from buildings, the weeping aspen, **Populus tremula** 'Pendula', is a most attractive small weeping tree, particularly in late winter when the twigs are draped with long, purple-grey, male catkins. It is suited to wet soils and atmospheric pollution, but avoid shallow chalk.

One of the most popular small weeping trees is **Pyrus salicifolia** 'Pendula', the weeping silver pear, with silvery willow-like leaves. Due to its colour, this tree is excellent for helping to create a sense of distance in a small garden. Easily grown in any fertile soil, it tolerates cold conditions and atmospheric pollution.

The branches of **Robinia pseudoacacia**

The Chusan palm, **Trachycarpus fortunei**, makes a good focal point and can be especially recommended if an exotic effect is required. It needs a sheltered position (*Overbecks, Devon, National Trust*)

'Rozynskyana' droop at their tips, and the large pinnate leaves also droop, making this small tree highly distinctive and creating a weeping effect. Excellent for dry sunny places and tolerant of atmospheric pollution. The wood is brittle, so provide a sheltered position to prevent damage.

Many people like weeping willows and one of the best is **Salix bablyonica** 'Pendula' (syn. **matsudana**), a cultivar of the Pekin willow. It is a medium-size tree with long, narrow, pointed green leaves with glaucous undersides. This cultivar shows resistance to the diseases scab and canker. Give it plenty of space – it is not recommended for small gardens. Willows thrive in any good loamy soil, especially if on the damp side.

It is difficult to know how to categorise **Tilia tomentosa** 'Chelsea Sentinel', a cultivar of the weeping lime named by Hillier's, as this large tree is of broadly columnar habit but has weeping branches. However, it makes a superb focal point in a large garden and thrives in any situation with fertile soil.

If an exotic effect is required try **Trachycarpus fortunei**, the Chusan palm, a small evergreen tree with large fan-shaped leaves up to 1.5m (5ft) across supported on top of a thick fibrous trunk. It needs a sheltered position to prevent winds from tearing its leaves, plus plenty of sun and good drainage, so it is ideal near a patio. Mature plants produce large pannicles of yellow flowers during early summer, followed by blue-black marble-like fruits, but only during long, hot summers.

WOODLAND GARDENS

To create light woodland conditions from scratch, plant trees 7.5–9m (25–30ft) apart each way. This will give them adequate space to develop, but if eventually they start to become overcrowded they can be thinned out. Generally it is best to choose small to medium-sized trees, unless you have an extremely large area to plant.

With their airy canopy of foliage and often white bark, birches are useful for creating light woodland conditions. However, they are rather thirsty trees, taking a lot of liquid from the soil during summer, so be sure to have a water supply nearby to prevent other woodland plants going short of moisture. Birches thrive in most soils, moist or dry, but are not ideal for shallow chalk.

Especially recommended are **Betula albosinensis septentrionalis**, a medium tree with orange-brown bark flushed pink and grey; **B. ermanii**, a large tree with cream peeling bark; **B. utilis** 'Jermyns', a medium tree named by Hillier's, with brilliant white bark, copper-coloured on branches; **B. papyrifera kenaica**, a medium tree with white bark tinted orange; and **B. pendula** 'Dalecarlica' (Swedish birch), a large tree with pendulous branchlets and attractively cut leaves. The white-stemmed species contrast beautifully with other woodland plants like rhododendrons.

Other trees that might be planted if space permits include **Fagus engleriana**, a medium-size beech with large glaucous leaves. The related nothofagus require acid or neutral soils and protection from cold winds; choose from **N. antarctica** (antarctic beech), a medium tree with shiny deep green rounded leaves; **N. betuloides**, a medium evergreen tree with small deep green shiny foliage; and **N. obliqua** (roblé beech), a big tree whose leaves are larger than those of most other species.

Oaks can be included, too, such as **Quercus canariensis** (Algerian oak) with very large, shiny deep green lobed leaves, and **Q. frainetto** (Hungarian oak) with long deeply lobed leaves, thriving in chalky soils. Both are large trees.

Related to elms, the zelkovas are well worth considering. They thrive in deep, moisture-retentive loamy soils and will take some shade. **Z. carpinifolia** is a large tree, although slow-growing, with attractive smooth, grey bark and rough, coarsely toothed leaves.

The alnus or alders can help to create woodland. The cut-leaved form of the common alder, **Alnus glutinosa** 'Imperialis', is particularly recommended as the feathery foliage is most attractive. A small tree, it thrives in moist soils but shallow chalk is best avoided.

If space permits, among the trees forming the main framework should be planted others of a more ornamental nature, especially flowering or fuiting kinds, including sorbus and prunus species for autumn/winter interest. All these are described elsewhere in this chapter.

Davidia involucrata (pocket-handkerchief tree) is an excellent medium-size tree for woodland planting, thriving in any fertile soil and carrying large pendulous white bracts in late spring.

Snowdrop-like flowers are borne in late spring, before the leaves, by the halesias. These make ideal companions for rhododendrons as they need the same acid soil conditions and the rhododendron foliage makes a good background for them. The flowers of **H. monticola** 'Rosea' are blush-pink and those of **H. m. vestita** are white, but may be tinted pink. Both are small trees. A problem with halesias, though, is that branches and even the trunk may twist off in high winds.

The related styrax or snowbells are also

Magnolia campbellii 'Darjeeling', with deep rose flowers, is one of many magnolias which are recommended for planting in woodland gardens (*Hillier Arboretum, Ampfield, Hampshire*)

of spring-flowering bulbs such as chionodoxas, scillas or bluebells (endymion).

Unfortunately larger tree magnolias spend many years growing before they condescend to flower. Magnolias enjoy a deep, fertile, moisture-retentive yet well-drained soil, including clay. Many revel in partial shade, and those which flower early in the year should be given shelter to protect the flowers from frosts and cold drying winds. Species with large leaves are particularly in need of wind protection. Woodland conditions, are, therefore, ideal for many magnolias.

There are some superb cultivars of **M. campbellii** (pink tulip tree), which produce large goblet-shaped flowers in late winter or early spring. They must be grown in acid soil. Try **M. c.** 'Charles Raffill', whose flowers are rose-purple on the outside; **M. c.** 'Darjeeling', deep rose; and **M. c.** 'Lanarth', cyclamen purple. All are large trees. **Magnolia loebneri** 'Merrill' is an outstanding small tree, with large white fragrant flowers in profusion during midspring.

Try these magnolias, too: **M.** 'Charles Coates', a small tree for acid soils which flowers cream-white with red stamens in late spring/early summer; **M.** 'Heaven Scent', a medium tree for acid soils flowering at an early age with large white goblet-shaped blooms, streaked purple on the outside of the petals, in spring; **M. hypoleuca**, another medium tree for acid soils,

worth including in woodland gardens and enjoy the same soil conditions, taking sun or partial shade. They have white, danging bell-shaped flowers in early summer. **S. japonica** has wide-spreading branches and **S. obassia** forms a rounded crown. Both are small trees.

The tree magnolias rank among the most beautiful flowering subjects for a woodland garden, combining superbly with rhododendrons and camellias. Spring-flowering species are enhanced by an underplanting

---

PLANTING SCHEME FOR WOODLAND GARDEN

Combine tree magnolias with rhododendrons and camellias, and underplant them with blue spring-flowering bulbs like chionodoxas, scillas or bluebells.

Magnolia 'Wada's Memory' is a small tree with scented flowers in spring, and is recommended for planting in a woodland garden

Sassafras are distinctive trees for lime-free woodland, enjoying the sheltered conditions. We recommend **S. albidum**, a medium-sized aromatic specimen of conical habit and bearing rather variable, often lobed and sometimes fig-like deep green leaves, with good autumn tints. It gives an exotic touch to the woodland garden.

The best stewartia in the Hillier Arboretum is **S. koreana**. It is a small to medium-size tree whose foliage takes on brilliant autumn tints. The flaking bark is another attraction, as are the white cup-shaped flowers produced in succession during mid to late summer. White-stemmed birches make a marvellous contrast for the autumn colour. Woodland provides the best conditions: ensure that there is moist, acid, loamy soil; semi-shade; and that the roots are shaded from strong sun.

BOLD FOLIAGE

The majority of garden plants have comparatively small leaves which can become monotonous *en bloc*. However, a few plants with large bold leaves will relieve this monotony and should be included in planting schemes. If an exotic atmosphere is required, plants with such foliage can oblige.

There are numerous trees with large pinnate leaves, including **Meliosma veitchiorum**. This is a small, very rare 'architectural' tree whose leaves are carried on stiff thick branches. In late spring large panicles of cream-white flowers are produced, which emit a pleasant fragrance and are followed by violet-coloured fruits. A marvellous specimen tree for associating with a modern building, perhaps in the vicinity of a patio. It is best grown in deep, slightly acid to neutral soil (although it tolerates alkaline conditions), and in a sunny position.

bearing cream-white fragrant flowers with red stamens in early summer; **M.** 'Peppermint Stick', a large tree for acid soils, flowering when young, with an erect habit of growth and white goblet-shaped flowers with a purple flush at the base; **M. sprengeri**, a medium tree for acid soils, growing well in full sun and producing rose-carmine flowers in midspring, or its cultivar 'Claret Cup'; **M. × veitchii** 'Peter Veitch', a medium to large-size tree for acid soils whose flowers are goblet-shaped and white with a purple-pink flush, blooming in midspring; and **M.** 'Wada's Memory', a small tree with white, scented flowers in spring.

A tree that makes a good lawn specimen is the large **Carya cordiformis** (bitter nut), whose leaves are composed of about seven leaflets – the number may vary from five to nine – and turn yellow in autumn. The yellow buds are conspicuous in winter, as is the brown scaly bark. An adaptable tree.

Pterocarya fraxinifolia (wing nut), a large tree of wide-spreading habit which also makes a fine specimen for a lawn, has large pinnate leaves up to 60cm (2ft) long and dangling catkins of greenish flowers during summer. Female catkins may be up to 50cm (20in) in length, and are followed by winged fruits. Best grown in moist soil and ideal near a lake or river.

Another tree with pinnate leaves is **Toona sinensis** (syn. **Cedrela sinensis**), a medium-size species of rapid growth, with panicles of white fragrant flowers in mid-summer. The foliage turns yellow in autumn. It is best grown in fertile, well-drained soil and full sun, and makes an attractive patio or lawn specimen.

Phellodendron amurense (amur cork tree) also has pinnate foliage coloured yellow in autumn. More mature trees have distinctive corky bark. A medium-size tree which thrives in alkaline soils, it too makes a fine lawn specimen.

Gymnocladus dioica (Kentucky coffee tree) has large bipinnate leaves which become yellow in autumn. This medium-size tree is very hardy, thriving in a deep, fertile, well-drained soil and open sunny position. Ideal for a lawn or adjacent to a patio.

Of the trees with other leaf shapes, the wide-spreading catalpas make fine specimen trees for large lawns. **C. bignonioides** (Indian bean tree) is of medium-size with large, heart-shaped, pale green leaves and, in mid to late summer, white foxglove-like flowers marked with yellow and purple. The cultivar **C. b.** 'Aurea' (golden Indian bean tree) has pale yellow foliage. This is often best as a large bush, which is achieved by annual hard pruning in early spring. **C. fargesii duclouxii** is a medium-size tree but its leaves are not so big as those of **C. bignonioides**. Corymbs of lilac-pink foxglove-like flowers are produced in late summer. Catalpas do not flower when young and need sheltered conditions to avoid leaf damage, but will thrive in any well-drained soil.

Paulownia tomentosa (syn. **P. imperialis**) is a medium, round-headed tree with large, lobed leaves of medium green. The tree is even more spectacular in late spring when it produces upright panicles of heliotrope-coloured foxglove-like flowers, but young ones do not bloom. This tree makes a superb lawn specimen, provided there is space for its wide spread, and it needs a deep well-drained soil, shelter from strong winds and full sun. Try planting it where flowers are seen from above.

Privets generally have small leaves but an exception is **Ligustrum lucidum** 'Latifolium', a small evergreen tree with large, shiny, camellia-like foliage. In autumn panicles of white flowers are produced. This privet is best seen in isolation and would make a good lawn specimen. It will tolerate any soil, in sun or shade, but is very slow growing at the start.

One of the largest-leaved poplars is **P. lasiocarpa**, a medium tree with heart-shaped leaves up to 30cm (12in) in length. They are bright green with a red central vein and petiole. This species makes an attractive specimen tree but keep it well away from buildings. It is suited to wet soils and atmospheric pollution, but avoid shallow chalk.

The large evergreen or holm oak, **Quercus ilex**, has quite bold elliptic evergreen leaves, dark green and shiny above and often grey-felted on the undersides. Another attractive feature is the corrugated bark. Although very slow growing, the tree makes a superb lawn specimen and flourishes on all well-drained soils, including chalk, and on the coast, but it is not recommended for extremely cold inland areas.

Some of the limes, which make stately lawn specimens, have quite big leaves. Examples include **Tilia henryana**, a rare tree of medium size whose wide oval leaves may be almost 15cm (6in) in length. They are covered in soft down and have toothed edges. Unfortunately this tree is slow to become established, but nevertheless it thrives in any fertile soil and any situation.

COLOURED FOLIAGE

Many deciduous trees have coloured foliage which is at its best in the spring and/or summer. A few evergreen trees have variegated leaves which, of course, create interest all the year round.

Some of these species, especially those with bright yellow or golden foliage and those with purple or reddish leaves, have to be used carefully in gardens for they create a rather exotic atmosphere. This is fine in towns, cities, and suburban gardens, where colour may be needed to relieve the monotony of concrete, but it may not be the ideal choice for natural or country gardens. Here more subdued native trees are generally a better proposition.

However, in the right situation trees with colourful leaves are most attractive, and it is possible to plan some striking plant combinations with dramatic contrasts in colour. Possibly subtly variegated foliage is easier to use, as it seems to blend better with other plants and usually does not look out of place in country gardens.

Yellow or gold foliage

This creates a 'sunshine' atmosphere in a garden and is useful for brightening up sombre parts. However, do bear in mind that most yellow or gold plants only produce their best colour if grown in a sunny position, although there are a few which are better grown in partial shade. For dramatic contrast, trees with yellow or gold foliage could be combined with purple or reddish trees or shrubs. More subtle would be a combination of yellow and grey foliage.

Quercus rubra 'Aurea', a cultivar of the red oak, is a small slow-growing tree whose leaves open bright yellow. However, this colour does not remain all season, for the foliage eventually turns yellow-green and then wholly green. This tree would make a fine lawn specimen but it needs shelter and, to prevent the leaves from being burned by hot sun, a position in partial shade. It can only be grown in acid soils.

Popularly called the golden oak, **Quercus robur** 'Concordia' is a small round-headed tree with golden-yellow leaves throughout the spring and summer. A very slow-growing subject, it would be suitable for a mixed border.

Acer cappadocicum 'Aureum' is a most striking medium-size tree for any well-drained soil. The large lobed leaves open red in the spring but then they turn deep yellow, this colour lasting for a number of weeks. It is another tree that is best grown in partial shade to prevent the leaves from being scorched by hot sun.

Perhaps one of the best-known golden-leaved trees is **Gleditsia triacanthos** 'Sunburst' (cultivar of the honey locust), a medium-size tree best grown in full sun. It makes a marvellous lawn specimen, looks good near a patio and contrasts dramatically with purple-leaved trees or shrubs. This tree grows in any well-drained soil and

Catalpa bignonioides 'Aurea', the golden Indian bean tree, contrasting beautifully with blue agapanthus or African lilies. It also makes a fine lawn specimen (*Coates Manor, Sussex*)

takes atmospheric pollution in its stride – hence it is invariably planted in towns and cities. The leaves are pinnate and bright yellow when young, this colour fading as the season progresses. Unlike the species, this cultivar does not produce thorns.

Equally popular as 'Sunburst', and invariably used in the same way, is **Robinia pseudoacacia** 'Frisia', a small to medium-size tree with brittle wood and rich golden-yellow pinnate leaves. The colour is retained until the autumn. Provide full sun and well-drained soil for this cultivar of the common acacia, which makes a fine lawn specimen or could be grown in a shrub border with purple or grey-leaved shrubs, when it should be cut back hard each spring. A popular companion shrub is **Cotinus coggygria** 'Royal Purple', with dark purple foliage.

One or two of the limes have yellow foliage, including **Tilia × europaea** 'Wratislaviensis', a medium-size cultivar of the common lime which makes a fine lawn specimen. The foliage is golden yellow when it opens but unfortunately changes to green as the season progresses. 'Wratislaviensis' is easily grown in any fertile soil and any situation.

A cultivar of the whitebeam, **Sorbus aria** 'Chrysophylla', is a very conspicuous tree with large, oval, yellowish leaves. The best colour is seen in late spring but it is held reasonably well throughout summer, and in the autumn the foliage turns bright yellow before it falls. This small tree looks especially pleasing when grouped with evergreens or large shrubs such as laurels. It grows especially well in chalky soils.

Silver, grey or white foliage

These are easy colours to use in gardens and help to create a sense of distance. Invariably only the undersides of the leaves are one of these colours.

This is certainly the case with **Populus × candicans** (Ontario poplar, balm of Gilead poplar), whose broadly oval balsam-scented leaves have grey-white undersides. This is a stately medium-size tree with a broad crown and can be recommended as a lawn specimen for large gardens. Suitable for all types of soil.

With intense silvery leaves, ideal for creating a sense of distance, is **Salix alba sericea**, a cultivar of the white willow. This is a medium-size, slow-growing, round-headed tree which associates particularly well with golden-leaved trees or shrubs and is excellent for moist or wet soils and coastal gardens.

Several sorbus in the aria section come into this colour category. These have simple leaves and are particularly recommended for growing in chalky soils, although they grow just as well in acid conditions. **Sorbus aria** 'Lutescens', a cultivar of the white-beam, has dense cream-white tomentum on the upper surface of the leaves. This is most striking in spring; the leaves change to grey-green in the summer. It is a small tree, ideal for a shrub border.

Sorbus thibetica 'John Mitchell' (syn. **S.** 'Mitchellii') is a medium to large, round-headed tree with exceptionally big leaves up to 15cm (6in) in length and width, which are covered with white tomentum on the undersides, the upper surface being green. Equally striking is **S.** 'Wilfred Fox', a medium-size tree of broadly columnar habit when young but which eventually develops

Robinia pseudoacacia 'Frisia' makes a fine
specimen either in a shrub border or in a lawn.
Provide full sun for the best leaf colour, and a
well-drained soil (*Merrist Wood Agricultural
College, Surrey*)

a rounded crown. The large elliptic leaves
attain a length of up to 20cm (8in), being
shiny deep green above and covered with
grey-white tomentum on the undersides.

The broad oval leaves of **Tilia oliveri**
are deep green on the upper surface but

covered in silver-white tomentum on the
undersides. This distinctive medium to
large tree with slightly drooping shoots
makes a pleasing lawn specimen, succeeding in any well-drained fertile soil.

Variegated foliage

Here the leaves are often irregularly
marked with white and green. Variegated
trees, being light in colour, can help to
brighten gloomy parts of the garden. Think-
ing in terms of plant combinations, those

55

A small variegated tree, suitable for a shrub border or for planting as a lawn specimen, is **Cornus controversa** 'Variegata', a dogwood with branches held in horizontal layers

with variegated foliage often associate pleasingly with purple-leaved kinds.

This certainly applies to the privet **Ligustrum lucidum** 'Excelsum Superbum', a small evergreen tree whose leaves are edged and speckled with cream-white and deep yellow. In the autumn large panicles of white flowers are produced. A good companion for this privet would be a purple-leaved cultivar of **Cotinus coggygria**.

Populus × **candicans** 'Aurora' is a very striking medium-size tree with large, broadly oval leaves which are variegated with cream-white and often tinted with pink. As the leaves age they become green; and often the variegation does not appear at all the first year after transplanting. If desired, this tree can be grown as a shrub by cutting it hard back in late winter each year. In this form it is an excellent addition to the shrub border, perhaps combined with a purple-leaved cotinus, berberis or corylus. It is easily grown in any soil but not recommended for shallow chalk, and should be kept well away from buildings.

Very effective as a lawn specimen is the variegated form of the Turkey oak, **Quercus cerris** 'Variegata', a medium-size, slow-growing tree whose leaves have cream-white margins. When young this tree has a narrow habit but eventually it forms a spreading crown. Well suited to alkaline soils and maritime areas.

A small, slow-growing tree suitable for a shrub border or for planting as a lawn specimen is **Cornus controversa** 'Variegata', a dogwood with branches in horizontal layers whose leaves are variegated with silver and green. Excellent companions for this cornus are purple-leaved cotinus or corylus.

Pink leaves

Some trees have bright pink young foliage which is very attractive in the spring. Perhaps one of the best trees in this respect is **Aesculus** × **neglecta** 'Erythroblastos', a slow-growing medium-size tree whose new leaves are bright shrimp-pink. Eventually they change to light yellow-green and in the autumn take on orange and yellow shades. Grow it in any well-drained soil; it thrives in partial shade; but the young growth is frost-tender, so try to protect it from spring frosts.

With the same foliage colour in spring and summer is **Acer pseudoplatanus** 'Brilliantissimum', a cultivar of the sycamore, a slow-growing tree, usually top grafted, suitable for a shrub border.

Purple foliage

Purple, especially deep purple, is not a colour to be used too freely as it can be rather heavy and sombre. So use it in moderation,

Aesculus × neglecta 'Erythroblastos' is a slow-growing medium-size tree whose new leaves are bright shrimp-pink. Eventually they change to light yellow-green, and in the autumn they take on orange and yellow shades

PLANTING SCHEME FOR AUTUMN LEAF COLOUR

For autumn leaf colour try **Prunus sargentii** with shrubs such as **Cotinus** 'Flame', **Rhus typhina** and **Euonymus europaeus** 'Red Cascade'. Then for dramatic contrast plant some pampas grass, **Cortaderia selloana**.

ideally combining it with lighter-coloured trees or shrubs such as those with variegated, grey/silver or yellow foliage.

Several **Prunus cerasifera** cultivars have purple foliage, for example the ubiquitous 'Pissardii' (purple-leaved plum) which dominates so many small front gardens, and 'Nigra'. Both of these are small trees with very deep purple leaves; rather more subtle is **P. c.** 'Rosea' whose new foliage is bronze-purple. Later this turns bronze-green, and by late summer the leaves are plain green. The early spring blossom is clear salmon-pink, carried on purple shoots. 'Rosea' is a small tree which is easily grown in any fertile well-drained soil, including chalk, and in a sunny position.

Where large purple-leaved trees are required some of the cultivars of the common beech, **Fagus sylvatica**, can oblige. **F. s.** 'Riversii' has large, deep purple foliage, while **F. s.** 'Rohanii' is a medium-size slow-growing tree of great beauty. It is the fern-leaved beech with purple foliage, the leaves being attractively cut. Both of these trees make superb lawn specimens. The beeches thrive in extremely alkaline or acid soils, provided the earth is well drained and not clayey.

AUTUMN LEAF COLOUR

Some of the most dramatic leaf colour is found in the autumn, when the foliage of many deciduous trees changes to brilliant tints before it falls.

Every garden should, if possible, have at least one tree noted for autumn leaf colour. These show up best against a dark background, for example a group of conifers with deep green foliage. Although not within the scope of most people, a lake makes a marvellous setting for trees which produce good colour in autumn.

Some of these trees also look superb in a woodland setting. Here they might, for instance, contrast beautifully with the white stems of birches. Or they might stand out sharply against a background of dark green rhododendron or camellia foliage.

It is possible to create some superb planting schemes featuring a tree or trees chosen

for their autumn foliage, say in a mixed bed or border. Start with a specimen of **Prunus sargentii**, for instance. Next choose a few shrubs noted for colourful autumn leaves, such as **Cotinus** 'Flame' or **Rhus typhina**, plus berrying kinds like **Euonymus europaeus** 'Red Cascade'. To contrast dramatically with this group plant a clump or two of pampas grass, **Cortaderia selloana**, with its majestic plumes of silky silvery flowers and fountain or arching foliage. This makes a perfect planting to herald the autumn. However, there are many other possible combinations – just let your imagination run free!

One of the most important genera for providing autumn leaf colour is **Acer**. The red maple, **Acer rubrum**, is one of the best. This is a large tree with dark green palmate leaves which turn deep red and scarlet in the autumn. The cultivar 'Scanlon', a medium-size tree of broadly columnar habit suited to smaller gardens, provides equally rich colour. With both the species and cultivar the best colour is achieved on acid soils, although the trees will tolerate some lime.

Although not very well known, and indeed quite a rare tree, **Acer triflorum** consistently produces the most brilliant autumn foliage. It is a small slow-growing tree with deep green trifoliate leaves, which in autumn turn bright orange-red, and with attractively furrowed, deep brown bark. This acer will grow in any well-drained soil and prefers a sunny spot.

An almost essential medium-size tree for autumn colour in a woodland garden is **Cercidiphyllum japonicum**. Against a dark background, such as rhododendron or

Acer rubrum 'Scanlon', a medium-size tree, can be recommended for providing brilliant autumn leaf colour in smaller gardens due to its columnar habit

camellia foliage, the pale yellow or smoky-pink autumn leaves show to great advantage. In autumn the rounded leaves have a pungent, sweet fragrance, likened by some to burnt sugar or toffee.

This is really a foliage tree, the flowers being inconspicuous, and is of vigorous, spreading habit. It may also be grown in a mixed border, perhaps with other trees or shrubs with red or fiery leaf tints in autumn, and with a background of tall evergreen conifers. Cercidiphyllum thrives in any fertile soil, provided it is of reasonable depth, and possibly the autumn colour is better in acid conditions. Positions in partial shade or sun are suitable.

One does not normally associate the ashes or fraxinus with autumnal hues, but one which colours particularly well is **Fraxinus angustifolia** 'Raywood' (claret ash). This is a large yet compact, round-headed tree, whose narrow pinnate foliage turns purple in the autumn. It is a little-known tree which makes a handsome lawn specimen where space permits and, like other ashes, it will thrive in any soil, take atmospheric pollution in its stride and tolerate windy localities, including coastal regions.

On the other hand, the liquidambars are planted primarily for their autumn foliage – they are certainly among the finest sources of colour available, their maple-like or palmate leaves taking on brilliant tints in the autumn. They are often grown individually as lawn specimens but also look good in a group of trees, especially if it includes large conifers. Unfortunately sweet gums, to use their popular name, are suitable only for lime-free or neutral soil. They prefer moisture retentive yet well-drained conditions.

The best-known species is **Liquidambar styraciflua** but we would recommend the clone 'Lane Roberts', a large-growing, broadly columnar tree whose five to seven-lobed foliage turns the deepest possible

An almost essential medium-size autumn-colouring tree for a woodland garden is **Cercidiphyllum japonicum** (*Winkworth Arboretum, Surrey, National Trust*)

crimson-red before it falls. It is considered to be the most reliable for autumn colour and, unlike the species, has comparatively smooth bark.

We also recommend **Liquidambar formosana monticola**, a small, broadly columnar tree and useful where space is limited. It has large three-lobed leaves which turn red in the autumn. This form is much hardier than the species and the colour is better, too.

The genus **Nyssa** is also mainly grown for brilliant autumnal leaves. As a suggestion for a dramatic plant combination, try growing a nyssa with one of the blue spruces such as **Picea pungens** 'Hoopsii' with silvery-blue foliage. Alternatively, plant on the edge of woodland or use as a lawn specimen. The nyssas must be grown in moisture-retentive lime-free soil and as they do not like disturbance, plant a small specimen.

A well-known species is **N. sylvatica** (tupelo), a slow-growing medium-size tree of broadly columnar habit with somewhat oval leaves which turn scarlet, yellow and orange in the autumn. However, we recommend a selection which originated in the Hillier Arboretum and is named 'Jermyn's Flame'. This is of similar size and shape, and its foliage takes on brilliant orange and flame shades.

Although most malus or ornamental crabs are grown for their decorative fruits, several are noted for superb leaf colour in autumn. Possibly there is none better than **Malus tschonoskii**, a medium-size tree of conical habit. In the autumn the oval toothed leaves are tinted with shades of scarlet, orange, purple and yellow. The tree is attractive in spring, too, when laden with white, pink-tinged blossoms. These are followed by globular yellow-green fruits which are flushed red-purple. It makes a fine lawn specimen and can also be highly recommend for street planting.

Another malus giving good autumn colour is **M. coronaria** 'Charlottae'. The large oval, lobed or toothed leaves of this small, broadly columnar tree turn rich red in the autumn. In late spring and early summer it is laden with large, semi-double pale pink blossoms which possess the scent of violets. These malus thrive in any well-drained fertile soil.

An excellent autumn-colouring large shrub or small tree for woodland, thriving in partial shade or sun, and associating particularly well with rhododendrons as it needs the same moisture-retentive lime-free soil, is **Oxydendrum arboreum** (sorrel tree). This produces pendulous racemes of white flowers in late summer and then, in the autumn, the oblong-lanceolate leaves colour crimson and yellow.

Parrotia persica has the reputation of being one of the finest trees for autumn colouring, but it cannot be considered reliable in this respect. In some years the colour is superb, in others decidedly disappointing, the foliage simply turning a rather dull yellow shade. It is a small tree or large shrub with leaves shaped rather like those of beech, which in a good year turn to shades of crimson and gold before they fall. The bark of more mature trees flakes off, resulting in a patchwork effect.

Parrotia has a marvellous habit of growth, being a low, wide-spreading tree which contrasts well with conical or round-headed specimens in a group. Alternatively it makes a distinctive, isolated lawn specimen. Although it is in the witch hazel or **Hamamelidaceae** family parrotia is lime-tolerant, thriving in moisture-retentive yet well-drained soil. However, the best autumn leaf colour is achieved in acid conditions. It should be planted in a position which receives full sun.

Photinias look good on the edge of a woodland garden, or they can be planted in a mixed border with shrubs and other plants for autumn interest. **Photinia beauverdiana** is a small tree bedecked in late spring or early summer with corymbs of white flowers, which resemble those of crataegus or hawthorn. Another superb show takes place in the autumn when the tree sports deep red fruits and its lanceolate leaves take on red tints. This species tolerates a moderate amount of lime but is better grown in acid soil if possible.

Perhaps a better-known species is **Photinia villosa**, a small tree or large shrub with similar flowers to **V. beauverdiana**. In autumn the obovate leaves become gold and scarlet, and small ovate bright red berries hang from the tree. This species is not suitable for thin alkaline soils.

Although most of the prunus are grown for spring blossoms, there are a few best known for their autumn leaf colour. Undoubtedly the winner in this respect is **Prunus sargentii**, a medium-size round-headed tree which produces single pink blossoms during early or mid spring. The young foliage is bronze-red. But the real show comes in early autumn, when the leaves take on brilliant flame shades. The bark is rich brown. This species makes a magnificent lawn specimen; try underplanting it with autumn-flowering crocuses.

Another prunus worth growing for its autumn leaves is **P. verecunda** 'Autumn Glory', a small to medium-size tree. Blush blossoms create a feast for the eyes in midspring but even more spectacular in autumn is the foliage, which turns dark crimson-red. This form of the Korean hill cherry was selected by that great cherry authority, Captain Collingwood Ingram, for consistent autumn colour, and was named by Hillier's. The prunus thrives in any ordinary soil, especially if it contains lime or chalk.

One does not usually associate pears with leaf colour, but one of the ornamental kinds certainly tints well in autumn. This is **Pyrus calleryana** 'Chanticleer', a small tree with shiny foliage which turns red-purple. White blossoms are produced in midspring by this narrowly conical tree, which makes a fine lawn specimen. Easily grown, it is suitable for any well-drained soil and thrives in areas with atmospheric pollution.

Several of the oaks from eastern North America are notable for their rich crimson or red, autumn foliage. Perhaps best known is **Quercus coccinea** 'Splendens', a form of the scarlet oak. It is a large tree (but supplied as a small plant) with wide, deeply lobed, dark green shiny leaves which turn scarlet in the autumn.

Quercus rubra (red oak) is another large tree, of vigorous habit, whose lobed leaves, which are oval or obovate in shape, become red in the autumn and then change to reddish brown. However, the colour is rather variable and the leaves of some trees become ruby red, or a mixture of yellow and brown.

Somewhat like the scarlet oak, **Quercus palustris** (pin oak) also has deeply lobed leaves which are shiny green and in the autumn become rich crimson. It is a large tree whose branches have pendulous tips. This and the other two oaks make fine lawn specimens in large gardens, or they may be incorporated into woodland. None of them is suitable for alkaline conditions and best growth is achieved in a deep fertile soil.

Many of the sorbus are grown for decorative autumn berries but some are also notable for rich autumn colour. For instance, the oval leaves of **Sorbus folgneri**, which in summer are dark green with white or grey tomentum on the undersides, turn to fiery shades in the autumn before they fall. This is a small tree of pleasing habit whose branches often arch, and it bears pendulous clusters of somewhat oval fruits which are deep red or purple-red in colour.

Sorbus sargentiana is also a small tree but with large pinnate leaves, often 30cm (12in) in length and with seven to eleven leaflets, which turn red in the autumn. The petioles are red. This sorbus is also conspicuous in the winter on account of its large, sticky red buds. The small scarlet fruits are carried in large clusters and ripen quite late in the season.

Sorbus scalaris is another small tree with pinnate foliage; indeed, the leaves are ferny in appearance, being composed of twenty-one to thirty-three narrow leaflets. These are deep, shiny green on the upper surface and covered with grey down on the undersides. They are attractive in spring and summer and even more so during autumn when they take on deep red and purple shades. Dense flat heads of small red fruits are an added attraction in the autumn.

The sorbus can be incorporated into a woodland garden, are ideal for mixed borders, or make fine specimen trees in small lawns. If you want to group them with other trees, they look particularly pleasing with white-stemmed birches. All are of easy culture in any fertile, well-drained soil. Those with pinnate leaves may not live to a great age if planted in shallow alkaline soils.

Finally a lime for autumn leaf colour, **Tilia mongolica**, popularly known as the Mongolian lime. The deep shiny green leaves are broadly heart-shaped, coarsely

The leaves of **Quercus coccinea** 'Splendens', a form of the scarlet oak, turn crimson in autumn.

toothed or lobed and up to 8cm (3in) in length, and become bright yellow in autumn. This is altogether a most attractive small tree of compact, rounded shape, thriving in any fertile soil and any situation, and particularly recommended as a lawn specimen. A good lime for the owner of a smaller garden.

TREES WITH NOTABLE FLOWERS

As we have seen, trees can provide sufficient interest in gardens with foliage alone, but we should not overlook the many trees which provide notable displays of flowers. There are numerous gardeners who, for instance, would not be without an ornamental cherry to herald the spring, nor indeed a winter-flowering cherry to keep the display going in the dark months.

One of the problems with trees grown for their blossoms is that some can be decidedly dull for fifty weeks of the year, when they are out of flower. This applies to some of the ornamental cherries, but so welcome is their flamboyant display of blossom that many gardeners tolerate lack of interest for the rest of the year simply to enjoy the very essence of spring for a couple of weeks.

Obviously trees with fleeting floral beauty are not recommended for smal gardens, where there may be space for only one tree, but they are fine for larger plots especially if they can be grown somewhere that is hidden from the rest of the garden, so that they are not in full view all the year round – perhaps in a spring garden, with spring-flowering shrubs, bulbs and perennials.

For small gardens a tree with interest during more than one season is recommended. However, if you already have, say, an established cherry with but fleeting floral beauty, you could ensure colour in the summer by growing a clematis up through it, such as one of the large-flowered cultivars.

PLANTING SCHEME WITH CHERRY AND CLEMATIS

An established ornamental cherry can have a large-flowered clematis growing up through it to provide colour in the summer, when the cherry is decidedly dull.

Or you might prefer an autumn-flowering clematis, such as **Clematis tibetana vernayi (orientalis)** or **C. tangutica**.

SPRING

To many gardeners flowers are most welcome in the spring. The ornamental cherries (prunus) come into their own at this season and indeed are often among the first plants to herald the return of the sun.

Some delightful scenes can be created by growing other spring-flowering plants with the cherries, such as forsythias and appropriate magnolias. Around these, install drifts of spring-flowering bulbs, especially blue chionodoxas, muscari and scillas. One can either aim for all plants to flower at the same time, season permitting, or, which would perhaps be more sensible in a small garden, plan for a succession of flowers. Cherry blossom benefits from a dark background such as that provided by a group of tall green conifers.

There are many ornamental cherries to choose from, so let us first take a look at the popular Japanese cherries. Most of these

SPRING PLANTING SCHEME FEATURING CHERRY

For spring, try a flowering cherry with a forsythia and magnolia, and plant drifts of blue bulbs like chionodoxas, muscari and scillas around them.

are small trees, some of which have bronze young foliage, the leaves often taking on yellow or orange shades in the autumn. These, as with all the prunus described here, require an open sunny position and thrive in any ordinary soil, especially if it contains lime or chalk. Unfortunately birds may damage the dormant buds of Japanese and other cherries, so to ensure a good display of blossoms bird repellents have to be used in many areas: the spray-on type, based on repellent scent.

Prunus 'Pink Perfection' is a very lovely Japanese cherry with long pendulous trusses of double blossom during mid and late spring. The new leaves are bronze.

In mid to late spring **P.** 'Shogetsu' (syn. **P.** 'Shimidsu Sakura') is bedecked with large, double white flowers which emerge from pink-tinted buds. These hang in clusters all along the branches, suspended on long

Prunus 'Shogetsu' (syn. **P.** 'Shimidsu Sakura') is one of the finest ornamental cherries, flowering in mid to late spring. The copper-coloured young leaves contrast beautifully with the white blossoms (*Hillier Arboretum, Ampfield, Hampshire*)

stalks. At the same time the young leaves are opening and, being copper in colour, contrast superbly with the blossoms.

Prunus 'Shirofugen' is a medium-size tree with wide-spreading branches. The large, long-lasting double flowers are produced in late spring and are purple-pink in bud, but white when fully open, ageing to purple-pink. The blossoms have lengthy stalks and hang in clusters, contrasting beautifully with the new foliage which is copper coloured.

A highly distinctive Japanese cherry is **Prunus** 'Mount Fuji' (syn. **P.** 'Shirotae'). It is a small tree of vigorous habit whose horizontal or slightly pendulous branches

A highly distinctive Japanese cherry of spreading habit is **Prunus** 'Mount Fuji' (syn. **P.** 'Shirotae'), a small tree flowering during midspring. The blossoms are fragrant (*Savill Gardens, The Great Park, Windsor, Berkshire*)

spread widely, often sweeping the ground. The large, fragrant, pure white flowers are either single or semi-double and are carried in pendulous clusters during midspring.

The great white cherry, **Prunus** 'Tai Haku', is a magnificent medium-size tree. In midspring it is laden with huge single flowers of the purest white, contrasting dramatically with the new copper-red foliage. Many gardeners consider this to be the best white Japanese cherry and it was made popular by the great cherry authority, Captain Collingwood Ingram.

Last but not least, as there are many other excellent Japanese cherries that one could include here, is **Prunus** 'Ukon'. This is a medium-size spreading tree which in mid-

The great white cherry, **Prunus** 'Tai Haku', is a magnificent medium-size tree laden with huge flowers in midspring. The young foliage is copper-red in colour

66

spring clothes itself with semi-double flowers of a light yellowish shade tinted with green, or sometimes flushed with pink, contrasting superbly with the new leaves which are deep bronze. This cherry has particularly good autumn leaf colour (rust-red or purple-brown), so it is a good dual-season tree.

Other good cherries include **Prunus** 'Accolade', a small tree with a spreading habit of growth. In early spring it is laden with pendulous clusters of semi-double deep pink blossoms, each 38cm (1½in) across. **Prunus** 'Kursar' was raised by Captain Collingwood Ingram. It is a small tree which covers itself with small deep pink blossoms in early or mid spring. The young foliage is red-bronze and may appear with or just after the flowers.

Prunus 'Pink Shell' is a small spreading tree named by Hillier's, with masses of palest pink blossoms in midspring, which appear with the new light green foliage.

Finishing with a miscellaneous selection of prunus, one which is especially recommended for the woodland garden is **P. avium** 'Plena', the double gean, which has a profusion of pendulous double white flowers during mid or late spring. It is a medium-size tree.

Prunus × **blireana** is an ornamental plum, a most beautiful large shrub or small tree highly recommended for the mixed border. In early to mid spring it produces, with the metallic copper-purple foliage, large double rose-pink blossoms which are slightly scented.

With flowers which are quite different from those of other prunus is **P. padus** 'Watereri', a cultivar of the bird cherry, with pendulous racemes of white fragrant flowers up to 20cm (8in) in length during late spring. It is a medium-size tree suitable for the woodland garden or for specimen planting in a lawn.

The spring cherry, **Prunus subhirtella**, has a number of forms including 'Pendula Rubra'. It is a small tree with, as the name suggests, a weeping habit and in early to midspring bears small, single, deep rose-coloured flowers. This would make a pleasing specimen tree in a lawn, or it could be used as a focal point.

This selection of prunus should please any discerning gardener but, of course, there are other trees which herald the spring with their flowers. For instance, there is an unusual acer, **A. negundo violaceum**, a medium-size tree which would make an attractive lawn specimen. In the spring the tree is bedecked with pendulous tassels of dark reddish-pink flowers up to 15cm (6in) in length. They are quite conspicuous set against a background of well-kept lawn. The shoots start off purple or violet and are covered with white 'bloom'; the pinnate leaves are composed of five to seven leaflets. An easily grown tree given a well-drained fertile soil.

Amelanchiers or snowy mespilus are almost as popular as ornamental cherries. A particularly good species for flowers is **A. lamarckii**, a small tree massed with starry white flowers in mid to late spring. The oval leaves are attractive, too, being copper-red when they unfurl in spring and becoming scarlet in autumn before they fall – a perfect dual-season tree. This species may be grown on the edge of a woodland garden where its flowers would show up well, or it may be incorporated into the mixed border. A particularly pleasing companion plant would be a blue-flowered rhododendron, such as **R. augustinii**. The two go well together from a practical point of view, too, for the amelanchier is best grown in acid soil and the rhododendron definitely needs lime-free conditions.

Cornus nuttallii is a medium-size, broadly columnar tree which sports large

Cornus nuttallii, a medium-size tree, starts flowering from a comparatively early age. The autumn foliage is yellow, or sometimes red (*Hillier Arboretum, Ampfield, Hampshire*)

white bracts (these surround the tiny flowers) in late spring. Sometimes the bracts are tinted with pink. Flowering starts from a comparatively early age. This is another dual-season tree, for the autumn foliage is yellow, or sometimes red. Grow it as a lawn specimen, ideally against a dark background so that the floral bracts show to advantage. It is not a particularly adaptable tree and cannot be recommended for thin chalky soils.

The Ornus Group of the genus **Fraxinus**,

the so-called flowering ashes, are notable for their flowers and make attractive lawn specimens. **F. ornus** itself, the manna ash, is a medium-size tree which freely produces panicles of fragrant cream-white flowers in late spring. The leaves consist of five to nine deep green leaflets. Like other ashes, it will thrive in any soil, ignore atmospheric pollution and tolerate windy localities, including coastal regions.

The genus **Malus** (the ornamental crabs) is indeed versatile. It gives us some of the best ornamental fruiting trees as well as some excellent species and cultivars for spring flowers. All make first-class lawn specimens, or they can be grown in mixed borders. They thrive in any well-drained fertile soil.

Among the spring-flowering kinds, **Malus floribunda** (Japanese crab) is considered by many to be one of the most beautiful. It is a small tree of arching habit which, in mid to late spring, produces white or palest pink blossoms from crimson buds. These are followed by small red and yellow fruits. Beautiful when underplanted with golden-yellow trumpet daffodils.

Malus × atrosanguinea is a small tree with a mushroom-shaped crown, quite useful for creating a focal point in a garden. In late spring it produces rose-pink blossoms from crimson buds. These are followed by small, yellow, red-flushed fruits. The shiny leaves are plain green.

Malus 'Hillieri' is a small tree named by Hillier's. The semi-double bright pink blossoms from crimson buds clothe the arching branches in late spring. **M. hupehensis** is a small tree with rather upright branches and in late spring or early summer it produces masses of white blossoms from pink buds. These are followed by yellow fruits with a red flush.

In midspring **Malus** 'Katherine' produces semi-double pink blossoms from

deeper pink buds and as the flowers age they turn white. Bright red fruits, with a yellow flush, follow. This is a small tree with a dense, globular crown, best grown as a bush. Flowering in late spring and early summer is **M.** 'Prince George's', a small tree which originated in the Arnold Arboretum, USA. The large, scented double flowers are pale pink. Crimson flowers are produced by **M.** 'Royalty' in midspring, followed by small deep red fruits. This small tree has attractive reddish-purple foliage.

SUMMER

Eucryphias are among the highlights of summer, being very distinctive broadly columnar evergreen or deciduous trees and shrubs which are best grown in partially shaded, sheltered positions with moisture-retentive, ideally acid, soil. Light woodland provides suitable conditions, as would a sheltered mixed or shrub border. Hot sun should not be allowed to reach the root area,

which could be shaded by lower-growing plants.

Eucryphias perform in late summer or early autumn, sporting white flowers each containing a conspicuous boss of stamens.

Of the tree species, **E. glutinosa** can be particularly recommended. It is a small tree with pinnate foliage which colours particularly well in the autumn. The flowers are over 5cm (2in) across.

The evergreen **E. × intermedia** 'Rostrevor' is a small tree which is extremely free-flowering, bearing large fragrant blooms. It was raised at Rostrevor, Co Down. **E. milliganii**, also a small evergreen tree, is slow-growing and has a narrow habit of growth. The small leaves are deep green and glossy, the flowers cup-shaped and freely produced, even by young specimens. It is on the tender side and needs ample protection.

The medium evergreen tree **E. × nymansensis** 'Nymansay' is a fast grower, bearing flowers well over 5cm (2in) in diameter. It was raised early this century at Nymans Garden, Handcross, West Sussex.

One has to be patient for cladrastis to flower, because young specimens will not oblige. **C. lutea** (yellow wood) has long pendulous panicles of white flowers which are well scented and rather like those of wisteria in shape, appearing in early summer. This is a medium-size dual-season tree, whose foliage turns yellow in autumn. It would make a fine lawn specimen, being hardy and requiring a sunny spot with impeccably drained, moderately fertile soil. Strong winds could damage old trees if they are not sufficiently protected, as the wood is brittle.

Fraxinus mariesii is one of the flowering ashes (in the Ornus Group of this genus), a small, slow-growing tree or large shrub producing panicles of fragrant cream-white flowers in early summer. The leaves are made up of three to five deep green, oval leaflets. It would make a handsome lawn specimen. Like other ashes it will thrive in any soil, take atmospheric pollution in its stride and tolerate windy locations, including coastal areas.

Koelreuteria paniculata (golden rain tree) is a distinctive medium-size tree, best used as a lawn specimen. The pinnate foliage, which consists of up to fifteen leaflets, is an attractive feature and in autumn turns yellow before it falls. In mid to late summer large panicles of yellow flowers are produced, especially when the season has been hot and dry. Bladder-like fruits follow the flowers. The golden rain tree is easily grown in any well-drained soil and needs full sun.

A very large lawn could have **Liriodendron tulipifera** (tulip tree) as a specimen. This large tree has three-lobed leaves which are 'cut off' somewhat squarely at the tips. They turn deep yellow in the autumn. The large tulip-shaped flowers, produced in early or midsummer only by well-established trees, are yellow-green and marked with orange on the inside. There are several forms of the tulip tree, including **L. t.** 'Aureomarginatum' whose leaves are edged with green-yellow or yellow. This is a medium-size tree. Tulip trees grow well in any deep, fertile, well-drained soil.

Robinia × slavinii 'Hillier' was raised on the Hillier Nurseries and is a shapely small tree with a rounded crown, especially recommended for small gardens, perhaps as a lawn specimen or as a feature in a mixed border. It would also look good planted near a patio. It has pinnate foliage and in early summer produces pendulous racemes of lilac pink, slightly scented pea-shaped flowers. Easily grown in any well-drained soil, tolerating hot dry situations and atmospheric pollution. It has brittle wood, so choose a sheltered spot to avoid wind damage.

AUTUMN AND WINTER

There are few trees flowering during autumn and winter. However, **Prunus subhirtella** 'Autumnalis', the autumn cherry, flowers on and off from late autumn to early spring. The semi-double white flowers appear whenever there is a mild spell of weather. Providing a little more colour is **P. s.** 'Autumnalis Rosea' with semi-double pale pink blossoms.

These small trees definitely need a dark background to ensure the flowers show up well, such as a group of tall dark conifers or other evergreens. In a large garden autumn cherries could be planted on the edge of a woodland area. In smaller gardens they are

Prunus subhirtella 'Autumnalis', the autumn cherry, flowers on and off from late autumn to early spring. It is a small tree (*Denmans, West Sussex*)

TREES NOTED FOR FRUITS

A number of trees are noted for their ornamental fruits, which are useful for providing colour in the autumn garden. A few other trees of an ornamental nature bear edible fruits and are therefore useful dual-purpose specimens.

The fruits of some trees, such as sorbus and crataegus, may be taken by birds almost as soon as they ripen and in some gardens, particularly those in the country, a lasting show of berries is never achieved. Therefore it is worth noting any trees whose fruits persist for long periods, as these are possibly the ones that are not touched by birds.

Some fruits can stain paving so make sure fruiting trees do not overhang the patio, nor indeed the pavement or neighbours' gardens. For this reason fruiting trees are not the ideal choice for planting in streets, shopping precincts, etc.

Among the most widely planted trees for ornamental autumnal fruits are the sorbus, especially those in the Aucuparia Section. These have pinnate leaves and large bunches of colourful berries. They are ideal for including in woodland gardens and mixed borders, or for use as lawn specimens, and look especially attractive when grouped with white-stemmed birches, plus pines and other conifers. All are of easy culture in any fertile, well-drained soil but they may not live to a great age if planted in shallow, alkaline ground.

We recommend the following sorbus: **S.** 'Apricot Lady', raised by Hillier's, a small tree with apricot-yellow fruits and rich autumn leaf colour; **S. aucuparia** 'Cardinal Royal', medium tree of upright habit, with large clusters of dark red fruits; **S. a.** 'Fastigiata', slow-growing small columnar tree with red berries in dense clusters; **S. cashmiriana**, small tree with clusters of white berries which persist long after leaf

ideal for incorporating into mixed borders.

A tree could form the centrepiece of a winter group. This might include such winter-flowering shrubs as hamamelis (witch hazel), **Viburnum tinus** (laurustinus) cultivars and mahonias. Cover the ground around these shrubs with winter-flowering heaths such as **Erica carnea** and **E.** × **darleyensis** cultivars and you have a group with an extremely long period of interest.

PLANTING SCHEME FOR WINTER

Use **Prunus subhirtella** 'Autumnalis' as a centrepiece for a winter group containing hamamelis, **Viburnum tinus** and mahonias with a ground covering of winter-flowering heathers.

fall; **S.** 'Eastern Promise', a small tree which originated on the Hillier Nurseries, producing rose-pink fruits in large clusters, purple and flame autumn foliage; **S.** 'Embley', small to medium-size tree of upright habit named by Hillier's, with orange-red fruits in heavy bunches, red autumn foliage; **S.** 'Ethel's Gold', a small tree which originated on the Hillier Nurseries, whose fruits are golden-amber and persist well into the New Year provided they are not stripped by birds; **S. hupehensis**, small tree with long-lasting, white, sometimes pink-flushed berries, and red autumn foliage; **S.** 'Joseph Rock', small tree with long-lasting cream-yellow berries which mature to amber, its autumn foliage red, orange, copper and purple; **S. × kewensis**, a small tree raised at Kew Gardens, with large clusters of orange-red fruits which unfortunately are relished by birds; **S.** sp. Ghose, a small upright tree introduced by Hillier's from the Himalayas, with dark green foliage and large bunches of long-lasting small rose-red berries; **S. vilmorinii**, small tree with pendulous clusters of rose-red fruits which later become white flushed with pink, and ferny foliage which turns red and purple in autumn; and **S.** 'White Wax', a small tree which originated on the Hillier Nurseries, with white fruits carried in pendulous clusters.

Another important group of trees for ornamental autumn fruits are the crataegus or thorns, whose red fruits follow the white late-spring flowers. Often the leaves take on colourful tints in autumn. These are extremely tough and highly adaptable small, spreading trees, thriving in exposed windy areas, including maritime gardens, tolerating industrial pollution and putting up with both extremely dry and moist soils. Grow crataegus either as lawn specimens or in mixed borders.

The following crataegus are especially recommended for their fruits: **C. laciniata**, with deeply cut greyish leaves and large fruits; **C. × lavallei** 'Carrierei', which has long, shiny, deep green leaves and orange-red berries which persist all winter; **C. pinnatifida major**, with large lobed leaves which turn deep red in autumn and shiny crimson berries; and **C. prunifolia**, producing oval leaves which colour extremely well in autumn and long-lasting fruits.

Many of the malus or ornamental crabs are grown for their decorative autumn fruits. They make pleasing lawn or mixed-border specimens and thrive in any well-drained fertile soil.

We can recommend the following: **M.** 'Crittenden', a small tree with large scarlet fruits which remain for a very long period; **M.** 'Golden Hornet', a small tree with masses of yellow crab-apples which last well into the winter; **M.** 'John Downie', a small tree with large cone-shaped bright red and orange fruits which are often used for preserves; **M. × robusta** 'Red Siberian', a medium-size tree with cherry-shaped red fruits; **M. × robusta** 'Yellow Siberian', a medium-size tree with cherry-shaped yellow fruits; and **M. transitoria**, a small slender tree with rounded yellow fruits and good autumn leaf colour.

The strawberry trees are notable for their fruits which, of course, resemble strawberries. They are small evergreen trees with shiny deep green foliage and are also attractive in flower, producing panicles of white urn-shaped blooms. A particularly attractive strawberry tree is **Arbutus unedo** 'Rubra', whose flowers are flushed with pink and which fruits copiously. The blooms and fruits are produced together in late autumn. The shredding dark brown bark is also attractive.

This tree can be grown in alkaline soils and is tolerant of windy maritime conditions. It makes an impressive lawn specimen or could be grown in a mixed border. Good companion plants are small trees or shrubs noted for their autumn leaf colour (such as **Acer triflorum**, photinias and **Cotinus coggygria** cultivars), which contrasts dramatically with the dark evergreen foliage of the strawberry tree.

There are several trees grown mainly for their edible fruits but which are also ornamental. This certainly applies to **Morus nigra**, the black mulberry, which makes a superb shade tree for the lawn. It is a small tree of distinctive habit, with a wide spread and becoming gnarled as it matures. This was once a very popular tree with cottage gardeners, and if you have inherited a mature tree you are indeed lucky. It has large heart-shaped leaves and loganberry-shaped, very dark red fruits which ripen in the summer. Mulberries can be grown in any well-drained soil but best results are achieved by planting in deep fertile earth. They are suitable for maritime and town or city gardens.

A large garden is needed for **Castanea sativa**, the sweet chestnut, the best fruiting clone of which is 'Maron de Lyon', which produces fruits while still young. This is a large fast-growing tree with long, lance-shaped, toothed leaves and long yellow-green catkins in summer. A drought-resistant tree, it is suitable for well-drained soils, ideally on the light side, and succeeds in moderately alkaline conditions but is not suitable for thin chalky soils. Good crops of nuts are produced only in hot summers.

The fig, **Ficus carica**, is an exotic-looking tree so it has to be carefully placed. It looks particularly good in the vicinity of a patio, where it creates a Mediterranean atmosphere with its large lobed leaves. This small but wide-spreading tree generally produces a crop of fruits in the autumn in the UK, where it is best grown against a warm sunny wall and will thrive in any well-drained soil. The cultivar 'Brown Turkey', with brown-purple fruits, can be recommended for outdoor culture.

ORNAMENTAL BARK

The value of bark is often not recognised sufficiently by gardeners, which is a pity for it can create a great deal of interest in a garden, especially during winter when it is particularly noticeable due to reduced competition from other plants.

It is important to ensure a suitable background for trees with ornamental bark. Many are used as lawn specimens, where light-coloured or red-brown stems show up particularly well. A dark background can also be recommended for trees with light-coloured stems, such as a group of large deep green conifers or other evergreens. A sufficiently dark background is also provided by a woodland garden.

There are several prunus with ornamental bark but one of the very best is **P. serrula**, a small tree with shiny red-brown bark. The unusually narrow willow-like leaves and small white blossoms, produced with the leaves in midspring, combine to make this a most attractive tree for the small garden.

Some of the most striking bark is found among the acers, especially the 'snakebark maples' whose green trunks and branches are striped with white. **Acer davidii** is possibly the best known of these, a small tree whose oval leaves take on brilliant tints in autumn. The fruits are also conspicuous in autumn, being green and often flushed with red. The form most generally grown is 'George Forrest'.

Another snakebark is **Acer pensylvanicum**, a small tree best grown in acid soil whose trunk is striped white and light jade-green when the tree is young. The three-lobed leaves become bright yellow in

Arbutus × andrachnoides, a strawberry tree, is a small evergreen with the most beautiful reddish bark. It is lime-tolerant and quite hardy (*Royal Botanic Gardens, Kew, Surrey*)

The white urn-shaped flowers are produced in late autumn and winter. A lime-tolerant hybrid, it is quite hardy.

Many of the eucalyptus or gum trees have beautiful bark, including **E. dalrympleana**, a fast-growing medium-size evergreen tree with patchwork bark in cream, brown and grey, and grey-green adult leaves. It is one of the hardiest eucalypts, as is **E. niphophila** (snow gum) which is also recommended. This is a small evergreen tree of slow growth, with grey-green foliage and grey, green and cream patchwork bark. Also extremely hardy is **E. parviflora**, a medium-size evergreen tree with narrow blue-green foliage and smooth grey bark which is particularly suited to chalky soils. The eucalypts are best planted in the spring as pot-grown seedlings about 0.3m (1ft) high, as they then establish rapidly. They grow in a wide range of soils but thin chalky types are best avoided. Plant eucalypts in sheltered positions.

Ashes are not normally regarded as having distinctive bark, but an exception is **Fraxinus excelsior** 'Jaspidea' (golden ash). This large tree has deep yellow young shoots and the branches are also yellowish, making it conspicuous in the winter. In the autumn the pinnate leaves turn pure yellow before they fall. Like other ashes it thrives

autumn before they fall. **Acer** 'Silver Vein' is a truly beautiful snakebark, a small tree with yellow autumn foliage which originated on the Hillier Nurseries.

The paperbark maple, **Acer griseum**, is a small, slow-growing tree whose older bark on the trunks and main branches peels and flakes away to expose reddish underbark. It is also one of the finest maples for autumn leaf colour, as the trifoliate leaves become red and scarlet before they fall. All of these acers are easily grown in any well-drained soil.

One of the strawberry trees **Arbutus × andrachnoides**, is a small evergreen specimen with the most beautiful reddish bark.

PLANTING SCHEME FEATURING BARK

Stooled plants of **Salix alba** 'Chermesina' with orange-scarlet shoots, or **S. a.** 'Vitellina' with deep yellow shoots, combine beautifully with other plants which have ornamental bark such as birches, snakebark maples, **Prunus serrula, Rubus cockburnianus** and **Cornus alba** 'Sibirica'.

in any soil, and tolerates atmospheric pollution and windy, maritime localities.

Some of the willows have coloured bark which shows up particularly well in the winter. Two forms of the white willow, **Salix alba**, can be especially recommended: 'Chermesina' (scarlet willow) with brilliant orange-scarlet shoots, and 'Vitellina' (golden willow) with deep yellow shoots. The former is a large tree, the latter is of medium size.

We recommend growing both as stooled plants, cutting hard back every other year in early spring to produce thickets of young shoots which have the best colour. These trees are particularly suitable for damp soils

Fraxinus excelsior 'Jaspidea', the golden ash, has deep yellow young shoots which are conspicuous in winter. Here it is seen displaying its autumn foliage (*Hillier Arboretum, Ampfield, Hampshire*)

and look especially good alongside pools, lakes or rivers. One can create an especially pleasing winter scene by planting with these willows white-stemmed birches, snakebark maples, **Prunus serrula** with its shiny red-brown bark, **Rubus cockburnianus** (white-washed bramble) and **Cornus alba** 'Sibirica' (Westonbirt dogwood) with crimson stems. If space permits, this group would form a marvellous basis for a winter garden.

CHAPTER 5

SHRUBS FOR
FLOWERS AND FOLIAGE

Shrubs form the next highest layer in planting schemes to trees (except, that is, prostrate or dwarf kinds), and like the latter they help to create the permanent framework of a garden. Other kinds of smaller plants are grown around and under them, such as hardy perennials and bulbs.

In the past, particularly in Victorian times, many shrubs were decidedly dull and, indeed, there was no more sombre feature than the Victorian shrubbery, heavy with dark evergreens such as aucubas and privets.

However, the range of shrubs has considerably increased since the last century – indeed, there is a bewildering choice available today to provide colour and interest all the year round. New shrubs from around the world are being introduced all the time. Not new genera, but certainly cultivars and, to a lesser extent, species. At every Chelsea Flower Show we now expect to see a good sprinkling of new cultivars.

WHAT CAN SHRUBS OFFER?

There is a vast choice of shrubs which flower in the spring and summer, and a good selection for autumn and winter, two seasons which still see many gardens drab and bare. Many flowering shrubs are fragrant and therefore make a particularly valuable contribution to the garden.

But flowers are not the only attractions of shrubs today: many have bold or otherwise distinctive foliage. These are most useful for incorporating into planting schemes to provide contrast in shape and texture. And never before have there been more shrubs with coloured foliage which, again, can be used for creating contrast in groups and for brightening up various parts of the garden. There are shrubs with gold, yellow, grey, silver, purple, red and variegated leaves.

We have already said that many gardens are still dull and devoid of colour and interest in autumn and winter. There is no excuse for this as there are many shrubs noted for their autumn leaf colour, crops of colourful berries and even coloured stems. But why aren't more gardeners stocking their plots with autumn and winter shrubs? A possible reason is that many people visit garden centres, nurseries and

A popular, fragrant, spring-flowering shrub is **Choisya ternata**, the Mexican orange blossom. This evergreen has clusters of sweetly scented orange-blossom-like flowers and shiny, deep green aromatic foliage (*Greys Court, Oxfordshire, National Trust*)

76

gardens only in spring and summer, and therefore stock their gardens with whatever is creating colour and interest during these seasons. By failing to visit such places in autumn and winter, people are missing out on plants which have much to offer during these seasons.

WHERE TO GROW SHRUBS

Shrubs can be grown in all parts of a garden in conditions ranging from shady with dry or moist soils, to hot and sunny with dry soil. Many thrive in maritime gardens, withstanding salt-laden winds, and others can be grown in cold exposed sites.

There are prostrate or low-growing shrubs suitable for creating ground cover, and much larger shrubs for borders. Today many people grow their plants in mixed borders and here shrubs are essential to form the 'framework' around and among which other plants are grown, like hardy perennials, bulbs, annuals and so on.

Of course, if space permits, there is no reason why a pure shrub border should not be a feature of a garden – certainly with careful choice of shrubs it will provide colour and interest all the year round, and it can be considered a labour-saving feature.

Plants can be grouped in various ways in mixed or shrub borders. For instance, you might like to have seasonal groups, each comprising a collection of plants which provide colour during a particular season. Alternatively, groups could comprise plants which flower during different seasons so that in any one part of a border you have a long succession of colour and interest.

INCREASING ONE'S KNOWLEDGE

Despite the incredible range of shrubs available today it comes as a surprise to learn that there are still many which are not known by amateur gardeners. This is a great pity, for the gardeners are missing out on some fine plants. Undoubtedly the reason is that the shrubs are not seen in the garden centres.

This chapter is intended to introduce a wide range of shrubs which deserve to be more widely grown, but it also includes many garden-worthy kinds that are already great favourites. By growing only a fraction of the shrubs described here, your garden will be all the richer and a major attraction not only for yourself but also for plant-loving friends.

SHRUBS RECOMMENDED FOR FLOWERS

A large proportion of shrubs flower in the spring and indeed there is generally no shortage of spring-flowering kinds in most gardens, even if they are nothing more adventurous than forsythias and ribes (although even with these there are some species and cultivars which deserve to be more widely grown).

Countless suburban gardens filled with philadelphus and weigela belie the fact that there are many summer-flowering shrubs from which to choose. However, even these two should not be despised provided one has sufficient space to devote to them, so that they do not dominate the garden and fade into the background when out of flower.

Deciduous hybrid azaleas flowering in the Hillier Arboretum, Ampfield, Hampshire. They bloom during late spring and early summer, many being fragrant. Azaleas look good underplanted with hostas

There are fewer autumn-flowering shrubs but those that are available are among the most distinctive of garden plants, an accolade that is certainly deserved by the mahonias which commence their display during that season.

The mahonias' display continues into winter and their flowers are beautifully scented, as are those of numerous other winter-flowering shrubs, such as chimonanthus, various daphnes, lonicera species and viburnums. Sometimes winter flowers are not very conspicuous but invariably they make up for that by emitting a powerful fragrance.

Let us now take a look at flowering shrubs for each season of the year and discuss their particular uses.

SPRING

Among the most aristocratic of spring-flowering shrubs are the magnolias. Because of their appearance many people think they are difficult to grow, but this is certainly not true provided they are planted in suitable conditions. The most widely grown, possibly because it tolerates atmospheric pollution and clay soils (but it is not recommended for very alkaline conditions), is **Magnolia** × **soulangeana**, or rather forms of it. This is a large spreading shrub, which can be grown against a wall, with tulip-shaped flowers before the leaves in mid to late spring, and even young plants flower well. Good forms include 'Brozzonii', with extra-large white flowers flushed purple at their base; 'Lennei', rose-purple outside, cream-white flushed purple within; and 'Lennei Alba', ivory white.

Other good magnolias include **M.** 'Elizabeth', a large shrub with pale yellow flowers before the leaves; and **M.** 'Jane', a medium but compact shrub whose purple-red flowers are white within. Both need lime-free soils and look especially good in light woodland conditions.

Other important shrubs

Evergreen ceanothus are often too tender for exposed conditions and are frequently grown against warm walls. They would make good companions for **Magnolia** × **soulangeana**. They need plenty of sun and very good drainage, are reasonably tolerant of alkaline soils and thrive by the sea. They are valued for their blue spring flowers and among the best of medium size are **C. arboreus** 'Trewithen Blue' with deep blue flowers; **C.** 'A. T. Johnson', rich blue; **C.** 'Delight', rich blue; and **C.** 'Puget Blue', deep blue. The dwarf **C.** 'Blue Mound', selected by Hillier's, with middling-blue flowers, and the prostrate **C. prostratus**, bright blue, would be most suitable for a garden of Mediterranean-climate plants, although these are among the hardier kinds.

Earlier we said that there are some ribes which deserve to be more widely grown. Too many gardens have only **R. sanguineum** 'King Edward VII', a medium-size flowering currant with crimson flowers. This is certainly a good cultivar, but for a change try **R. s.** 'Tydeman's White', a medium shrub with white flowers. Both bloom in midspring and are useful additions to the mixed border, underplanted with spring bulbs. **R. sanguineum** cultivars are not much to look at when out of flower, so plant something with summer interest in front of them or grow a summer-flowering clematis through them.

Other ribes to try are **R. laurifolium**, a dwarf evergreen shrub for the front of the border or rock garden, with pendulous racemes of green-white flowers in early spring; and **R. speciosum**, a medium semi-evergreen shrub with bristly reddish stems and drooping clusters of deep red fuchsia-like flowers in midspring, followed by bristly fruits. It needs warm-wall protection in cold parts of the country. All ribes grow in any well-drained soil.

Forsythias are found in almost every suburban garden, where they create a bright splash of yellow which announces that spring has arrived. Almost certainly the cultivar will be **F.** × **intermedia** 'Lynwood', with large wide-petalled flowers covering every inch of the stems. 'Golden Nugget', raised by one of Hiller's foremen and named by the nursery, is equally floriferous, bearing extremely large canary-yellow blooms. Similar is 'Beatrix Farrand', with an upright habit of growth. All make medium-size shrubs which flourish in any well-drained soil. Unfortunately forsythias are decidedly

---

PLANTING SCHEME WITH FORSYTHIA AND CLEMATIS

Grow a **Clematis viticella** cultivar through a mature, spring-flowering forsythia to provide late summer and autumn interest.

Evergreen ceanothus make good companions for **Magnolia** × **soulangeana**, both requiring a warm sheltered wall. This is the deep blue **Ceanothus** 'Puget Blue' (*Hillier Arboretum, Ampfield, Hampshire*)

dull when out of flower, so make sure they are set towards the back of a border and have something of interest planted in front of them to take over in the summer. Also you could grow **Clematis viticella** cultivars through mature specimens to provide late summer and autumn interest.

Chaenomeles form another important group of shrubs for early spring colour, especially in partially shady situations. Like forsythias, they grow in any well-drained soil. The flowers are rather like apple blossom in shape and are followed by yellow quince-like fruits, hence the common name: ornamental quince. They can be grown as free-standing specimens in a border or be trained against a wall. There are many forms of **C. speciosa**, a medium-sized shrub, for example 'Moerloosei' in pink and white and the beautiful white 'Nivalis' which shows up so well in partial shade. Among the best of the **C.** × **superba** cultivars are 'Pink Lady', a small spreading shrub in rose-pink, and 'Rowallane', a medium spreading cultivar with huge flowers of deepest red. Chaenomeles are insipid when out of flower so provide interest at other seasons as suggested for forsythia.

One can have mahonias in flower from autumn through to spring by careful selection of species. These evergreen shrubs with pinnate foliage and yellow flowers in various formations, followed by blue-black berries, thrive in any well-drained soil and are good on chalk. They associate well with lots of plants including coloured-stemmed cornus (dogwoods), hellebores such as **Helleborus orientalis** (Lenten roses), bergenias and bulbs like galanthus (snowdrops). Such groups look superb on the edge of a woodland garden.

Spring-flowering mahonias include the **M. aquifolium** (Oregon grape) cultivars 'Apollo', a low spreading shrub with deep yellow blooms, and 'Atropurpurea', a small shrub whose foliage turns a deep reddish-purple in winter and spring; the dwarf, suckering **M. nervosa**, best in acid or neutral soils; **M. trifoliolata glauca**, a medium shrub with bluish-green foliage, best planted in front of a warm wall; and **M. × wagneri** 'Undulata', also of medium size but with deep green wavy leaves.

Viburnums are an important group for late spring blooms. Many have fragrant flowers and have therefore been described under that heading. Very fragrant and a worthy border kind is **V. × carlcephalum**, a medium-size yet compact shrub with large globular heads of white flowers opening from pink buds.

Needing a lot of lateral space are the **V. plicatum** cultivars, medium shrubs with a wide-spreading habit and white flowers. 'Grandiflorum' has globe-shaped heads; 'Mariesii' holds its branches horizontally in layers, which look as though they are covered with snow when the plant is in flower; the blooms of 'Pink Beauty' become flushed with pink as they age; 'Rowallane' forms layers of horizontal branches, fruits well, has good autumn foliage colour and is compact in habit, ideal for smaller gardens; and 'Nanum Semperflorens' is of similar habit, with flat heads of flowers which start to appear in summer. The plicatums look especially lovely on the woodland edge, perhaps combined with deciduous azaleas and underplanted with bluebells (**Hyacinthoides non-scriptus**). All viburnums grow in any well-drained soil, including chalk.

For woodland planting

There are numerous spring-flowering shrubs which look lovely planted in woodland gardens, but failing that combine them with, say, a small specimen tree such as a birch in a shrub or mixed border.

Plant **Embothrium coccineum lanceolatum** (Chilean fire bush) in partial shade and lime-free, moisture-retentive yet well-drained soil. Then in late spring and early summer this large, hardy evergreen shrub will reward you with exotic-looking orange-scarlet flowers. Provide a dark green background.

Enkianthus need the same conditions and indeed make suitable companions for embothriums, and also for rhododendrons. They bear clusters of pendulous urn or cup-shaped flowers in late spring, and provide a bonus of spectacular autumn leaf colour. Perhaps best known is **E. campanulatus** with pale yellow-bronze flowers, but try also **E. cernuus rubens** with dark red blooms and the white **E. perulatus**.

With lime-free moisture-retentive soil one can also grow kalmias, which may be planted in groups with enkianthus and rhododendrons. They too enjoy partial shade, but also grow well in full sun. The cup-shaped pink or red flowers in late spring or early summer show up well against the evergreen rhododendron-like foliage. **K. latifolia** is the best-known species, but there are now several cultivars such as 'Ostbo Red' with bright red blooms. Both make medium-size shrubs.

The evergreen pieris also need moist lime-free soil and are often used in groups of the above calcifuge shrubs. **P. japonica**

Pieris japonica 'Blush' in a woodland garden, contrasting superbly with a yellow corylopsis and white narcissi. It needs a moist lime-free soil (*Savill Gardens, The Great Park, Windsor, Berkshire*)

cultivars are among the best for a display
of pendulous trusses of white lily of the
valley-like flowers in early to midspring.
Try 'Purity' for the purest white or, for
something a little different, 'Blush' with
palest pink blooms from deeper pink buds.
Both make medium-size shrubs and look
lovely underplanted with a mixture of the
miniature bulbs **Narcissus cyclamineus**
(yellow) and **Crocus tomasinianus** (lilac).

As **Sycopsis sinensis** needs a sheltered
position with moist, humus-rich soil, in sun
or partial shade, it could be considered for
woodland planting. It is a large shrub with
thick, evergreen lance-shaped leaves and in
late winter and early spring produces petal-
less flowers consisting of tufts of yellow
stamens with red anthers.

Ideal for carpeting the ground around
spring-flowering shrubs in partial shade or
sun are the prostrate periwinkles, **Vinca
minor** cultivars, with starry flowers set
against evergreen foliage. These are blue in
'Bowles' Variety' and white in 'Gertrude
Jekyll'.

A miscellany for the mixed border

There is no shortage of good shrubs for providing spring colour in the mixed border.
Some are best grown against a warm sunny
wall at the back of the border, where they
will enjoy the protected conditions; an
example is **Acacia dealbata**, the mimosa or
silver wattle, which is recommended for
outdoor cultivation only in the mildest

areas. Best grown in well-drained neutral to
acid soil, this large evergreen shrub with
silver-green ferny foliage generally starts to
flower in winter and continues into spring,
with large heads of fluffy yellow globular
flowers.

Coronilla glauca also needs the protection of a warm wall, and well-drained soil. It
is a medium evergreen shrub with glaucous
foliage and heads of yellow pea-shaped
flowers in spring, with further flushes
throughout the year. It makes a good companion for evergreen ceanothus with blue
flowers, creating a striking contrast in shape
and colour.

Crinodendron hookerianum is also
best grown against a wall and is recommended only for the mildest areas. It is also
suitable for woodland planting. Grow it in
moisture-retentive acid soil and partial
shade. It makes a large evergreen shrub
with pendulous, crimson, lantern-shaped
flowers in late spring and early summer, set
against dark green lanceolate leaves.

Although it may be grown in the open,
Piptanthus nepalensis is recommended
for growing beside a warm sunny wall. It is a
large evergreen shrub with trifoliate leaves
and large pea-shaped flowers in bright
yellow, carried in abundance during late
spring. Grow this shrub in any well-drained
soil, including chalky types.

A warm wall getting good sunshine is also
needed by **Rhaphiolepis × delacourii**, its
other requirements being rich soil with very
good drainage. This small shrub has oval,
shiny, evergreen leaves and in spring or
summer carries upright panicles of rose-
pink flowers. The blooms are rose-crimson
in the cultivar 'Coates Crimson' and apple-
blossom pink in 'Spring Song', which
flowers through to the autumn.

Grow the New Zealand Kowhai, **Sophora
tetraptera** 'Grandiflora', against a sunny
south-west wall where in late spring it will

produce yellow, pea-shaped, yet somewhat tubular flowers. This is a large evergreen shrub of spreading habit with pinnate foliage, which will grow in any reasonably rich, well-drained soil.

There are numerous berberis (barberry) for spring flowers, including one named by Hillier's: 'Goldilocks', a large evergreen shrub which bears pendulous clusters of golden-yellow flowers with red stalks, set against shiny deep green foliage. Also a large evergreen shrub, **B. linearifolia** 'Jewel' has conspicuous orange flowers from scarlet buds, set against deep green, shiny leaves. The berberis grow in any well-drained soil and are particularly good on chalk.

The spring-flowering dogwoods or cornus are noted not for their actual flowers, but for the conspicuous bracts that surround them. Some are large shrubs, like the American 'Eddie's White Wonder' with white bracts, while of medium size is **C. florida** 'Cherokee Chief', a cultivar of the North American flowering dogwood, whose bracts are dark rose-red. Neither is recommended for shallow alkaline soils, while both have good autumn leaf colour.

Every border should have a cytisus (broom) or two, which produce sprays of pea-shaped flowers, mainly in late spring. **Cytisus** 'Mrs Norman Henry' is a medium-size shrub bearing small white flowers with deep lilac wings which from a distance appear pink, making a refreshing change from the bright yellow colour of most cytisus. Position some lower-growing shrubs or perennials in front of it to provide interest when the broom is out of flower. Brooms need very well-drained soil and are short lived shrubs.

There are numerous daphnes for spring colour and, as many are highly fragrant, they have been included in the next section. Without scent, though highly desirable, is the small-growing **Daphne genkwa**, ideal for a partially shady spot in the front or middle of a border, where it will produce lilac-blue flowers on bare stems during mid to late spring. It is not easy to establish, but well worth trying, and is suitable for any well-drained soil.

Another small shrub is **Exochorda × macrantha** 'The Bride', which has a low mound-like arching habit and in late spring bears masses of white flowers. Other white-flowered shrubs of somewhat similar habit are **Spiraea × cinerea** 'Grefsheim', a medium-size shrub which blooms early to late spring, and **Spiraea thunbergii**, a small to medium-size shrub performing in early to midspring. All of these are noted for the sheer profusion of their flowers and, of course, look lovely when underplanted with spring bulbs. Try muscari, scillas or chionodoxas with the spiraeas. These three shrubs need a fertile well-drained soil.

Kolkwitzia amabilis 'Pink Cloud' is a lovely cultivar of the beauty bush, with masses of pink foxglove-like flowers in late spring and early summer. This medium-size shrub has peeling brown bark and is effectively combined with purple-leaved cotinus or berberis. Can be grown in any well-drained soil, including chalk.

Related to hamamelis or witch hazel, and requiring lime-free soil, is **Fothergilla major** which bears white flowers shaped like bottle-brushes in the spring before the leaves unfurl, and in autumn boasts brilliant leaf colour. An excellent dual-purpose shrub of medium size, it is much enhanced by a carpet of heaths and heathers around it.

Another shrub with somewhat unusual flowers in **Neillia thibetica**, a medium-size species in the rose family which bears pink tube-shaped flowers in pendulous racemes during late spring and early summer, against a background of quite attractive lobed leaves. Very easily grown in any soil

Cytisus 'Porlock' is a large semi-evergreen shrub which produces masses of scented, yellow, pea-like flowers in racemes during midspring. An excellent companion for blue ceanothus (*Hillier Arboretum, Ampfield, Hampshire*)

provided conditions are not excessively dry, this shrub would make a contrasting companion for philadelphus, which should be in flower at the same time.

Tree paeonias are handsome additions to the mixed or shrub border and could be combined with tall bearded irises, which flower at the same time. For instance, **Paeonia lutea ludlowii** with large golden-yellow saucer-shaped flowers would contrast beautifully with blue irises. This medium-size shrub is easily grown in any soil which is well drained.

Several of the flowering prunus add to the spring scene in a mixed or shrub border. **P. glandulosa** 'Alboplena', a double-flowered cultivar of the Chinese bush cherry, is a small shrub with weeping stems clothed with white blossoms in late spring. **P. g.** 'Rosea Plena' is also a small shrub with double blossoms, but they are bright pink. Both have good autumn leaf colour. **P. tenella** 'Firehill', a cultivar of the dwarf Russian almond, has become very popular in recent years. In midspring this dwarf shrub bears masses of bright rose-red flowers on upright stems.

A much larger prunus, developing into a large shrub or even a small tree, is **P. incisa** 'Praecox', a cultivar of the Fuji cherry. It bears a profusion of small white blossoms from pink-tinted buds in early spring, and is excellent for incorporating into a spring group containing such shrubs as forsythia and ribes.

Making first-class ground cover, or a specimen at the front of a mixed or shrub border, is the evergreen **Prunus laurocerasus** 'Otto Luyken'. This is a cultivar of the cherry laurel, a small dome-shaped shrub with slim, deep green shiny leaves, but noted for its profusion of white flowers in erect racemes during midspring. This shrub is much enhanced by yellow daffodils growing through and around it.

All these prunus thrive in any well-drained fertile soil.

Rubus 'Benenden' (syn. **R.** 'Tridel') is a sophisticated bramble. This is a large shrub for the back of a border, whose spineless stems arch over and carry lobed leaves. In late spring there are large, single, white rose-like flowers, each with a boss of yellow stamens. Easily grown in any well-drained soil.

Salix or willows are synonymous with spring, many of them being the first shrubs to come into flower. They carry catkins (a cluster of petal-less flowers), these being very conspicuous in many species. The following willows make good companions for evergreen shrubs such as cherry laurels and hollies.

SPRING PLANTING SCHEME FOR MIXED BORDER

Willows noted for spring catkins can be effectively planted with evergreen shrubs such as cherry laurels (**Prunus laurocerasus** cultivars) and hollies.

Salix fargesii is a medium to large shrub for the back of a border, whose green catkins emerge from conspicuous buds with or soon after the foliage. The shoots are red-brown. Most attractive during the winter are the polished, red-brown shoots.

Among the small to medium willows for the front or middle of borders, one of the most attractive is **Salix hastata** 'Wehrhahnii', a spreading species. The conspicuous male catkins start silvery-grey then change to yellow. **S. gracilistyla** 'Melanostachys', a large shrub, has very distinctive catkins, which appear in early spring before the leaves. They are almost black, as are the surrounding scales, and the anthers are brick-red but eventually turn yellow. These willows will grow in any soil which does not dry out excessively.

Stachyurus chinensis is a rather aristocratic medium to large shrub which has pendulous but rigid racemes of yellow cup-shaped flowers in late winter and early spring. These contrast beautifully with the shoots, which are purple-brown in colour. Underplant it with equally aristocratic hellebores, especially pale green flowered species like **H. foetidus** (stinking hellebore). Stachyurus is easily grown in any fertile soil.

Staphylea holocarpa 'Rosea' (bladder nut) is particularly distinctive in mid to late spring when it bears pink blossoms in hanging clusters, followed by inflated seed capsules which look, as the name suggests, like bladders. The newly opened leaves are bronze and follow the flowers. This is a large shrub, or even a small tree, suitable for the back of a border and easily grown in any fertile moisture-retentive soil, and in sun or partial shade.

As a change from the hybrids, try species of weigela, which undeservedly are inclined to be neglected, such as **W. middendorffiana**, a small shrub with peeling bark producing pale yellow, campanulate flowers marked with orange during mid to late spring. It is best grown in a sheltered spot with partial shade but is suited to any well-drained soil. Try an under-planting of blue **Muscari armeniacum** (grape hyacinth).

One should not grow unusual shrubs purely for the sake of it – they must have some attractive quality to earn their place in a garden. This certainly applies to our final two subjects for spring. **Xantheroceras sorbifolium** is a large shrub noted for its upright panicles of white flowers, each with a red centre, produced in late spring. The pinnate foliage is quite attractive, too. It can be grown in any fertile soil and is particularly recommended for chalky earth.

Xanthorhiza simplicissima (yellow root) is a small shrub of suckering habit which forms dense thickets of stems. The tiny, star-shaped, purple early to midspring flowers are carried in pendulous panicles and the attractive leaves are pinnate, taking on bronzy purple tints in the autumn. The roots are bright yellow, hence the common name. This shrub must have a moisture-retentive soil and is excellent in clay, but shallow chalk soils are not recommended. It is suitable for shade or partial shade.

SUMMER

There is a huge range of shrubs which flower in the summer. Some of these we consider essential to most gardens, as they epitomise the season.

Some essentials

Deutzias are mainly early summer-flowering shrubs, although some bloom in midsummer, which are generally grown in mixed or shrub borders. They produce a mass of five-petalled flowers and flourish in any fertile soil which has good drainage. Try associating some early summer perennials, such as irises or digitalis, with deutzias. Due to the flower colours, deutzias contrast pleasantly with purple-leaved shrubs such as **Cotinus coggygria** 'Velvet Cloak'.

We recommend the following deutzias: **D. chunii**, a medium shrub with pink and white flowers in midsummer; **D. chunii** 'Pink Charm', medium shrub with pink flowers, raised on the Hillier Nurseries; **D. compacta** 'Lavender Time', medium shrub, lilac, changing to lavender, midsummer flowering, named by Hillier; **D. × elegantissima** 'Rosealind', medium shrub, dark carmine-pink; **D. longifolia** 'Veitchii', medium shrub, blooms tinted with lilac-pink; **D. monbeigii**, medium shrub, small white starry flowers in midsummer; **D. × rosea** 'Carminea', small shrub, flushed with rose-carmine; and **D. setchuenensis corymbiflora**, medium shrub, small star-shaped white flowers, mid to late summer.

Hydrangeas are noted for their long flowering period in summer and autumn. Essentials for their success are moisture retentive soil, as they are rather thirsty shrubs, and, for the large-leaved species

---

PLANTING SCHEME FOR SUMMER FLOWERS

Deutzias are among the essential early summer flowering shrubs. Combine them with perennials which bloom at the same time, like irises and digitalis. Also include a purple-leaved shrub such as **Cotinus coggygria** 'Velvet Cloak'.

PLANTING SCHEME FOR HYDRANGEAS

Excellent companion plants for hydrangeas are hostas (plantain lilies). They like the same conditions (moisture and shade) and provide dramatic contrast with their large, bold foliage and spikes of lily-like flowers.

especially, dappled or partial shade such as that provided by light woodland conditions.

Flowerheads may be dome-shaped or flat. There are two kinds of flowers – tiny rather inconspicuous fertile ones, and larger sterile flowers with showy coloured sepals, referred to as ray florets. The ray florets may be situated on the outside of a head, surrounding the fertile flowers (as in the lace-cap hydrangeas), or the entire flower head may be composed of them (as in the Hortensia group of **Hydrangea macrophylla**).

Excellent companion plants for hydrangeas are hostas (plantain lilies). They like the same conditions and provide dramatic contrast with their large bold foliage and spikes of lily-like flowers.

Too many people plant only the Hortensias but there are many more interesting hydrangeas from which to choose, such as **H. aspera**, a medium shrub with bold foliage and light blue fertile flowers, with mauvy pink or white sterile flowers in early to midsummer. Grow it in partial shade. **H. involucrata** 'Hortensis' is a small shrub with double cream-white flowers which are flushed with pink; it too prefers partial shade.

Hydrangea paniculata 'Kyushu' is a medium-size shrub suitable for a position in full sun, with spikes of cream-white sterile florets. **H. p.** 'Tardiva' makes a large specimen which will also thrive in full sun and, during early and mid autumn, carries heads of white ray florets.

The oak-leaved hydrangea, **H. quercifolia**, has deep-green, deeply lobed leaves, and heads of white flowers from midsummer until the middle of autumn. Also in autumn, the foliage becomes red and purple. This is a bushy medium-size shrub for a position in partial shade.

With equally attractive foliage is **H. sargentiana**. The large leaves of this medium-size shrub have a velvety texture and the shoots are densely covered with hairs. The flower heads are blue with white ray florets and are produced in mid and late summer. Grow this hydrangea in sheltered conditions with partial shade, such as a woodland garden.

Hydrangea villosa also has attractive leaves. These and the stems are covered with hairs. The flower heads are mauve-blue and appear in late summer. This is a medium spreading shrub which thrives best in partial shade.

There are some attractive cultivars of **H. serrata**, which have mainly flat heads of flowers surrounded by ray florets. In 'Bluebird' the fertile flowers are blue and surrounded by showy reddish-purple ray florets. However, if the soil is lime-free they are blue. This is a small shrub, as is 'Preziosa' which has globe-shaped bright pink flower heads which take on a red-purple flush in the autumn. The stems are purple-red and the young foliage is tinted with this colour. Both cultivars should be grown in partial shade.

If you want to grow some of the lace-cap cultivars of **H. macrophylla** there are few finer than 'Blue Deckle', a dwarf, compact, slow-growing shrub with blue flowers; 'Blue Wave', which is of medium size and whose fertile flowers are blue with the ray florets varying from pink to blue according to the soil pH (blue in acid soils); 'Geoffrey

Chadbund', a small shrub with red fertile flowers and deep red ray florets; and 'Miranda', a dwarf shrub with deep blue flowers on acid soils. All of these need positions in partial shade.

Border miscellany

Here we consider a wide range of shrubs of diverse habit which are excellent candidates for mixed or shrub borders. Some are common and need little introduction, while others are classed as unusual but deserve to become better known.

Abelia × grandiflora is one of the longest-flowering shrubs, producing its pink and white tubular blooms non-stop from midsummer to early autumn, so it can take pride of place in a border. This small to medium shrub is semi-evergreen and grows in any fertile well-drained soil. A good companion is a purple leaved **Cotinus coggygria**.

One does not immediately think of horse chestnuts for summer colour in shrub borders, but there are actually several shrubby kinds, with upright panicles of flowers and bold compound palmate leaves, like **Aesculus parviflora**, a medium-size shrub bearing white flowers with red anthers in mid to late summer. The foliage becomes yellow in autumn. **A. × mutabilis** 'Induta' is a large shrub or small tree with apricot-coloured flowers in early summer. The foliage is very handsome. **A. pavia** 'Atrosanguinea' (red buckeye) is of similar stature, with dark crimson flowers in early summer set against bold foliage. These aesculus would also make fine specimens, say in a lawn, or could be used as focal points in a garden.

Caragana arborescens 'Lorbergii' is a large, very tough shrub, succeeding in very exposed positions and any well-drained soil. It has compound leaves and yellow pea flowers in early summer, and would make a good specimen in a lawn or border.

An excellent small shrub for the front of a border, perhaps in association with shrub roses, is **Caryopteris × clandonensis** 'Heavenly Blue' which gives a long display of deep blue tubular flowers in late summer and autumn set against lanceolate grey-green foliage. It grows in any well-drained soil and is especially recommended for chalky conditions.

A rather similar small shrub, needing the same conditions, is **Ceratostigma willmottianum** with deep blue flowers from midsummer until autumn, when the leaves take on red shades. Another excellent blue-flowered shrub is the deciduous **Ceanothus** 'Topaz', of medium size with light blue flowers (also see ceanothus under the Spring section, this chapter).

The easily grown **Chionanthus virginicus** (North American fringe tree) is a large shrub for any fertile, well-drained yet moisture-retentive soil, whose abundant midsummer flowers have white strap-shaped petals.

Several cornus (see Spring, this chapter) flower in the summer. **C. kousa** is a large shrub for the back of a border or for use as a lawn specimen, with white bracts in early summer followed by red strawberry-like fruits; **C. k. chinensis** is somewhat larger in all its parts; and **C.** 'Norman Hadden' is a superb large semi-evergreen shrub or small tree, with white flowers over a long period in early summer which later turn pink, followed by red strawberry-like fruits. All are suitable for any well-drained soil, other than shallow chalk.

Very different in habit, except for the white bracts, is **Cornus canadensis**, a prostrate ground-cover shrub which thrives in a semi-shaded position, such as under larger shrubs or on the woodland edge. It is ideal for drifting around rhododendrons in lime-free soil.

Cornus 'Norman Hadden' is a large semi-evergreen shrub with white flowers in early summer, followed by red strawberry-like fruits (*Hillier Arboretum, Ampfield, Hampshire*)

Best grown against a warm south-facing wall for protection, or in woodland, is **Desfontainia spinosa**, a medium-size evergreen shrub with holly-like leaves and, in late summer, scarlet, yellow-tipped tubular flowers. It is easily grown given a lime-free soil and partial shade.

Among the longest-flowering shrubs for summer are the hardy fuchsias. They bloom in summer and autumn, grow in any well-drained soil and are excellent for planting near the sea. Combine them with, say, blue-flowered shrubs like caryopteris and ceratostigma, and silver or grey-leaved perennials such as artemisias. **Fuchsia** 'Lady Thumb' is a dwarf shrub with carmine and white flowers; **F.** 'Tom Thumb' is of similar

PLANTING SCHEME WITH HARDY FUCHSIAS

The summer and autumn-flowering hardy fuchsias combine beautifully with blue-flowered shrubs like caryopteris and ceratostigma, and silver or grey-leaved perennials such as artemisias.

dimensions, with scarlet and violet flowers; **F. magellanica** 'Versicolor' is a small shrub noted for its grey-green and cream variegated foliage and red flowers; and **F.** 'Prosperity' is also a small shrub but with large double flowers in white and deep pink.

With an equally long flowering period are the hebes or shrubby veronicas from New Zealand, which also combine well with hardy fuchsias. All are evergreen and grow in any well-drained soil. Many are not very hardy and may not survive severe winters inland, but they stand more chance in mild coastal gardens. Among the most desirable are **H.** 'Blue Clouds', a small shrub with blue flowers from early summer until the end of the year; **H. youngii** (syn. 'Carl Teschner'), a dwarf shrub for ground cover with violet and white blooms in early and midsummer; **H. hulkeana**, a small shrub with pale lilac-blue flowers in late spring and early summer; **H. macrantha**, a dwarf shrub which needs protection in colder areas, with large white star-shaped flowers; **H.** 'Marjorie', one of the hardiest types, a small shrub with violet and white flowers from midsummer to early autumn; **H. rakaiensis**, a dwarf shrub bearing white flowers in midsummer; **H.** 'Mrs Winder', a medium shrub of moderate hardiness, its flowers bright blue, foliage purple; and **H.** 'Spender's Seedling', a small shrub with masses of white flowers in early to late summer.

Hibiscus provide welcome colour in late summer and early autumn with their large, trumpet-shaped flowers and deserve a place in every border, thriving in any well-drained fertile soil. We recommend the **H. syriacus** cultivars 'Blue Bird', single flowers in violet-blue; 'Diana', single, pure white; and 'Pink Giant' with large single, deep pink flowers. All make medium-size shrubs and are much enhanced when combined with silver foliage shrubs or perennials.

Hoherias are large shrubs with an abundance of white flowers in summer but in cold areas they need warm-wall protection. Otherwise they are easily grown in any well-drained fertile soil and look particularly beautiful when combined with red or pink shrub roses. **H. lyalli** blooms in midsummer and bears attractive heart-shaped silver-grey leaves, while **H. sexstylosa** has evergreen grey-green foliage and is best grown in partial shade.

Hypericums are good value on account of their long season of yellow cup-shaped blooms, which combine well with shrubs bearing blue flowers, such as various hebes or caryopteris. **H. kouytchense** is a small semi-evergreen shrub with golden-yellow flowers from early summer to mid autumn, followed by bright red seed pods; **H. × moserianum** is a dwarf shrub often used for ground cover which blooms in the same period, the flowers having red anthers; and **H.** 'Rowallane' is a medium semi-evergreen shrub which needs protection in cold areas, with large golden-yellow blooms. All thrive in any well-drained soil.

Everyone, it seems, has fallen for **Lavatera thuringiaca** 'Barnsley', a medium-size evergreen tree mallow with white hollyhock-like flowers each with a pink centre, which age to pink. Blooms are produced all summer and growth is extremely vigorous. Tends to revert, so cut out branches producing pink flowers. Suited to any well-drained soil.

Leycesteria formosa, the flowering nutmeg, although very common is nevertheless worthy of the space it takes up in a border, and it grows in any fertile, moist, yet well-drained soil. From early summer to early autumn it produces pendulous panicles of white flowers surrounded by striking wine red bracts. These are followed in autumn by red-purple berries. The green stems are quite conspicuous in winter. Try combining it with a purple-leaved berberis or cotinus.

The privets are inclined to be neglected, possibly because the common hedging kinds, which are rather boring, are seen in so many gardens. Yet numerous species are very attractive when in flower and make handsome additions to the shrub or mixed border. Try the medium-size **L. quihoui**, one of the best for flowers, which has large panicles of white blooms in late summer and early autumn.

Phygelius, although frost-hardy, need to be planted in sheltered positions where they will produce their attractive tubular flowers in late summer and autumn. Stems may be cut down to the ground by frosts and should be pruned back in spring. The soil should be fertile, well-drained yet moisture-retentive. **P. aequalis** 'Yellow Trumpet', named by Hillier, is one of the most spectacular, a small shrub with yellow flowers. **Phygelius × rectus** cultivars introduced by Hillier include 'Devil's Tears', bright orange-red; 'Moonraker', light cream-yellow; 'Pink Elf', dwarf, light pink; 'Salmon Leap', salmon pink; and 'Winchester Fanfare', dwarf, dusky red, yellow inside. All these are small shrubs, unless otherwise stated.

Although it takes up quite a lot of space with its spreading branches, **Sorbaria aitchisonii** is well worth considering for the shrub or mixed border, or as an elegant poolside shrub. Of medium size, it has attractive pinnate foliage, reddish young stems, and in mid to late summer bears large panicles of white flowers, like those of spiraea. It grows best in fertile, moisture-retentive soil.

Coming to spiraeas, **S. nipponica tosaensis** (syn. **S.n.** 'Snowmound') is one of the best kinds for flowering in early summer, forming a small dense mound and covering itself with white blooms.

Weigelas for early-summer colour (see also Spring, this chapter) include **W. hortensis** 'Nivea', a medium white-flowered shrub which could be effectively under-planted with **Ajuga reptans** 'Burgundy Glow', a ground-cover perennial with purple foliage.

Hot and dry

Many summer-flowering shrubs relish hot and dry situations – in other words, sheltered positions in full sun with extremely well-drained soil which is inclined to dry out. Some are on the tender side so are more likely to flourish in such places than in other parts of the garden. Here one could create a layout which includes Mediterranean-climate plants.

The evergreen summer-flowering cistus or sun roses, like **C. × pulverulentus**, are ideally suited to hot dry areas and in warm weather give off a pleasant scent from their foliage

93

The evergreen callistemons, whose bottle-brush-like flowers give the shrub its common name, immediately come to mind, including **C. citrinus** 'Splendens' with showy scarlet flowers, and the light yellow **C. salignus** which is hardier than other species. Both are medium-size shrubs.

The evergreen cistus or sun roses (which really do come from the Mediterranean region) are ideally suited to hot dry areas and in warm weather give off a pleasant scent from their foliage. Most do not tolerate very hard frosts but thrive in mild maritime areas and grow well in alkaline conditions. There are many from which to choose, like **C. × aguilari** 'Maculatus', small shrub with white, crimson-blotched flowers; **C. × corbariensis**, small shrub with white blooms from crimson buds, hardy; **C.** 'Peggy Sammons', medium shrub bearing light pink blooms, grey-green foliage; **C. × pulverulentus**, dwarf shrub, cerise; **C.** 'Silver Pink', small shrub, silvery pink, extremely hardy; and **C. × skanbergii**, small shrub, pink flowers.

Another plant from the Mediterranean region is **Dorycnium hirsutum**, a dwarf sub-shrub covered with silvery hairs and bearing white, pink-flushed pea flowers in late summer and autumn followed by red-brown seed pods. The stems die down each autumn.

The escallonias like warm, sunny, well-drained conditions. Some are not fully hardy although they thrive in mild coastal areas, where they are very wind resistant, and they grow well in chalky soils. All have evergreen glossy foliage and produce masses of five-petalled flowers during summer and into autumn. Try the following: **E.** 'Apple Blossom', medium shrub, pink and white blooms; **E. rubra** 'Crimson Spire' (syn. **E.** 'Crimson Spire'), medium, crimson; **E.** 'Donard Beauty', medium, rose-red; **E.** 'Donard Seedling', medium, white, from

Genista aetnensis, the Mount Etna broom, revels in hot dry conditions and in midsummer produces masses of yellow, pea-like flowers. It is a large slender shrub (*Coldham, Kent*)

pink buds; **E.** 'Iveyi', large shrub, needs protection, white, autumn; **E.** 'Langleyensis', medium, rose-pink; and **E. rubra** 'Woodside', small spreading shrub, crimson.

Many genistas, with their yellow pea-like flowers, revel in hot dry conditions and are best grown in acid or neutral soils, although they will tolerate alkaline conditions. **Genista aetnensis**, the Mount Etna broom, a large slender shrub, performs in mid summer, but starting a few weeks before is **G. tenera** 'Golden Shower', also a large shrub but with arching branches. Try growing genistas with cistus for contrast in shape and colour.

From Australia and Tasmania are the

grevilleas, which must be grown in acid soils and given protection in colder areas. They have small honeysuckle-like flowers. These are crimson in **G. rosmarinifolia**, set against dark green rosemary-like foliage, and yellow in **G. juniperina sulphurea**, which has similar but bright green foliage. Both are medium-size evergreen shrubs.

× **Halimiocistus wintonensis (Halimium × Cistus)** is something like a cistus, a dwarf evergreen shrub needing protection in exposed areas and bearing white flowers marked with yellow and maroon, which are set against a background of grey foliage. It originated in the Hillier Nurseries. The cultivar 'Merrist Wood Cream' has light yellow flowers with a maroon centre, and attractive grey leaves. Flowering period is early summer. **Halimium ocymoides**, one of the parents, is a dwarf evergreen shrub from southern Europe with bright yellow flowers, each petal being marked at the base with dark brown, set against grey foliage.

Although very hardy, since it comes from Mongolia, **Hedysarum multijugum** is nevertheless at home in hot dry conditions. The pinnate foliage of this small shrub forms a lacy background for the red-purple pea-shaped flowers, which are carried in long racemes all through the summer.

Also with pinnate foliage is **Indigofera heterantha** (syn. **I. gerardiana**), a small shrub which bears racemes of showy purple-pink flowers all summer and well into autumn.

The evergreen Australasian daisy bushes revel in hot dry conditions, including chalky soils, and tolerate windy sites, particularly in seaside areas. They produce daisy-shaped, generally white flowers in profusion. **Olearia × scilloniensis** is a compact medium-size shrub with grey foliage, which needs protection in exposed areas, as does **O. phlogopappa** 'Splendens', a small species which bears little flowers resembling

Michaelmas daisies, in shades of blue, lavender or pink.

From the Mediterranean region is **Ononis fruticosa**, whose leaves are composed of three leaflets and which produces clusters of showy, rose-pink pea-shaped flowers all summer long. It grows well in chalky soils, although it is adaptable.

The shrubby potentillas or cinquefoils revel in well-drained soils and very sunny conditions, and combine well with cistus, as there is good contrast in flower and foliage shape and colour. The potentillas, with single-rose-like blooms, have an extremely long flowering period and will still be in bloom when the cistus are over – indeed the display continues well into autumn. Of the many available, we can recommend **P. arbuscula** 'Beesii', dwarf, deep yellow, silvery leaves; **P. dahurica** 'Abbotswood', dwarf, white, deep green foliage; **P. dahurica** 'Manchu', dwarf ground-cover shrub, white, grey foliage; **P.** 'Eastleigh Cream', dwarf, cream, Hillier-produced hybrid; **P.** 'Elizabeth', small shrub, large canary-yellow flowers, raised on the Hillier Nurseries; **P.** 'Goldfinger', small shrub, rich yellow; **P.** 'Katherine Dykes', medium shrub, large yellow flowers; **P.** 'Longacre', dwarf, for ground cover, large bright yellow flowers; **P.** 'Primrose Beauty', small shrub, primrose-yellow; **P.** 'Tangerine', dwarf, light copper-yellow; and **P.** 'Vilmoriniana', medium shrub, cream, silvery foliage.

Robinia kelseyi is a large shrub or small tree, useful for creating height in planting schemes, with attractive pinnate foliage and pea-shaped mauve-pink flowers in early summer, followed by bristly seed pods. The branches are rather brittle.

Many of the shrubby salvias are on the tender side and can be grown outside only in mild areas. They produce their tubular two-lipped flowers in whorls during late summer and early autumn. **S. involucrata**

'Bethellii' is a medium shrub with magenta-crimson blooms against a background of bold heart-shaped foliage; and **S. microphylla neurepia** (syn. **S. neurepia**) is a small shrub with rose-red flowers. Neither should be grown in exposed positions without some protection.

An essential shrub for a hot dry position is **Spartium junceum**, the Spanish broom, a medium-size shrub from the Mediterranean region with yellow pea-shaped flowers on erect, green rush-like stems throughout the summer and into autumn. Excellent for coastal planting, it makes a fine centrepiece for a group of sun-loving shrubs.

The fuchsia-like **Zauschneria californica** (Californian fuchsia) is a dwarf sub-shrub with loose spikes of red and scarlet tubular flowers in late summer and autumn, and grey-green foliage. It needs protection in exposed areas.

AUTUMN

We have already seen that many summer-flowering shrubs continue their display into autumn, but there are some which bloom only during that season. An example is **Hibiscus sinosyriacus** 'Autumn Surprise', a medium-size shrub with large white trumpet-shaped flowers with cerise feathering. Grow it in any well-drained soil.

Lespedeza thunbergii (bush clover) is a small shrub suited to partial shade, with trifoliate leaves and, in early autumn, red-purple pea-shaped flowers borne in large panicles on arching stems.

WINTER

We cannot understand why so many gardens are devoid of flowers in winter, especially after Christmas, for there is no shortage of shrubs which bloom during that season. Many are scented and so will be found under that section.

The hamamelis or witch hazels are essen-

PLANTING SCHEME FOR WINTER FLOWERS

Combine a witch hazel or hamamelis with winter-flowering rhododendrons and camellias. The foliage of large rhododendrons will provide a suitable background for the witch hazel's flowers.

---

tial winter-flowering shrubs, producing a profusion of spidery flowers with strap-shaped petals on the bare branches. Hamamelis are superb in the woodland garden, where they enjoy the dappled shade and could be combined, perhaps, with winter-flowering rhododendrons and camellias because they need a dark background. Of course, similar groups could also be created in a shrub or mixed border. Hamamelis grow best in fertile, leafy soil with good drainage, ideally acid or neutral, although soil over chalk is acceptable provided it is deep.

Most hamamelis are fragrant and will be found under that heading, but not so the **H. × intermedia** cultivars 'Diane', with copper-red flowers, and 'Jelena', whose yellow blooms are heavily flushed with copper-red. Both of these large shrubs have striking autumn leaf colour.

Another shrub which should be in every garden is the evergreen **Viburnum tinus** (laurustinus). Indeed, the deep green shiny leaves would make a good background for hamamelis. It produces flat heads of small white flowers between late autumn and early spring, these being followed by metallic blue berries. Laurustinus is a large shrub, thriving in any well-drained soil, and is especially recommended for seaside gardens. We suggest the cultivars 'Eve Price' whose pink-tinted flowers emerge from red buds, and 'Gwenllian' with pink and white flowers. Both are medium-size shrubs.

FRAGRANT FLOWERING SHRUBS

The flowering shrubs we have recommended so far have no fragrance (or at best only very slight, almost unnoticeable scent), but there are many with strong perfume. This is an essential element in gardens as far as most people are concerned.

Hamamelis or witch hazels are essential winter-flowering shrubs, superb in a woodland garden. **H. × intermedia** 'Jelena' makes a change from the normal yellow cultivars

To get the best from fragrant shrubs, grow them in sheltered positions so that the scent lingers on the air instead of being blown away by the wind. And try to place the

97

Corylopsis are popular spring-flowering shrubs with fragrant flowers. This species is **C. veitchiana**, a large shrub whose yellow flowers have conspicuous brick-red anthers. They are produced in large racemes (*Savill Gardens, The Great Park, Windsor, Berkshire*)

plants where they are easily accessible, such as alongside a path, by a summerhouse or other sitting area, or near the house.

Some of the genera included here have already been discussed (see Shrubs recommended for flowers, this chapter) in which case they are generally cross-referenced to avoid repetition regarding cultural requirements and the like.

SPRING

One of the most popular fragrant spring shrubs is **Choisya ternata** (Mexican orange blossom), a medium-size evergreen shrub with clusters of white, sweetly scented orange-blossom-like flowers continuing into early sumer, and handsome,

shiny, deep green aromatic foliage. Suitable for sun or shade, and any fertile well-drained soil. New on the scene is the Hillier introduction **Choisya** 'Aztec Pearl', a small shrub with deeply cut aromatic evergreen foliage, and white almond-scented flowers opening from pink buds in spring and late summer. It needs full sun.

Another very popular shrub is **Corylopsis pauciflora**, a small species with yellow flowers which smell of cowslips in early spring. It must be grown in acid soil and you could try planting cultivars of **Erica carnea** around it, especially those which continue flowering into spring. This shrub is not very attractive after flowering, so do not give it a very prominent position.

Cytisus 'Porlock' is a large semi-evergreen shrub which thrives in sun and well-drained soils, producing scented, yellow, pea-shaped flowers in racemes during midspring. It must have protection in cold exposed areas and is an excellent companion for the blue evergreen ceanothus.

There are several daphnes to scent the
spring garden including **D. × burkwoodii**,
a small semi-evergreen shrub with clusters
of small light pink flowers in late spring; **D.
mezereum**, a small shrub (prone to virus)
with purple-red flowers in early spring
(especially good in chalky soils), and its
cultivars 'Alba' (white) and 'Rosea' (rose
pink); and **D. odora** 'Aureomarginata', a
small evergreen shrub with purple-pink
flowers in early spring and cream-edged
leaves. Try underplanting **Daphne mezer-**

There are several daphnes to scent the spring
garden including **D. mezereum**, a small shrub
which is especially good for chalky soils. It has
several equally desirable cultivars (*Hillier
Arboretum, Ampfield, Hampshire*)

eum with hellebores, especially green-
flowered species.

Deserving to be more widely planted is
the weigela-like **Dipelta floribunda**, with
masses of light pink funnel-shaped flowers
each with a conspicuous yellow throat. It

blooms in late spring, giving off a delightful fragrance. It is a large shrub for the back of a shrub or mixed border, thriving in fertile well-drained soil.

Several magnolias for the shrub or mixed border have fragrant flowers (see also Shrubs recommended for flowers, this chapter). With a very powerful scent from its deep purple flowers is **M. liliiflora** 'Nigra', a medium shrub which needs acid to neutral soil and an open aspect, making a good lawn specimen. Try also **M. × loebneri** 'Leonard Messel', a large adaptable shrub for full sun, with starry lilac-pink flowers in midspring; and **M. stellata** 'Water Lily', a medium shrub with starry white flowers in early to midspring, suitable for limey soil. Try underplanting the latter with dwarf bulbs, such as yellow cyclamineus hybrid daffodils and blue scillas.

Osmanthus delavayi is a medium evergreen shrub which emits a powerful fragrance from its small, white, jasmine-like flowers in midspring, and the bi-generic hybrid **Osmanthus × burkwoodii**, also a medium-size evergreen shrub, has white, tubular, equally fragrant blossoms from mid to late spring. Both are easily grown in any fertile, well-drained soil.

Another evergreen osmanthus producing small but very fragrant white flowers in spring, is **O. decorus** (syn. **Phillyrea decora**), a very tough medium-size shrub with handsome shiny foliage, thriving in any well-drained soil. It makes a good background for smaller flowering shrubs.

Be careful when savouring the sweetly scented, orange-blossom-like white flowers of **Poncirus trifoliata** (Japanese bitter orange), as it has potentially dangerous spines. These are green, the same colour as the stems. The blooms are followed by tiny 'oranges'. It makes an impenetrable hedge and thrives in any fertile, well-drained soil.

Ribes odoratum, the buffalo currant, is

FRAGRANT PLANTING SCHEME

Rosemaries, with their aromatic evergreen foliage and blue flowers in spring, make excellent companions for red or pink, fragrant shrub roses, and provide interest when the roses are out of flower.

---

one of the more distinctive medium-size currants (see also Shrubs recommended for flowers, this chapter), with pendulous deep yellow clove-scented flowers and glossy foliage which takes on showy tints in autumn.

Everyone loves rosemaries for their aromatic evergreen foliage and blue flowers in spring. As they revel in hot dry conditions they are ideal for a garden devoted to Mediterranean-climate plants – indeed, the rosemaries come from southern Europe. **R. officinalis** 'Prostratus' (syn. **R. lavandulaceus**) is a prostrate shrub which must be protected in exposed positions. The various other cultivars of the common rosemary, **R. officinalis**, are variable in habit. 'Miss Jessop's Upright' (syn. 'Fastigiatus') is a medium shrub of upright habit; 'Severn Sea' is a dwarf arching shrub and 'Tuscan Blue', also dwarf, has broader leaves than the species. Rosemaries make excellent companions for red or pink shrub roses and provide interest when the roses are out of flower.

Flowering in late spring and early summer, the lilacs are among the best-loved fragrant shrubs. However, it is a pity that most are so dull after blooming, particularly the cultivars of the common lilac, **Syringa vulgaris**. It is a good idea to grow large-flowered clematis through mature lilacs for summer colour, or the late summer/autumn-flowering **Clematis viticella** cultivars. Also, bear in mind that lilacs are space-consuming shrubs and take a lot of moisture from the ground in summer. They grow in any well-drained soil and are good on chalk.

Some of the more distinctive lilacs include **Syringa × josiflexa** 'Bellicent', a large shrub with huge panicles of rose-pink flowers; **S. × laciniata**, a small shrub with pinnately cut foliage and lilac blossoms in loose panicles; **S. microphylla** 'Superba', a medium shrub with rose-pink flowers in late spring, with further flushes until mid autumn; **S. × persica** (Persian lilac), a medium shrub with lilac flowers, or white in the cultivar 'Alba'; **S. sweginzowii** 'Superba', a medium shrub offering palest pink flowers in long open panicles; and **S. meyeri** 'Palibin' (syn. **S. velutina**) (Korean lilac), a small to medium shrub with pale lilac or lilac-pink flowers set against a background of deep green velvety foliage, one of the best lilacs for small gardens.

An ideal shrub for hot dry places with acid soils, including coastal gardens, is **Ulex europaeus** 'Plenus', a double-flowered form of the common gorse. It produces a mass of bright yellow flowers on small, very spiny, evergreen bushes. It also looks good in association with heaths and heathers, birches and pines.

Several spring-flowering viburnums (see also Shrubs recommended for flowers, Spring, this chapter) have fragrant blooms, including **V. × burkwoodii** 'Anne Russell', a medium evergreen shrub with heads of white flowers emerging from pink buds; **V. carlesii** 'Diana', another medium shrub but with flower buds opening red and turning to pink, late spring; **V. × juddii**, a medium shrub whose pink-flushed flowers in mid to late spring are sweetly scented; and **V. × burkwoodii** 'Park Farm Hybrid', a strongly growing medium-size evergreen shrub with white flowers from pink buds in mid to late spring. All of these viburnums are for the shrub or mixed border and, for striking contrast in leaf and flower shape and colour,

underplant them extravagantly with bergenias.

SUMMER

Early summer in English gardens is not complete without mock orange (philadelphus). These are among the most highly fragrant shrubs available, and for that quality alone are dearly loved. They bear white four-petalled flowers in profusion. As with many lilacs, it is such a pity that these popular shrubs are so insipid when their flower display is over. But, as with lilacs, use the 'clematis treatment' and also plant some tallish, later summer-flowering perennials in front of them to ensure continued interest, such as campanulas, echinops, eryngiums and scabious. If you want to create a pleasing group purely for early summer, then plant herbaceous paeonias and tall bearded irises with the philadelphus. Mock oranges are easily grown in any well-drained soil and thrive in chalky conditions.

The following philadelphus are especially recommended: **P.** 'Beauclerk', medium shrub, cerise-centred flowers; **P.** 'Belle Etoile', medium, large blooms with maroon centres; **P. delavayi calvescens,** large vigorous shrub, big leaves, large flowers in substantial trusses, each with a purple calyx; **P.** 'Manteau d'Hermine', dwarf compact shrub, double cream-white flowers; **P. microphyllus**, small shrub, tiny leaves and

---

PLANTING SCHEME FEATURING PHILADELPHUS

The highly fragrant shrub philadelphus, or mock orange, produces its white blooms in early summer. Combine it with contrasting perennials which flower at the same time, particularly herbaceous paeonias and tall bearded irises.

flowers, the best for small gardens; and **P.** 'Sybille', small shrub, arching habit, flowers stained purple.

Having covered the essential fragrant shrubs for summer, let us now consider others for this season, including a few unusual kinds. Valued for its late summer and autumn flowers is **Clerodendrum bungei**, which produces domed heads of small rose-red blossoms. This medium-size suckering shrub with bold heart-shaped leaves is suitable for a position in partial shade and for any well-drained soil.

Clethra alnifolia 'Rosea', a cultivar of the sweet pepper bush, produces sweetly scented, white, pink-tinted bell-shaped flowers in late summer. This medium-size shrub needs acid, humus-rich, moisture-retentive soil in partial shade, and is therefore ideal for woodland gardens. **C. barbinervis**, of similar size and needing the same conditions, has white flowers in long racemes and red and yellow autumn leaf tints.

Very spiny is **Colletia hystrix** 'Rosea', so be careful when sniffing the fragrance of its small tubular flowers. These develop from pink buds in late summer and autumn. A medium-size, almost leafless shrub, needing a sheltered position in full sun and suitable for any well-drained soil, it would be at home in the hot, dry garden.

Best grown against a high sunny wall is **Cytisus battandieri** 'Yellow Tail', a large shrub from the Hillier Nurseries with long spikes of yellow pineapple-scented pea flowers in midsummer, and laburnum-like silky-grey leaves. Any well-drained soil is suitable. Try associating this cytisus with red climbing roses for striking contrast in colour and form.

Several hoherias have already been recommended (see Shrubs recommended for flowers, Summer, Border miscellany, this chapter), but **H. glabrata** must be included too, for the sake of its fragrant white flowers borne in profusion during early and mid summer. Provide a position in full sun for this large shrub.

Itea ilicifolia is an unusual evergreen shrub with handsome shiny holly-like leaves and, in late summer, long thin catkin-like racemes of tiny green-white, fragrant flowers. This medium-size shrub flourishes in partial shade and any well-drained soil, provided it is not too dry.

Old English lavender is among the best-loved aromatic shrubs but some of the other species also deserve garden space, including **Lavandula stoechas**, the French lavender, a dwarf evergreen shrub with deep purple flowers in summer and narrow foliage. Needing very sunny well-drained conditions, this species is ideal for the garden devoted to Mediterranean-climate plants (it does in fact originate from that region).

A rather unusual shrub is **Lomatia myricoides**, a medium-size evergreen shrub with narrow lanceolate foliage and highly fragrant white flowers, consisting of four twisted petals, in midsummer. The foliage is good for flower decorations. Grow it in moisture-retentive acid soil and partial shade. This Australian shrub is not recommended for outdoor cultivation in the coldest parts of the country.

One of the shrubby honeysuckles, **Lonicera syringantha**, with small sea-green leaves, has very fragrant flowers. They are tubular, lilac in colour, and produced in early summer on a small bush. This plant is suited to any well-drained fertile soil.

We have already discussed magnolias (see Shrubs recommended for flowers, Spring, this chapter) but now we come to the fragrant kinds, which include **M. sinensis**, a large shrub for a sunny position whose pendulous, cup-shaped, white flowers with red stamens smell of lemons. They appear in early summer. **M. × thompsoniana** is a large spreading shrub which needs plenty of sun. At intervals throughout summer it bears large, beautifully scented, creamy globular flowers, even when young.

The genus **Olearia** (already discussed under Shrubs recommended for flowers, Summer, Hot and dry, this chapter) has some scented species including **O. avicenniifolia**, a medium-size evergreen shrub with white daisy-type flowers in late summer and early autumn, with leaves that have white undersides. This makes a good hedge.

Ozothamnus rosmarinifolius (Helichrysum rosmarinifolium) has scented white flowers from conspicuous red buds in early summer, narrow deep green leaves and white woolly stems. This medium-size Australian evergreen is suited to hot dry places and recommended only for the mildest areas.

Romneya coulteri (tree poppy) is a truly spectacular plant, sporting large, white, fragrant poppy-like flowers, with a boss of yellow stamens, carried singly from midsummer to midautumn. It is a small to medium-size sub-shrub with deeply cut grey foliage, which is also attractive. Best grown in well-drained deep soil, it is difficult to establish but when settled often spreads rapidly. It does not take kindly to disturbance. In very cold areas you should protect the roots from frost during winter.

The flowers show up best against a background of dark green foliage. For contrast, try companion plants with bold spikes of flowers, such as delphiniums or verbascums.

For the woodland garden, where it enjoys lime-free moisture-retentive humus-rich soil and partial shade, we recommend **Zenobia pulverulenta**, a fairly unusual medium semi-evergreen shrub of open

Mahonias start flowering in autumn and continue into winter. These evergreens are among the aristocrats of garden shrubs, sporting fragrant yellow flowers. **Mahonia** 'Charity' is shown here, a medium upright-growing shrub (*Hillier Arboretum, Ampfield, Hampshire*)

habit. It displays hanging, white, bell-shaped flowers, which smell of aniseed, in early and midsummer and looks lovely underplanted with green or bluish-leaved hostas.

AUTUMN

We can include mahonias in autumn because some start flowering then, but remember that they continue into winter and indeed many are at their best during that season. These evergreens are among the aristocrats of garden shrubs. They are handsome in all their parts – bold pinnate foliage and yellow, sweetly fragrant flowers which are carried in various bold forma-

AUTUMN AND WINTER PLANTING SCHEME FEATURING MAHONIAS

Combine winter-flowering mahonias with coloured-stemmed dogwoods – **Cornus alba** cultivars and **C. stolonifera** 'Flaviramea' – together with **Rubus cockburnianus** and **Prunus subhirtella** 'Autumnalis'.

tions. Mahonias are ideally suited to the shrub or mixed border and look superb on the edge of a woodland garden. They flourish in any well-drained fertile soil, including alkaline conditions.

One can create some wonderful groups featuring mahonias. For instance, try combining them with coloured-stemmed dogwoods – **Cornus alba** cultivars and **C. stolonifera** 'Flaviramea' – together with **Rubus cockburnianus** and **Prunus subhirtella** 'Autumnalis' (the winter-

flowering cherry), to provide interest throughout autumn and winter.

We recommend the following mahonias: **M. × media** 'Buckland', with long leaves and long drooping flower racemes; **M. japonica**, which is very popular and has superb dark green foliage with lemon-yellow flowers in long dangling racemes, starting after Christmas; **M. × media** 'Lionel Fortescue', bearing upright racemes of bright yellow blooms, starting in late autumn; and **M. × media** 'Winter Sun', with dense upright flower racemes. All are medium-size shrubs.

Osmanthus armatus is a large holly-like evergreen shrub which produces small, sweetly fragrant white flowers in autumn. The thick leaves have spiny edges. Suitable for any well-drained fertile soil and a position in sun or shade.

Vitex agnus-castus (chaste tree) is a medium-size shrub with aromatic compound foliage, woolly grey shoots and scented violet flowers carried in slim racemes during early and mid autumn. The form 'Silver Spire' has white flowers. Ideally it should be grown against a wall which receives full sun, and you should ensure very well-drained soil. Of Mediterranean origin, it is a suitable candidate for the hot, dry garden.

WINTER

Some winter-flowering shrubs do not have very conspicuous blossoms but often make up for this with intense fragrance. This is certainly true of the shrubby honeysuckles, **Lonicera × purpusii** 'Winter Beauty' (a cross made by one of Hillier's foremen) and **Lonicera setifera**. Both are medium-size shrubs, the former being semi-evergreen

The winter flowers of **Chimonanthus praecox** 'Grandiflorus' (winter sweet) emit a very honeyed scent. Best grown against a sunny wall

Daphnes with fragrant winter flowers include **D. bholua** 'Jacqueline Postill', a medium-size evergreen raised by Hillier, which looks superb with an underplanting of snowdrops

with a long succession of creamy flowers. **L. setifera** has pink and white tubular flowers in winter and early spring. Both are ideal for winter groups of shrubs but need a dark background if the flowers are to show up. Any well-drained soil is suitable.

Better known is **Chimonanthus praecox** 'Grandiflorus' (winter sweet), whose yellow flowers with red centres have a waxy texture and emit a very sweet scent. This medium-size shrub is best grown against a wall which receives plenty of sun. Any soil, including chalk, is suitable, provided drainage is good. It is a boring shrub when out of flower so, for spring interest, grow a slender climber through it such as the violet-blue **Clematis alpina**, and make sure the shrub is partly masked by summer-flowering perennials. Also worth growing is **C. p.** 'Luteus', which is later coming into flower.

Daphnes with fragrant winter flowers are **D. bholua** 'Gurkha', a medium shrub with purple-rose flowers throughout winter, named by Hillier's, and **D. b.** 'Jacqueline Postill', a medium-size evergreen with

witch hazels, with sweetly fragrant light yellow flowers and yellow autumn foliage. It eventually makes a large specimen and its flowers show up best against a background of dark evergreen shrubs or conifers.

Although they produce only small white flowers in late winter, the sarcococcas (Christmas box) emit a powerful fragrance which can be detected from some distance. Generally these small, shiny-leaved evergreens are planted in woodland gardens where they enjoy the partial shade, but they would also be candidates for the front of a shrub or mixed border. Any well-drained soil, including chalk, is suitable.

We recommend **S. confusa**, with a spreading habit of growth and long slim leaves, and **S. hookerana digyna** with narrow lanceolate leaves. Black berries follow the flowers.

Viburnum × bodnantense 'Charles Lamont' is a medium to large shrub whose white flowers, flushed with pink, are very fragrant. This is highly recommended, as is the better known **V. farreri (V. fragrans)**, also medium to large, with sweetly fragrant white flowers from pink buds, starting in late autumn and continuing through winter. The leaves are bronze when they first unfurl (see also Shrubs recommended for flowers, Spring, this chapter). These two viburnums are most effective when underplanted with hellebores of various kinds, which can be interplanted with snowdrops.

white and mauve flowers, raised by Hillier's. They look superb underplanted with snowdrops and flourish in any well-drained soil.

Related to daphne, and very unusual, is **Edgeworthia chrysantha**, a small shrub with clusters of tubular yellow flowers in late winter and early spring, which are liable to be damaged by frost. You had best grow it against a warm sunny wall in well-drained soil.

Hamamelis were discussed previously (see Shrubs recommended for flowers, Winter, this chapter), but here we consider **H. mollis** 'Pallida', the most popular of all

Winter-flowering **Viburnum × bodnantense** 'Charles Lamont' has very fragrant blooms. It is a medium to large shrub, effectively underplanted with hellebores and snowdrops (*Coates Manor, Sussex*)

CAMELLIAS

These aristocratic shrubs are considered separately because they are among the most important flowering evergreens. Their often flamb~~ ~~wers may be produced in autumn, winter or spring, according to species, but even when they are not in bloom their handsome, shiny, often deep green foliage can be enjoyed.

Acid, moisture-retentive, humus-rich soil is essential for their well-being. Camellias enjoy the dappled shade of light woodland, but may produce more flowers when grown in full sun. However, avoid siting them where they will receive early morning sun, because rapid thawing of frozen flower buds will result in the buds being damaged or killed. In the woodland garden camellias can be combined with rhododendrons, hamamelis, pieris and various other woodland shrubs, together with suitable perennials for summer interest candelabra primu-

Camellia × williamsii 'Debbie' is a medium-size shrub whose large semi-double clear pink flowers are sometimes produced in time for Christmas but may well continue until early summer. A very reliable and vigorous cultivar

Camellias are among the most important flowering evergreen shrubs for moist, lime-free soils. **C. sasanqua** produces scented blooms in the autumn and winter. The cultivar 'Narumi-gata' is shown here

PLANTING SCHEME FEATURING CAMELLIAS

In the woodland garden, camellias can be combined with rhododendrons, hamamelis and pieris, together with perennials such as candelabra primulas, meconopsis and hostas for summer interest.

The best camellias for garden planting in Britain are cultivars of **C. × williamsii** and the most popular of these is undoubtedly 'Donation', a large shrub (*Hillier Arboretum, Ampfield, Hampshire*)

las, meconopsis and hostas. Similar arrangements could be created in shrub borders, too.

There are hundreds of cultivars available, but the following are especially recommended and flower in spring unless otherwise indicated.

Camellia 'Cornish Snow', medium shrub, small white flowers in profusion.

C. 'Inspiration', medium shrub, large flowers, semi-double, deep pink.

C. japonica, the common camellia, offering many cultivars which flower during late winter to late spring. Try the following: 'Adolphe Audusson', medium shrub, semi-double, rich red; 'Betty Sheffield Supreme', medium shrub, semi-double or paeony-form flowers, white, edged deep pink; 'Magnoliiflora', medium shrub, semi-double, palest pink; and 'Rubescens Major', medium shrub, double, crimson.

C. sasanqua, medium shrub, flowering in autumn and winter and into early spring. Small white fragrant flowers. Needs shelter so grow against a warm wall. Seldom if ever grown, but rather the forms 'Crimson King', with small single red flowers, and 'Narumigata', cream and pink, and scented.

C. 'Spring Festival', large shrub, tiny semi-double pink flowers.

C. × williamsii cultivars. The best camellias for garden planting in Britain. They flower within the period from late autumn to late spring, and do so in profu-

sion. These camellias were raised by J. C. Williams at Caerhays Castle, Cornwall, early this century, by crossing **C. japonica** with **C. saluenensis**. The following are recommended: 'Anticipation', medium shrub, paeony-form deep pink flowers; 'Brigadoon', medium shrub, semi-double, deep pink; 'Debbie', medium shrub, semi-double, pink; 'Donation', large shrub, very large semi-double, rich pink; 'E. T. R. Carlyon', medium shrub, semi-double to double, white, late in season; and 'St Ewe', medium shrub, single, deep pink.

RHODODENDRONS

The genus **Rhododendron** is extremely large and diverse and therefore deserves a section to itself.

Rhododendrons enjoy the same conditions as camellias – that is, an acid humus-rich soil which retains moisture and the dappled shade of a woodland garden. The large-leaved species need protection from cold winds, but the hardy hybrids can be grown in full exposure to sun and wind.

Rhododendrons can be effectively combined with all kinds of shrubs which enjoy the same conditions, such as camellias, pieris, kalmias, hamamelis, enkianthus, halesia and Japanese maples, and with suitable perennials and bulbs such as hostas, candelabra primulas, meconopsis and lilies. Birches with white trunks contrast superbly with rhododendrons and can therefore be used to help create woodland conditions.

Of course, rhododendrons are equally at home in a shrub border so long as suitable conditions can be provided, and the same plant combinations could be considered.

The main flowering period is midspring to early summer, but some bloom in winter and even in midsummer. Many are ever-green with handsome foliage, others are deciduous and often produce pleasing autumn leaf colour. The relative hardiness of rhododendrons is indicated in the descriptive lists as follows: H4, hardy anywhere in Britain; H3, hardy in the south and west, also along the coast and in sheltered inland gardens; H2, needs protection in very sheltered gardens.

Rhododendron species

R. albrechtii, medium shrub, deciduous, deep pink, mid to late spring, yellow autumn tints, H4.

R. argyrophyllum 'Chinese Silver', large shrub, evergreen, pink, late spring, foliage silver below, H4.

R. augustinii, large shrub, evergreen, blue, late spring to early summer, excellent for woodland, H3–4.

R. bureavii, medium shrub, evergreen, deep pink bells, mid to late spring, red tomentum on underside of leaves, H4.

R. calostrotum 'Gigha', small shrub, evergreen, wine-red, late spring to early summer, greyish foliage, H4.

R. dauricum 'Midwinter', medium shrub, semi-evergreen, purple, midwinter to early spring, a good companion for hamamelis, H4.

R. kaempferi 'Mikado', medium shrub, deciduous or semi-evergreen, orange-salmon, early to midsummer, H4.

R. lutescens, medium to large shrub, evergreen, pale yellow funnel-shaped flowers, late winter to midspring, H3–4.

R. luteum, the common highly fragrant yellow azalea, late spring, medium to large shrub, deciduous with good leaf colour in autumn, H4.

R. macabeanum, large shrub or small

PLANTING SCHEME FEATURING RHODODENDRONS

Rhododendrons, especially in the woodland garden, can be combined effectively with all kinds of shrubs which enjoy the same conditions of moist, acid soil and dappled shade. Examples of good companions are camellias, pieris, kalmias, hamamelis, enkianthus, halesia and Japanese maples, and perennials and bulbs like hostas, candelabra primulas, meconopsis and lilies.

Rhododendron yakushimanum, seen here with a pieris, is one of the best dwarf rhododendrons for small gardens. (*Hillier Arboretum, Ampfield, Hampshire*)

tree, evergreen, large pale yellow bell-shaped flowers, early to midspring, large leaves with white tomentum below, H3 to 4.

R. mucronulatum, medium shrub, deciduous, rose-purple, midwinter to early spring, good companion for hamamelis, H4.

R. orbiculare, medium to large shrub, evergreen, bright pink, early to midspring, rounded leaves, glaucous below, H4.

R. prunifolium, medium to large shrub, deciduous, intense orange-red, mid to late summer, H3 to 4.

R. rex fictolacteum, large shrub or small tree, evergreen, cream-white crimson-blotched bells, mid to late spring, large leaves with brown tomentum on undersides, H4.

R. schlippenbachii, large shrub, deciduous, light to deep pink or white, mid to late spring, good autumn leaf colour, H4.

R. vaseyi, large shrub, deciduous, pink shades or white, mid to late spring, fiery autumn leaf colour, H4.

R. viscosum, medium shrub, deciduous, fragrant sticky flowers, white sometimes flushed pink, early to midsummer, H4.

R. yakushimanum, small shrub, evergreen, pale pink flowers from deep pink buds, fading to white, late spring, young growth silvery, brown tomentum on underside of leaves, H4.

Rhododendron hybrids

All are evergreen. HH indicates an original hardy hybrid, very tough, tolerating full exposure to wind and sun.

'Arthur Stevens', medium shrub, light pink turning white, blotched deep pink, late spring to early summer, raised on the Hillier Nurseries, H3.

'Beatrice Keir', large shrub, lemon-yellow, midspring, H3.

'Betty Wormald', HH, medium shrub, deep rose, marked crimson, late spring to early summer, H4.

'Blue Peter', HH, medium shrub, violet blue, late spring to early summer, H4.

'Bow Bells', medium shrub, pale pink bells, mid to late spring, H4.

'Britannia, HH, medium shrub, crimson-scarlet, late spring to early summer, H4.

'Brocade', medium shrub, peach-pink bells, mid to late spring, H4.

'Cool Haven', medium, shrub, light yellow, flushed pink, late spring to early summer, named by Hillier, H3.

'Crest, medium shrub, pale yellow bells, late spring to early summer, H3.

'Cynthia', HH, large shrub, rose-crimson, late spring to early summer, H4.

'Doc', medium shrub, rose-pink, late spring, H4.

'Fastuosum Flore Pleno', HH, large shrub, double mauve, late spring to early summer, H4.

'Furnivall's Daughter', medium to large shrub, pale rose-pink, late spring to early summer, H4.

'Gomer Waterer', HH, large shrub, white, flushed mauve, blotched yellow, late spring to early summer, H4.

'Halfdan Lem', medium to large shrub, bright red, late spring to early summer, H4.

'Hotei', medium shrub, canary yellow, late spring to early summer, H3.

'Hugh Koster', HH, medium shrub, crimson-scarlet, marked black, late spring to early summer, H4.

'Kluis Sensation', medium shrub, bright scarlet with darker spots, late spring to early summer, H4.

Lady Chamberlain, large shrub, mandarin-red and orange-buff tubular flowers, late spring to early summer, H3.

Lady Chamberlain 'Exbury', large shrub, yellow and salmon-orange, late spring to early summer, H3.

'Lady Clementine Mitford', HH, large shrub, peach pink and white, late spring to early summer, H4.

Deciduous hybrid azalea 'Homebush' with semi-double deep pink flowers. It is a medium-size shrub

Lady Roseberry 'Pink Delight', large shrub, pink tubular flowers, late spring to early summer, H3.

'Lavender Girl', medium shrub, lavender, late spring to early summer, H4.

Loderi 'King George', large shrub or small tree, soft pink in bud, pure white, marked green within, lightly scented, mid to late spring, H3.

'Loder's White', HH, large shrub, mauve buds, pure white flowers, edged pink, crimson spots, late spring to early summer, H4.

'May Day', medium shrub, bright red or orange-red, late spring to early summer, H3.

'Mrs Charles E. Pearson', HH, medium shrub, light mauve-pink, ageing white, late spring to early summer, H4.

'Mrs G. W. Leak', HH, medium shrub, mottled rose-pink, marked crimson and brown-black, late spring to early summer, H4.

'Nobleanum', HH, large shrub or small tree, rose, flushed white, midwinter to early spring, a good companion for hamamelis, H4.

'Pink Pearl', HH, large shrub, lilac-pink, ageing white, marked crimson-brown, late spring to early summer, H4.

'Polar Bear', large shrub or small tree, fragrant, white, marked green within, early summer, H3.

'Purple Splendour', HH, large shrub, rich purple, late spring to early summer, H4.

'Sappho', HH, medium shrub, white, blotched purple-black, late spring to early summer, H4.

'Unique', small shrub, cream, spotted crimson, mid to late spring, H4.

'Vanessa Pastel', medium shrub, cream and pale pink, flushed scarlet, late spring to early summer, H3 to 4.

'Winsome', medium shrub, deep pink, wavy edges, late spring to early summer, H3 to 4.

'Yellow Hammer', medium shrub, tubular bright yellow flowers, midspring, H3 to 4.

Deciduous hybrid azaleas

These usually have trumpet-shaped flowers which are produced during late spring and early summer, many being fragrant. The leaves often take on striking tints in autumn. As a foil for the often strong colours, underplant with hostas; interplant with lilies to continue the display throughout the summer. Medium shrubs, unless otherwise stated.

'Berryrose', rose-pink, H4.

'Cecile', salmon-pink, H4.

'Coccinea Speciosa', fragrant, intense orange-red, excellent autumn foliage colour, H4.

'Daviesii', fragrant, white, flared yellow, H4.

'Gibraltar', brilliant orange, flushed yellow, H4.

'Homebush', semi-double, deep pink, H4.

'Irene Koster', fragrant, deep pink, blotched yellow, H4.

'Klondyke', orange-gold, flushed red, H4.

'Nancy Waterer', fragrant, deep yellow, superb leaf tints in autumn, H4.

'Narcissiflorum', fragrant, double, yellow shades, superb leaf tints in autumn, H4.

'Persil', white, flared orange, H4.

'Silver Slipper', white and pink, flared orange, H4.

'Spek's Orange', small shrub, orange, H4.

'Strawberry Ice', pale pink, flared gold, H4.

Evergreen hybrid azaleas

These low-growing shrubs with a spreading habit flower in mid or, more usually, late spring. They completely cover themselves with blooms and relish partial shade with protection from cold winds. They will flourish in full sun provided they are not allowed to dry out. The best effects are obtained when these azaleas are mass planted, perhaps in a patchwork of several contrasting or harmonising colours. They are ideal for the edge of a shrub border and light woodland, and lilies could be allowed to grow through them to provide colour in the summer.

Many were introduced from Japan earlier this century by plant hunter E. H. Wilson. All the following are small shrubs, unless otherwise stated.

'Addy Wery', dark orange-red, H4.

'Azuma-kagami', medium shrub, bright pink, H3.

'Blaauw's Pink', salmon-pink, H4.

'Blue Danube', blue-violet, H4.

'Fedora', light pink, H4.

'Hatsugiri', crimson-purple, H4.

'Hino Crimson', crimson-scarlet, H4.

'Hinodegiri', crimson, H4.

'Hinomayo', pink, H4.

'Hoo', light pink, white centre, H4.

'Ima-shojo', brilliant red, H4.

'Iro-hayama', white, edged lavender, H4.

'John Cairns', deep orange-red, H4

'Kirin', deep rose-pink, H4.

'Kure-no-yuki', white, H4.

'Leo', brilliant orange, late in the season, H4.

'Madame Van Hecke', rose-pink, H4.

'Mother's Day', rose-red, H4.

'Naomi', medium shrub, salmon-pink, late in the season, H4.

'Orange Beauty', salmon-orange, H4.

'Palestrina', white, H4.

'Purple Triumph', dark purple, H4.

'Rosebud', rose-pink, late in season, H4.

'Silver Moon', white, with frilly margins, H4.

'Suga-no-ito', lavender-pink, with white centre, H4.

'Vida Brown', rose-pink, H4.

'Vuyk's Rosy Red', dark rose-red, H4.

'Vuyk's Scarlet', carmine-red, H4.

HEATHERS

The majority of heathers are low, spreading, very long-flowering evergreen ground-cover plants, a collection of which can provide colourful blooms throughout the year. Many have coloured foliage too, which is attractive all year round, often becoming more intense in winter.

Heathers have many uses but are always mass planted for best effect. For instance, they can be used to create a heather garden, where numerous kinds are planted in a patchwork in informal beds or borders to create flower and foliage colour during the whole year. An interesting idea is to plant in bold drifts. Here, heathers are planted at the front of long informal borders whose edges curve gently, 'flowing' through the garden like a stream.

Of course, one can include other plants in a heather garden if desired, but be careful

---

PLANTING SCHEME FOR HEATHERS

Plants that can be effectively grown in a heather garden include betula (birches), pines, ulex (gorse), cytisus (brooms), cistus (sun roses), genistas and **Spartium junceum** (Spanish broom). One can also have beds of heathers and dwarf conifers; or dwarf rhododendrons could be combined with them.

---

about what you choose as not all plants associate effectively with heathers. Try to select those that occur with them in the wild, such as betula (birches), pines and ulex (gorse). Other plants that look at ease with heathers include cytisus (brooms), cistus (sun roses), genistas and **Spartium junceum** (Spanish broom).

Another idea, liked by some people, detested by others, is to devote informal beds to heathers and dwarf conifers. This certainly creates contrast in shape, texture and colour.

Dwarf rhododendrons combine well with heathers. Grown in an informal island bed, this combination could make an attractive feature in many gardens.

Alternatively, heathers may be used in more general plant groups. For instance in a winter group comprising, say, a **Prunus subhirtella** 'Autumnalis', hamamelis and **Viburnum tinus** (laurustinus), you might have at the front a carpet of winter-flowering **Erica carnea** or **Erica × darleyensis** cultivars, or coloured-foliage cultivars of **Calluna vulgaris**.

Autumn-flowering cultivars of **Calluna vulgaris** could be included in an autumn group comprising berrying shrubs like cotoneasters, euonymus and berberis, and shrubs with autumn leaf tints such as rhus and cotinus. Autumn crocuses could be

'Peter Sparkes', with double pink flowers from late summer to mid autumn, is one of the most popular cultivars of **Calluna vulgaris** (heather or ling) due to its prolific flowering habit (*Hillier Arboretum, Ampfield, Hampshire*)

allowed to flower through the callunas.

Do not forget that you can also let dwarf spring-flowering bulbs grow through heathers, especially crocus and galanthus species.

In a heather bed you could allow **Clematis viticella** cultivars to trail over winter-flowering heathers to create interest in late summer and autumn. Their thin stems and light foliage will not smother the heathers.

In whatever way you use heathers, remember that they must have open positions with plenty of sun (avoid planting under trees or other shrubs) and most need acid soil. We can thoroughly recommend the following small selection.

Calluna vulgaris (Heather, ling), dwarf shrub needing acid or lime-free, humus-rich, moisture-retentive soil. There are many cultivars including 'Beoley Gold', golden foliage, flowers white, late summer

PLANTING SCHEME FOR WINTER HEATHERS

In a heather bed you could allow **Clematis viticella** cultivars to trail over winter-flowering heathers to create interest in late summer and autumn.

Erica × **darleyensis** is a lime-tolerant winter-flowering heather. There are numerous cultivars, including the well-known 'Darley Dale' with pale pink flowers over a long period (*Hillier Arboretum, Ampfield, Hampshire*)

to early autumn; 'County Wicklow', double, light pink, late summer to early autumn; 'Gold Haze', golden foliage, white flowers, late summer to early autumn; 'H. E. Beale', double, bright rose, late summer to mid autumn; 'J. H. Hamilton', double, pink, mid to late summer; 'Kinlochruel', double, white, late summer to early autumn; 'Peter Sparkes'; double, pink, late summer to mid autumn; 'Silver Queen', light mauve, late summer to early autumn, foliage silver-grey; 'Sir John Charrington', crimson, late summer to early autumn, golden foliage; and 'Sister Anne', pink, late summer to early autumn, grey foliage.

Daboecia cantabrica (St Dabeoc's heath) is a dwarf shrub with large bell-shaped flowers from early summer to late autumn and hard, elliptic, dark green leaves. It needs to be grown in acid, moisture-retentive humus-rich soil. Cultivars are normally grown and we recommend 'Alba', white; 'Atropurpurea', deep red-purple; and 'Pragerae', deep pink.

Erica arborea 'Alpina' (tree heath), medium shrub for acid soil, flowers fragrant, white, early spring, bright green foliage.

Erica carnea (syn. **E. herbacea**), dwarf lime-tolerant shrub, winter flowering. The many excellent cultivars include 'Ann Sparkes', purple flowers, late winter to early spring, foliage golden; 'Eileen Porter', carmine-red, mid autumn to midspring; 'Foxhollow', light pink, foliage yellow, flushed red in winter; 'Myretoun Ruby', dark rose-pink, late winter to midspring, deep green foliage'; 'Pink Spangles', pink, throughout winter; 'Springwood Pink', rose-pink, midwinter to early spring; 'Springwood White', white, midwinter to early spring, foliage bronze-red in winter; 'Vivelli', carmine, midwinter to early spring; and 'Winter Beauty' (syn. 'King George'), rose-pink, starting in early winter.

Erica ciliaris (Dorset heath), dwarf shrub for acid soils, flowering period mid-summer to mid autumn. Recommended cultivars: 'Mrs C. H. Gill', red flowers; and 'Stoborough', white flowers.

Erica cinerea (bell heather), dwarf shrub for acid soils, flowering period early summer to early autumn. Good cultivars include 'Atrosanguinea Smith's Variety', scarlet flowers; 'C. D. Eason', dark pink; 'Eden Valley', mauve-pink'; 'Golden Drop', summer foliage gold-copper, winter foliage rust-red, few flowers produced; 'Golden Hue', foliage gold in summer, red in winter; and 'P. S. Patrick', purple.

Erica × darleyensis, a lime-tolerant dwarf shrub; flowering period late autumn to midspring. We recommend the cultivars 'Arthur Johnson', magenta flowers; 'Jack H. Brummage', deep pink, yellow and gold foliage, tinted red in winter; and 'Silber-schmelze' ('Molten Silver'), white, fragrant.

E. erigena (syn. **E. mediterranea**) (Mediterranean heath), small shrub, flowering period early to late spring. Tolerates lime in the soil. Recommended cultivars 'Brightness', rose-pink; 'Irish Dusk', pink, late autumn to late spring; 'Superba', medium shrub, pink; and 'W. T. Rackliff', white, brown anthers, deep green leaves.

Erica lusitanica (Portugal heath, tree heath), medium to large shrub for acid soils with fragrant white flowers from early winter to late spring and feathery light green foliage.

Erica terminalis (syn. **E. stricta, E. corsica**), (Corsican heath), medium shrub, suitable for chalky soils, flowers rose-coloured, late summer.

Erica tetralix (cross-leaved heath), a dwarf shrub for acid, moisture-retentive humus-rich soil. Foliage silvery grey. Flowering period early summer to mid autumn. There are numerous excellent cultivars including 'Alba Mollis', white; 'Con Underwood', crimson; and 'L. E. Underwood', light pink.

Erica vagans (Cornish heath), dwarf shrub for acid soils, flowering period mid summer to mid autumn. We recommend 'Lyonesse', white flowers, conspicuous brown anthers; 'Mrs D. F. Maxwell', dark cerise; 'St Keverne', rose-pink; and 'Valerie Proudley', white, foliage golden yellow.

DISTINCTIVE FOLIAGE

So far we have concentrated on shrubs notable for their flowers, but others have bold or otherwise distinctive foliage. Often these are referred to as 'architectural plants' because they associate particularly well with modern buildings. They can be used in and around patios, for instance, where they provide dramatic contrast to the paving with their sword-shaped, hand-shaped (palmate), pinnate or otherwise distinctive leaves.

The yuccas, with their evergreen sword-like leaves, demonstrate admirably what we have in mind. They help to create a subtropical atmosphere in the vicinity of a patio. Alternatively, they look good planted in a gravel area in association with kniphofias, phormiums and ornamental grasses. Established plants produce panicles of pendulous, white, bell-shaped flowers in summer. They need a very sunny site and extremely good drainage.

We recommend **Yucca filamentosa** 'Bright Edge', a dwarf shrub with stemless clumps of yellow-edged leaves; **Y. f.** 'Variegata', similar habit, yellow and green striped leaves; **Y. flaccida** 'Golden Sword', dwarf stemless shrub with tufts of leaves each with a wide yellow stripe in the centre; and **Y. f.** 'Ivory', grown for its cream-white flowers in large panicles.

Equally impressive architectural plants, also with tufts of sword-shaped evergreen leaves, are the phormiums or New Zealand flax. They are reasonably hardy but not recommended for the coldest areas: grow them in full sun and any well-drained soil.

Many shrubs have bold or distinctive foliage, including the yuccas. They have evergreen sword-shaped leaves, yellow-striped in some such as the dwarf **Y. flaccida** 'Golden Sword' (*Stream Cottage, Sussex*)

PLANTING SCHEME FOR BOLD FOLIAGE

Yuccas, with their sword-shaped leaves, look good planted in a gravel area in association with kniphofias, phormiums and ornamental grasses.

P. tenax cultivars 'Purpureum' with bronze-purple leaves, the red, pink and cream 'Sundowner', and white-edged 'Variegatum' are very popular. They are medium-size shrubs and, except for 'Sundowner', hardier than the more recent New Zealand introductions like 'Bronze Baby', a small shrub, bronze; **P. cookianum** 'Cream Delight', another medium shrub, cream central band; 'Dark Delight', small shrub, bronze-black; 'Dazzler', medium shrub, red shades; 'Maori Chief', small shrub, scarlet, crimson and bronze; and 'Maori Sunrise', small shrub, red, pink and bronze. **P. cookianum** 'Tricolor' is a popular medium shrub with cream and red-edged leaves, as is 'Yellow Wave', of similar stature but with yellow leaves edged green.

A very popular, almost over-used architectural plant is **Fatsia japonica**, a medium to large evergreen shrub with large palmate, shiny deep green leaves and, in midautumn, globe-shaped white flower heads in large panicles. A versatile shrub for any well-drained soil, it will thrive in partial shade and seaside gardens, contrasting beautifully with paving and modern concrete buildings. There is also a variegated form with white-tipped leaves.

Some of the salix or willows have quite dramatic foliage, but for some reason are inclined to be overlooked in this respect by landscape architects and garden designers. **Salix magnifica** is a large shrub or small tree with very big blue-green leaves resembling those of magnolias. Very long green catkins are produced in the spring with the leaves. It will grow in any soil and situation.

Trochodendron aralioides is a large evergreen shrub with distinctive foliage. The leathery, elliptic leaves are deep green and shiny and in spring and early summer racemes of petal-less green flowers are produced. This would make a handsome specimen shrub, but provide shelter from cold winds. Sunny or shady places with moisture-retentive yet well-drained soil offer the right conditions, but this shrub is unsuitable for very shallow chalky soils or dry situations.

We have already covered most of the viburnums (see section Shrubs recommended for flowers, Spring; and Fragrant flowering shrubs, this chapter) but there are several with very distinctive foliage: **Viburnum lantanoides** (syn. **V. alnifolium**) (hobble bush), for instance, a medium shrub whose large leaves have conspicuous veins and which turn red in autumn. Red berries follow the white hydrangea-like flowers. This is an excellent shrub for woodland, thriving in partial shade, but surprisingly for a viburnum it needs acid soil.

V. davidii is much better known, its large, conspicuously veined, deep green shiny leaves contrasting beautifully with paving. This small, evergreen, mound-forming shrub produces turquoise berries if several plants are grown together.

Decaisnea fargesii makes a handsome specimen shrub in association with architecture and paving. Of medium size, it has pinnate foliage up to 1m (3ft 3in) in length and blue seed pods, shaped like those of broad beans, follow the yellow-green flowers. It needs moisture retentive yet well-drained soil and will thrive in partial shade.

One does not often think of privets as having distinctive foliage. However, **Ligus-**

trum japonicum 'Rotundifolium' is worth growing purely for its rounded, black-green leathery leaves. This is a slow-growing medium evergreen shrub of compact habit, and would look good in the vicinity of a patio. It is suitable for any well-drained soil.

Very unusual is **Maytenus boaria**, a large, graceful evergreen shrub or small tree with narrow, oval, shiny leaves. This would make a fine specimen shrub but ensure that it is sheltered from cold winds. It will grow in sun or partial shade and any fertile well-drained soil.

Melianthus major is generally recommended only for the mildest areas of Britain and is suitable for the garden devoted to Mediterranean-climate plants, or a really warm sheltered corner of a patio, but it is hardier than many people imagine. This South African dwarf sub-shrub is notable for its long, pinnate, evergreen glaucous leaves, which create a sub-tropical atmosphere. In summer crimson tubular flowers are produced.

Olearias have already been discussed (see Shrubs recommended for flowers, Summer, Hot and dry, this chapter) but **O. macrodonta** 'Major' (New Zealand holly) must be included here for its bold holly-like leaves with silvery undersides. This medium evergreen shrub has fragrant white flowers in early summer, and the whole plant gives off a musky scent. It can be grown as a specimen and also makes a good hedge.

Phlomis 'Edward Bowles' is for the garden devoted to Mediterranean-climate plants, or a hot well-drained corner of the patio. It is a small sub-shrub with large, heart-shaped, woolly leaves. In summer and autumn whorls of hooded sulphur-yellow flowers are produced.

Sambucus racemosa 'Tenuifolia', a cultivar of the red-berried elder, is a small shrub forming a mound of very finely divided ferny foliage. It is a slow grower and ideal for a small patio, where it contrasts well with plants which have large, rounded leaves, such as bergenias. It would also look good with **Senecio monroi**, a small evergreen shrub forming a dome, with oval leaves which have wavy edges and white tomentum below. Yellow daisy-like flowers are produced in summer and any well-drained soil is suitable.

Britain is largely devoid of elms now due to Dutch elm disease, but we are still able to grow **Ulmus minor** 'Jacqueline Hillier', a medium shrub of dense, suckering, yet neat habit with small rough-textured leaves which have serrated edges. It may be grown as a specimen and is also suitable for forming a low hedge. This shrub was named by Hillier.

Hollies are suited to the woodland garden or shrub border, or make excellent lawn specimens, and enjoy well-drained soil and partial shade or full sun. Some have distinctive foliage, like **Ilex × altaclarensis** 'Camelliifolia', a large evergreen shrub or tree with bold, camellia-like, usually spineless glossy deep green leaves, purple stems and large deep red berries; and **I. latifolia** (Tarajo holly), a large shrub or small evergreen tree with very large, shiny, deep green saw-edged foliage and masses of dark red berries.

COLOURED FOLIAGE

Many deciduous and evergreen shrubs are noted for their coloured foliage, and are becoming increasingly popular for planting schemes as people realise that they represent really good value, with a very long or year-round period of interest. We are not here referring to autumn leaf colour – this is discussed in Chapter 6.

Coloured-leaved shrubs can, of course, be used with flowering specimens and other plants to create contrasts or harmonies. Some are ideal as lawn specimens, or as focal points in a garden. Plenty of examples of imaginative use are given throughout the following text.

Red/purple

Shrubs with red or purple foliage are numerous and, for striking contrast, can be associated with yellow or gold-leaved shrubs. A more subtle effect is obtained by combining them with white-variegated or grey/silver varieties. Shrub roses and other shrubs with red or pink flowers associate pleasingly with red or purple foliage.

Corylopsis willmottiae 'Spring Purple' has deep purple young foliage and yellow flowers in spring, and is a medium shrub for any well-drained soil. Making a large shrub or small tree is **Cercis canadensis** 'Forest

Shrubs with red or purple foliage can be used to create striking contrasts with other shrubs and plants. **Cotinus** 'Grace', introduced by Hillier, is one of the best shrubs with red-purple leaves

Pansy', with dark red-purple heart-shaped foliage all summer and pale pink pea flowers in spring. Provide well-drained soil.

Corylus maxima 'Purpurea' (the purple-leaf filbert) is a large shrub for any well-drained soil, with deep purple foliage. It makes an excellent companion for red shrub roses, although some people team it with **Corylus avellana** 'Aurea', the golden hazel. Also associating well with shrub roses, or other red-flowered shrubs, are **Cotinus coggygria** 'Velvet Cloak', a large shrub with wine-red foliage all summer, and **C.** 'Grace', also a large shrub with bold red-purple foliage, introduced by Hillier. Cotinus grow in any well-drained soil.

Sambucus nigra 'Guincho Purple' (syn. **S. n.** 'Purpurea') (cultivar of the common elder) with purple-flushed foliage showing its best colour when young, is a worthwhile addition to the woodland edge or shrub border, particularly if the soil is chalky. Try planting purple wild foxgloves around it (seeds are available from specialist wild-flower seedsmen).

Some pieris have been described already (see Shrubs recommended for flowers, Spring, this chapter) but there are others with an even greater attraction in spring – red young foliage. These include **P.** 'Fire-crest', medium evergreen and free-flowering, which takes more exposure than most; **P.** 'Flaming Silver', small evergreen, whose leaves develop silver-white edges as they mature, and which produces cream-white flowers; **P.** 'Forest Flame', medium evergreen, multicoloured young foliage, large pendulous panicles of flowers; and **P. formosa forrestii**, large evergreen with long cone-shaped flower panicles, and its forms 'Jermyns' (selected on the Hillier Nurseries) and 'Wakehurst'. **P. japonica** 'Variegata' is a medium evergreen with white-edged leaves which have a pink flush when newly opened.

COLOURED-FOLIAGE PLANTING SCHEME

Shrubs with red or purple foliage can be associated with yellow or gold-leaved shrubs; a more subtle effect is achieved by combining them with white-variegated or grey/silver shrubs.

Some of the photinias are also noted for their brilliant red young leaves and can be recommended for woodland garden or shrub border, especially where the soil is unsuitable for pieris, as photinias will grow in any well-drained soil. **Photinia × fraseri** 'Red Robin' and **P. × fraseri** 'Robusta' are large evergreen shrubs, while **P. glabra** 'Rubens' is a medium-size evergreen.

Leucothoe fontanesiana is a small evergreen ground-cover shrub for the woodland garden, where it enjoys shade or semi-shade and moisture-retentive, humus-rich acid soil. The lance-shaped, shiny, deep green leaves become tinted with red or purple in winter. In late spring white urn-shaped flowers appear. The cultivar 'Rainbow' is difficult to categorise as regards colour, because the leaves are variegated pink, yellow and cream.

Nandina domestica (sacred bamboo) is a handsome medium evergreen foliage shrub, needing a position sheltered from cold winds and any fertile, well-drained yet moisture-retentive soil. The large compound green leaves become flushed with red in autumn, winter and spring. Good contrast would be provided by bergenias, which are evergreen perennials with large rounded leaves.

Pittosporum tenuifolium 'Purpureum' is one of the few hardy evergreen shrubs with purple leaves. It is a large plant and, like all pittosporums, recommended only for mild areas, including sheltered coastal gardens. It will grow in any well-drained soil, and red-flowered escallonias make excellent companions. **P. t.** 'Tom Thumb' is a small shrub with deep purple foliage, green when young.

For a sheltered spot in a woodland garden, where it enjoys partial shade and moisture-retentive yet well- drained humus-rich acid soil, is **Pseudowintera colorata**, a medium evergreen with light yellow-green oval leaves which are flushed with pink and blotched and margined with deep red-purple.

An unusual viburnum (see Shrubs recommended for Spring, this chapter) is **V. × hillieri** 'Winton', raised on the Hillier Nurseries, a medium semi-evergreen shrub whose leaves become bronze-red in autumn and tinted with copper when they unfurl in spring. Creamy flowers are produced in early summer, followed by red berries which darken to black.

For sheltered positions with reasonable sun in the woodland garden or shrub border are the purple-leaved forms of the Japanese maple, **Acer palmatum**, with palmate foliage. They also make handsome specimen shrubs, say in a lawn. We recommend 'Bloodgood', a medium shrub with dark red-purple leaves, the best clone of 'Atropurpureum'; 'Corallinum', a very slow-growing dwarf shrub whose young leaves are a startling bright shrimp-pink; 'Crimson Queen', a small shrub with deep red leaves; 'Linearilobum Atropurpureum', a medium shrub bearing leaves with long narrow lobes, flushed with red; and 'Red Pygmy', a small mound-shaped shrub with red-maroon thread-like leaves, suitable for partial shade. These acers succeed in any well-drained yet moisture-retentive deep soil.

Several berberis (see also Shrubs recommended for flowers, Spring, and Miscellany for the mixed border, this chapter) have red foliage, including **B. × media** 'Red Jewel', a small semi-evergreen, and **B. thunbergii** 'Red Chief', small shrub of upright habit. These look good when planted with pink deutzias.

Yellow/gold

Shrubs with yellow or gold foliage, or whose leaves are variegated with these colours, help a great deal to brighten up parts of a garden. Generally, full sun is needed for the best colour. Some people combine these shrubs with purple-leaved varieties for dramatic contrast, but for a more subtle arrangement try a combination of yellow/gold and silver/grey.

One of the more distinctive ribes (see also Shrubs recommended for flowers, this chapter) has golden-yellow foliage: **R. sanguineum** 'Brocklebankii', a small shrub with pink flowers. Provide partial shade, as the foliage tends to burn in full sun. This bush is lovely with an underplanting of bluebells.

Acer shirasawanum 'Aureum' (syn. **A. japonicum** 'Aureum') is a medium-size, slow-growing Japanese maple with soft yellow foliage. It too needs a position in partial shade, plus shelter from cold winds, but any well-drained soil is suitable other than shallow chalk. In summer it helps to brighten up the woodland garden, for instance.

Rather like a tallish heath in habit is **Cassinia fulvida**, a small evergreen with very tiny leaves and yellow shoots; the whole shrub appears golden. A suitable candidate for the hot dry area.

Very conspicuous gold-edged leaves are sported by **Cornus alba** 'Spaethii' (red-barked dogwood), with red stems which show up in winter. Any well-drained but moisture-retentive soil will please this shrub.

SHRUBS FOR FLOWERS AND FOLIAGE

Shrubs with yellow or gold foliage, like
Philadelphus coronarius 'Aureus', very much
help to brighten up parts of a garden. This mock
orange also has white, fragrant flowers in early
summer and is best grown in partial shade (*York
Gate, Leeds*)

Corylus avellana 'Aurea' (yellow-leaved
hazel) has already been mentioned as a
companion for **Corylus maxima**
'Purpurea' (see Red/purple section). It is a
medium shrub with soft yellow foliage and it
thrives in partial shade on any well-drained
soil, including chalk.

The evergreen elaeagnus are invaluable
shrubs for the border and flourish in maritime areas, but they are not suited to shallow chalky soils. **E. × ebbingei** 'Gilt Edge'
is a large variety whose leaves are edged
with golden-yellow, and **E. pungens**
'Maculata' is of medium size with gold-
splashed foliage, which is particularly bright
in winter. For a pleasing winter effect try
associating them with red-stemmed dogwoods.

Several of the evergreen euonymus have
yellow or gold foliage. They are very adaptable, thriving in any well-drained soil and in

125

partial shade. For ground cover we recommend the small **E. fortunei** 'Emerald n' Gold' which has gold-variegated leaves, flushed with pink in winter, creating a superb effect when mass planted.

Myrtus luma 'Glanleam Gold' (myrtle) is a large evergreen shrub with gold-variegated aromatic foliage. It requires well-drained soil and is recommended only for mild areas, where it is best grown against a south or west wall, perhaps in association with blue evergreen ceanothus.

Undoubtedly the most popular golden-leaved shrub is **Philadelphus coronarius** 'Aureus' (mock orange, see also Fragrant flowering shrubs, this chapter), which offers the additional benefit of white fragrant flowers in early summer. It is used as a companion for many other plants and looks superb surrounded by blue-leaved hostas. The best location is in partial shade, to prevent the foliage becoming burnt.

Ptelea trifoliata 'Aurea' (hop tree) is a large shrub with soft yellow trifoliate leaves, which makes a handsome lawn specimen and is suitable for any fertile well-drained soil.

Sambucus nigra 'Aurea' (golden elder, see also the Red/purple section), is a medium shrub whose golden-yellow foliage helps to brighten up a shrub or mixed border in summer, as does **Weigela** 'Looymansii Aurea' which is best grown in partial shade to prevent burning of its pale gold foliage. Pink flowers are produced in early summer.

Especially welcome in winter is the gold-speckled foliage of **Aucuba japonica** 'Crotonifolia', a medium shrub which thrives virtually anywhere, including positions in shade or semi-shade, and on any well-drained soil. It is useful for a winter group containing red-stemmed dogwoods.

Several evergreen hollies have gold foliage, like **Ilex × altaclerensis** 'Golden King', a large shrub with gold-edged, almost spineless leaves, and **I. aquifolium** 'Golden Milkboy', a medium shrub whose leaves are splashed with gold. These two are suitable for woodland or shrub border or as specimens in lawns, growing in any well-drained soil.

Grey/silver

Many grey or silver-leaved shrubs relish sun-baked well-drained conditions, and so would be suitable for the garden devoted to Mediterranean-climate plants or for the patio. They also associate well with many other plants, like shrub roses and gold-foliage shrubs.

The salix or willows, though, generally prefer moister conditions. Several have grey or silver foliage, including the small shrubs **S. helvetica** with grey-green leaves, woolly young shoots and spring catkins; **S. lanata** (woolly willow), with silver-grey foliage and yellow-grey catkins in spring; and **S. repens argentea** (creeping willow), with silky silvery leaves. Of the larger willows, **S. exigua** (coyote willow) has narrow, lance-shaped, silky silvery leaves. It makes a large shrub or small tree.

Very useful for mixing with flowering shrubs is **Artemisia** 'Powis Castle', a small evergreen sub-shrub which forms a neat mound of feathery silver foliage. It needs plenty of sun and very good drainage. The dwarf sub-shrub **Ballota pseudo-dictamnus**, whose rounded leaves and shoots are covered with grey-white wool, needs the same conditions. Also revelling in very sunny well-drained situations are the silver-grey helichrysums, **H. italicum serotinum** (curry plant), a dwarf evergreen with aromatic leaves; and **H. splendidum**, a small evergreen shrub. Another useful small evergreen is **Ruta graveolens** 'Jackman's Blue' (rue), a compact bush with grey-blue foliage.

Grey-green feathery foliage is found on **Santolina pinnata** 'Edward Bowles' (syn. **S. neapolitana**), a dwarf shrub, while the small **Senecio compactus** has the leaf undersides and young shoots covered in white felt. Both are evergreen, needing full sun and very good drainage.

All the above small shrubs are useful for mixing with summer and autumn-flowering bulbs such as alliums, crinum and nerine.

Among the most interesting buddlejas for gardens are those with white foliage. **B. crispa** is a medium to large shrub with white-felted leaves and stems and, in early autumn, fragrant lilac flowers. **B fallowiana** is a medium shrub which needs

Several salix or willows have grey or silver foliage, including **S. exigua**, the coyote willow, which has narrow, lance-shaped, silky, silvery leaves that associate beautifully with many other plants (*Coldham, Kent*)

a sheltered site and thrives in partial shade. The leaves and shoots are covered in white wool and in late summer fragrant, light lavender flowers are produced. **B.** 'Lochinch', a medium shrub, has grey, hairy young shoots and the leaves have white undersides. Violet-blue fragrant flowers appear in late summer. All these thrive in any well-drained soil and are good on chalk.

Bearing pinnate blue-grey leaves is

Colutea orientalis (bladder senna), a medium shrub with copper-coloured pea flowers throughout summer followed by inflated seed pods. This is a shrub for sunny well-drained conditions.

Elaeagnus (see also Yellow/gold section) with silver foliage include **E. commutata** (silver berry), a medium shrub, and **E. macrophylla**, a large evergreen. These are excellent for coastal gardens, particularly in association with hardy fuchsias.

Also looking good with dwarf hardy fuchsias are **Hebe albicans**, a dwarf evergreen shrub with blue-grey leaves and white flowers, and **H.** 'Red Edge' with red-edged grey-green leaves and light mauve flowers.

Ozothamnus rosmarinifolius has been described before (see Fragrant flowering shrubs, this chapter), but we also recommend its cultivar 'Silver Jubilee', a medium shrub with silver-grey foliage and, in late summer, pink flowers.

One of the most widely used small grey-leaved sub-shrubs is **Perovskia atriplicifolia** 'Blue Spire', which has erect panicles of lavender-blue flowers from late summer until mid autumn. It has aromatic deeply cut foliage and looks good with many shrubs, including shrub roses, escallonias and hibiscus.

White variegated

Shrubs with white and green variegated foliage have a lightening effect in planting schemes and some can be used in gloomy corners since they take partial shade. They combine well with many other plants, including purple-foliage shrubs.

Aralia elata 'Variegata', a large architectural shrub, is ideal for planting in the vicinity of a patio or it can be used as a lawn specimen. The leaflets of the large compound leaves are edged with cream-white. It can be easily grown in any well-drained soil, but provide shelter from wind.

Several cornus are attractively white-variegated, including **C. alba** 'Elegantissima' (red-barked dogwood), a medium shrub which makes a marvellous companion for purple-leaved cotinus and which thrives in partial shade; **C. alternifolia** 'Argentea', a medium shrub with cream-edged leaves and spreading, horizontal branches, making a fine lawn specimen; and **C. mas** 'Variegata' (Cornelian cherry), a large shrub which produces small yellow flowers in late winter. These cornus grow in any well-drained soil.

The evergreen variegated euonymus are excellent for partial or even full shade and are therefore ideal for lightening up dark corners. They tolerate any well-drained soil. White-variegated **E. fortunei** cultivars include 'Emerald Gaiety', a small ground-cover shrub with white-edged leaves, and 'Silver Queen', a medium shrub with heavily variegated foliage which becomes flushed with pink in winter. **E. japonicus** 'Latifolius Albomarginatus' a large shrub ideal for coastal planting, has white-edged leaves.

Also highly recommended for seaside planting in the milder areas, and for partial shade, is **Griselinia littoralis** 'Dixon's Cream', a medium evergreen shrub with large, oval leathery leaves variegated cream-white, which enjoys any well-drained soil.

A handsome privet for the shrub border is **Ligustrum sinense** 'Variegatum' whose grey-green leaves are edged with white. This large shrub with sprays of white flowers in mid-summer makes a lovely companion for red or pink shrub roses. Any well-drained soil will do and this shrub is suitable for partial shade.

The holly-like **Osmanthus heterophyllus** 'Latifolius Variegatus' has broad silver-variegated leaves and fragrant white flowers in autumn. It is a medium evergreen for any well-drained soil.

Shrubs with white and green variegated foliage have a lightening effect in gardening schemes and combine well with many other plants. One such is **Pittosporum** 'Garnettii', whose grey-green leaves are edged white

Many pittosporums (see also Red/purple section) have white variegated foliage, including **P. eugenioides** 'Variegatum' (tatara), with wavy leaves edged cream-white; **P.** 'Garnettii', grey-green white-edged leaves; and **P. tenuifolium** 'Irene Paterson', marbled white. All are large evergreen shrubs.

Rhamnus alaternus 'Argenteovariegata' is a very vigorous medium evergreen shrub with grey marbled, white-edged leaves. It makes an excellent companion for vigorous purple-leaved berberis such as **B. × ottawensis** 'Superba' (syn. 'Purpurea'). This buckthorn succeeds in any well-drained soil, including chalk, in seaside gardens and in partial shade.

A very lightening effect is provided by **Sambucus nigra** 'Pulverulenta', an elder with white variegated foliage (see also Red/purple section).

Making another good companion for purple-leaved berberis is **Weigela praecox** 'Variegata', a medium shrub with cream-white variegation and pink flowers in late spring. Or try underplanting it with the purple-leaved ground-cover perennial **Ajuga reptans** 'Burgundy Glow'.

The **Acer palmatum** cultivar 'Butterfly' (see also Red/purple section) is a medium shrub, whose young leaves are pink but later become green and edged with cream. We recommend it for partial shade and as a good companion for purple-leaved Japanese maples.

Silver or white-variegated evergreen hollies (see also Yellow/gold section) include **Ilex × altaclerensis** 'Belgica Aurea', with cream-edged leaves, mottled grey, an almost spineless shrub of upright habit; **I. aquifolium** 'Handsworth New Silver' with purple stems; and **I. aquifolium** 'Silver Milkmaid', whose leaves are blotched with cream in the centre. All are large shrubs.

Best in full sun for colour is **Prunus laurocerasus** 'Marbled White', a cherry laurel named by Hillier whose leaves are marbled with grey-green and white, giving a very light effect. It is a large evergreen of slow growth, making a cone-shaped bush. Not recommended for shallow chalky soils, but particularly effective in winter groups which can include red-stemmed dogwoods and purple-flowered **Helleborus orientalis.**

CHAPTER 6

MORE SHRUBS FOR AUTUMN AND WINTER COLOUR

We have already indicated in the previous chapter that autumn and winter are the two seasons when many gardens are drab and bare. There is really no excuse for this. In Chapter 5 we have described many shrubs that flower during these seasons, and we have included shrubs with notable evergreen foliage which, of course, really come into their own once the deciduous kinds have shed their leaves. Any garden or border should be well-stocked with evergreens: about one-third evergreen shrubs to two-thirds deciduous is a good 'balance' in our opinion. Any more evergreens and planting schemes could start to become heavy.

So what shrubs remain to provide colour and interest in autumn and winter? Those which take on autumn leaf colour, berrying shrubs whose display may span both seasons, shrubs with coloured stems which show up really well in winter, and a few shrubs which contribute not colour but interesting shapes to the winter garden.

Where can we use shrubs for autumn and winter colour? Most people will want to create seasonal groups in a shrub border; or in a mixed border, where other subjects of the appropriate season such as perennials and bulbs can be included. Shrubs which enjoy dappled shade and shelter could be grouped together in a woodland garden, which can be ablaze with autumn leaf tints.

If you have sufficient space, why not create a winter garden with appropriate shrubs and other plants? This idea was once popular with owners of large gardens. It was a secluded area which would be visited only when the plants were in flower and ignored for the rest of the year (however, it would be maintained by the gardener!). For modern gardens, though, we suggest that the period of interest is extended with spring-flowering plants as this makes better use of the space. Traditional winter gardens can be seen in various places open to the public, such as Wisley Garden in Surrey.

AUTUMN LEAF COLOUR

To show up really well, shrubs with autumn leaf colour need a dark background, such as a group of large deep green conifers or evergreen shrubs. Some can be used as lawn specimens, in which case the grass itself generally makes a suitable background.

Garden designers often plan for groups of shrubs with autumn leaf colour to be near water, such as a lake or large pool, so that the reflections can be enjoyed.

Japanese maples should be grown in positions sheltered from cold winds, such as woodland gardens. Their autumn colour is best on acid soils (*The Old Rectory, Burghfield, Berkshire*)

Some conifers look good in these groups of shrubs, especially the 'blue' **Picea pungens** 'Hoopsii' and **Chamaecyparis lawsoniana** 'Pembury Blue'. Of course, autumn-berrying shrubs (see next section) may be included, too.

Various perennials may be incorporated in groups of shrubs with autumn leaf colour, particularly large clumps of pampas grass, **Cortaderia selloana** and its cultivars, since the tall silvery plumes of flowers provide dramatic contrast to the leaf tints. Also, in mixed borders, consider autumn-flowering **Anemone × hybrida** cultivars, Michaelmas daisies (aster), sedums and other perennials, plus autumn-flowering bulbs like colchicums, crocus species and **Nerine bowdenii**.

The Japanese maples, cultivars of **A. palmatum** and **A. japonicum** (see also Coloured foliage, Chapter 5), immediately come to mind when one thinks of autumn colour: especially acer glades in woodland

Japanese maples are, for many people, the epitome of autumn leaf colour. Seen here are **A. japonicum** 'Vitifolium', with red-crimson foliage, and **A. palmatum** 'Senkaki' (*Hillier Arboretum, Ampfield, Hampshire*)

gardens, as at Westonbirt Arboretum in Gloucestershire, for example. However a single maple, perhaps grouped with a conifer and white-stemmed birch, can be just as effective. It is usually considered that best colour is achieved in acid soils. **A. japonicum** 'Vitifolium', a large shrub, has deeply cut foliage which turns red-crimson. Of the **A. palmatum** cultivars we recommend 'Koreanum', a medium to large shrub especially good for partial shade, with crimson autumn foliage; 'Osakazuki', a large shrub, with seven-lobed leaves, turning orange-scarlet in autumn, perhaps the best; 'Ribesifolium', a large shrub of slow growth, upright habit and dark gold autumn foliage; and 'Seiryu', a medium shrub of erect habit,

PLANTING SCHEME FOR AUTUMN LEAF COLOUR

Include 'blue' conifers like **Picea pungens** 'Hoopsii' and **Chamaecyparis lawsoniana** 'Pembury Blue' in groups of shrubs noted for autumn leaf colour. Also incorporate suitable perennials, such as pampas grass (**Cortaderia selloana**), **Anemone × hybrida** cultivars, Michaelmas daisies (aster) and sedums, plus autumn-flowering bulbs such as colchicums, crocus species and **Nerine bowdenii**.

Very popular shrubs for autumn foliage are the cotinus or smoke bushes. **C.** 'Flame', a large shrub named by Hillier, is undoubtedly the best

best in partial shade, with fern-like foliage turning scarlet.

Some of the best autumn foliage colour is also provided by berberis (barberry) (see also Shrubs recommended for flowers, Spring, A miscellany for the mixed border, Chapter 5) such as **B. dictyophylla**, a medium shrub whose young stems are red and covered in white 'bloom', as are the red berries; and **B. × media** 'Parkjuweel', a small semi-evergreen shrub with almost spineless leaves.

High in the popularity charts for autumn leaf colour are the cotinus (smoke bushes), so-called because of their smoke-like inflorescences. **C.** 'Flame', a large shrub named by Hillier, is undoubtedly the best, whose leaves turn brilliant orange. With orange, red and purple tints is **C. obovatus** (**C. americanus**). The closely related rhus (sumachs) are also popular. Unlike cotinus, which have rounded leaves, rhus have long pinnate foliage. Being of distinctive shape they make fine lawn specimens. We recommend **R. glabra** (smooth sumach), a medium shrub with a wide spread, smooth stems and orange-red or orange-yellow autumn foliage; **R. g.** 'Laciniata', a ferny-leaved form; **R. typhina** (stag's-horn sumach), a large shrub or small tree, its stems covered in brown felt, whose leaves turn orange, red, scarlet and yellow in autumn; and **R. t.** 'Dissecta' (syn. **R. t.** 'Laciniata'), the cut-leaved form. Both genera grow in any well-drained soil.

No self-respecting woodland garden should be without **Disanthus cercidifolius**, provided the soil is lime-free. This medium shrub, which enjoys dappled shade, has heart-shaped leaves which become wine-red and crimson in autumn. Needing the same conditions is **Lindera obtusiloba**, a medium shrub whose aromatic lobed leaves turn butter-yellow in autumn. They show up best against a background of rhododendron or camellia foliage. Also include in the woodland garden a specimen of **Hamamelis vernalis** 'Sandra', a medium

Rhus or sumachs, with their long pinnate foliage, are among the best shrubs for colourful autumn leaves. This is **Rhus glabra** 'Laciniata', the fern-leaved form of the smooth sumach (*Hillier Arboretum, Ampfield, Hampshire*)

shrub whose young leaves start off purplish, then change to green with purple undersides and finally, in autumn, to flame shades. In winter bright yellow flowers are produced. This superb shrub was raised on the Hillier Nurseries.

Excellent for chalky soils is **Euonymus alatus** 'Compactus', a small shrub which has conspicuous corky wings on the shoots. In autumn the leaves become brilliant red.

Rhus typhina 'Dissecta' (syn. **R. t.** 'Laciniata'), the cut-leaved form of the stag's-horn sumach, contrasting superbly with **Fatsia japonica** which sports large evergreen leaves

Pleasing companion plants include **Anemone × hybrida** cultivars and schizostylis.

Noted for their brilliant autumn leaf colour, most of the nyssas are trees, but **N. sinensis** is a large shrub which turns to shades of red in autumn. It is a subject for moisture-retentive lime-free soil, and as a contrasting companion we suggest **Picea pungens** 'Hoopsii' with intense glaucous-blue leaves.

BERRYING SHRUBS

Berberis or barberries, which are so good on chalky soils, are among the main providers of autumn berries. Among the more unusual species which deserve to be better known are **B. × antoniana**, a small evergreen shrub, rounded in shape with virtually no spines on the leaves, and dark yellow blooms followed by blue-black berries, and **B. temolaica**, a vigorous medium-size shrub with glaucous shoots and stems and ovate red berries covered in white 'bloom'. **B. wilsoniae** is better known, a small shrub forming a mound of little grey-green leaves which colour well in autumn, and carrying heavy crops of coral-red berries.

Cotoneasters are indispensable autumn-berrying plants for shrub and mixed borders, where they combine well with various scale conifers such as junipers, Lawson cypress cultivars and thujas, including those with golden foliage. The ground-cover cotoneasters can be effectively planted with ground-cover junipers like **Juniperus horizontalis** cultivars, say in a patchwork design. Cotoneasters grow in any well-drained soil and are good on chalk.

We recommend the following: **C. nanshan** (syn. **C. adpressus praecox**), small vigorous ground-cover shrub, big orange-red berries; **C. conspicuus** 'Decorus', dwarf evergreen shrub, masses of bright red berries; **C.** 'Coral Beauty',

Cotoneaster horizontalis is a popular autumn-berrying shrub suitable for wall training or for use as ground cover. The leaves also colour well in autumn (*Private garden, Surrey*)

PLANTING SCHEME FOR BERRYING GROUND COVER

Berrying ground-cover cotoneasters can be effectively planted with ground-cover junipers, such as **Juniperus horizontalis** cultivars noted for their pleasingly textured evergreen foliage, say in a patchwork design. Both grow well on chalk.

shrub, tiny dark green leaves but large scarlet berries; **C.** 'Pink Champagne', large evergreen, heavy crop of yellow, flushed-pink berries, named by Hillier; **C.** 'Rothschildianus', large evergreen, cream-yellow berries; **C. floccosus**, medium evergreen, tiny red berries in profusion; **C.** 'Gnom', dwarf evergreen ground-cover shrub, masses of bright red berries; and **C. splendens** (syn. 'Sabrina'), medium shrub with copious orange berries.

The spiny evergreen pyracanthas or firethorns are as important in the autumn garden as cotoneasters, and are equally adaptable as regards soils. They are easily wall-trained (but do not trim too hard or berry production will be reduced), or they can be grown as free-standing shrubs in borders. We recommend **P.** 'Mohave', large shrub, orange-red berries in profusion (prone to scab disease); **P. rogersiana**, large shrub, masses of red-orange berries, small shiny leaves; **P. rogersiana** 'Flava', large shrub, yellow berries; and **P.** 'Soleil d'Or', medium shrub, orange-yellow. The latter can also be used for ground cover on banks, etc, perhaps in combination with ground-cover junipers.

The autumn-fruiting euonymus should be represented wherever possible. They thrive in any well-drained soil, including chalk. The best for fruits are **E. europaeus** 'Red Cascade', a medium shrub with heavy

dwarf, spreading evergreen ground-cover shrub, orange-red berries; **C.** 'Cornubia', large semi-evergreen shrub, masses of large red berries and one of the heaviest croppers; **C. sternianus**, medium semi-evergreen shrub, greyish foliage, arching habit. orange-scarlet berries in abundance; **C. serotinus**, large evergreen, red berries well into winter; **C. horizontalis**, popular for wall training or ground cover, masses of red berries and good autumn leaf colour; **C.** 'Hybridus Pendulus', which can be grown as a small weeping tree or as ground cover, evergreen, heavy crops of bright red berries which last well into winter; **C.** 'John Waterer', large semi-evergreen shrub, many bunches of red berries; **C. microphyllus**, dwarf evergreen ground-cover

Cotoneaster 'Rothschildianus' is a large evergreen shrub with cream-yellow berries, well worth growing where space permits (*Hillier Arboretum, Ampfield, Hampshire*)

crops of rose-red fruit capsules which split to reveal orange seeds, the leaves turning red in autumn; **E. hamiltonianus sieboldianus** 'Coral Charm', large shrub with light pink fruits which split to reveal red seeds, the leaves turning light yellow in autumn; and **E. planipes** (syn. **E. sachalinensis**), a large shrub, the fruits scarlet and splitting to reveal orange seeds, the leaves turning brilliant red before they fall.

Thriving in the same conditions are the autumn-fruiting viburnums, which produce bunches of translucent berries. One of the best is **V. betulifolium**, a large shrub with bunches of long-lasting red berries. Plant a group to ensure pollination. **V. opulus** 'Notcutt's Variety' is a large shrub with red berries which last for a long period. The leaves colour well in autumn. A small to medium shrub, **V. sargentii** 'Onondaga' has purple young foliage, red fruits and bronze-red autumnal leaf tints. **V. wrightii** 'Hessei' is a small shrub and has orange-red berries.

The skimmias are neat, compact, slow-growing evergreen shrubs which sport bright red berries in autumn and winter, preceded by white fragrant flowers produced in spring. Plant groups of male and female plants to ensure berry production (only the females produce berries, of course). **S. japonica reevesiana**, however, is hermaphrodite and can be planted singly. Suitable for seaside, town and city gardens, they thrive in any fertile, moisture-retentive yet well-drained soil and are best grown in shade or partial shade. Consequently they are ideal for woodland gardens. We recommend **S. × confusa** 'Kew Green', a small male shrub, with large clusters of

Ilex aquifolium 'Bacciflava' is a large holly displaying bright yellow berries. It makes a handsome addition to the woodland garden but needs a male holly to pollinate it

fragrant cream-white flowers; **S. japonica** 'Nymans', a small female shrub, bearing masses of large berries; **S. japonica** 'Rubella', another small male shrub with white flowers from red winter buds; and **S. reevesiana**, a dwarf hermaphrodite shrub needing an acid soil and producing crimson fruits which last all winter.

Several ilex or hollies (see also Coloured foliage, Chapter 5) are grown for their crops of autumn and winter berries. However, to obtain berries a male holly, such as **I. aquifolium** 'Golden Milkboy', should be grown with the berry-producing females to ensure fertilisation of the flowers. Hollies make handsome additions to the woodland garden, where their evergreen foliage is welcome in winter, and look especially good

when grouped with white-stemmed birches, and can also be used in shrub or mixed borders or as lawn specimens.

Of the **I. aquifolium** (common holly) cultivars, we suggest 'Bacciflava', a large shrub with bright yellow berries; 'Green Pillar', a medium shrub of columnar habit bearing red berries, named by Hillier; and 'J. C. van Tol', large shrub whose leaves have few or no spines and which produces huge crops of red berries. **I. cornuta** 'Burfordii' is a very free-berrying small shrub with interesting leaf shape, ideal where space is limited.

Other autumn-berrying shrubs include **Aucuba japonica** 'Salicifolia' (see also Coloured foliage, Chapter 5). To ensure aucubas produce their masses of red berries, grow a male plant with the females, such as **A. j.** 'Lance Leaf'. Both are medium evergreen shrubs with narrow leaves.

For unusually coloured berries try **Callicarpa bodinieri** 'Profusion', a medium shrub with masses of purple-blue berries in autumn. Group several plants together for best berry production; they are suitable for any well-drained soil and partial shade.

Equally spectacular blue berries, surrounded by crimson calyces, are produced in autumn by **Clerodendrum trichotomum fargesii**. These follow the starry, fragrant, white, late-summer flowers. This is a large shrub for the border and is suited to any humus-rich well-drained soil.

Raised on the Hillier Nurseries, **Photinia** 'Redstart' (syn. **Stranvinia** 'Redstart') is difficult to put into a pigeon-hole. An evergreen, it forms a large shrub or

Skimmia japonica 'Rubella' is a small male shrub with white flowers opening from red winter buds. It is useful for planting in groups of female skimmias to pollinate them, thereby ensuring crops of red berries in winter (*Hillier Arboretum, Ampfield, Hampshire*)

Pernettya mucronata is a dwarf, evergreen, berrying ground-cover shrub. There are lots of cultivars, such as 'Cherry Ripe', raised and named by Hillier's. Plant groups of male and female plants to obtain berries

small tree whose young leaves are flushed with copper-red. Some take on bright scarlet tints in autumn. The masses of white, early-summer flowers are followed by red berries tipped with yellow. A spectacular plant for the woodland garden or shrub border, it thrives in any fertile well-drained soil.

Danae racemosa (Alexandrian laurel) is an excellent berrying shrub for dense shade or sun and any moisture-retentive soil. It is a small evergreen with shiny, narrow, leaf-like shoots and orange berries in autumn. Excellent for the woodland garden or for underplanting trees or large shrubs, as is **Ruscus hypoglossum**, a closely related dwarf evergreen ground-cover shrub with flattened, leaf-like shoots and large bright red bérries on female plants. Grow males and females to obtain berries. This plant is excellent for very dry soil in shade.

Several members of the family **Ericacea**

are notable for their autumn berries, including × gaulnettya, pernettya and vaccinium. All need acid, humus-rich, moisture-retentive soil, are suitable for dappled shade and can be grown with rhododendrons, camellias and other lime-haters, say on the edge of a woodland garden.

× **Gaulnettya** 'Pink Pixie' (gaultheria × pernettya) is a dwarf evergreen ground-cover shrub raised and named by Hillier's, with white urn-shaped flowers followed by purple-red berries.

Pernettya mucronata is also a dwarf evergreen ground-cover shrub with white flowers in spring, followed by clusters of large berries the size and shape of marbles. These are produced only by female plants, which must have a male to pollinate the flowers. Recommended cultivars are 'Cherry Ripe', with cherry-red berries; 'Mulberry Wine', dark purple; 'Sea Shell', pale pink, deepening with age; and 'White Pearl', pure white. All of these were raised and named by Hillier's.

There are many vaccinium species, like **V. corymbosum** (swamp blueberry), a medium shrub with black edible berries whose leaves turn scarlet and bronze in the autumn; **V. cylindraceum**, a large semi-evergreen shrub, its berries blue-black, covered with white 'bloom'; **V. glauco-album**, a small suckering evergreen, the leaves grey-green with blue-white undersides and blue-black berries covered in white 'bloom'; **V. macrocarpon** (American cranberry), a prostrate evergreen shrub of creeping habit with edible red berries (needs very moist or boggy soil); **V. praestans**, another prostrate creeping species with edible red berries and brilliant autumn leaf colour (must have moist soil and cool conditions); and **V. vitis-idaea** (cowberry), a dwarf creeping evergreen with edible red berries (best grown in partial shade).

MORE SHRUBS FOR AUTUMN AND WINTER

COLOURED STEMS

Some shrubs with coloured stems can add even more colour than flowers to the winter garden. They are certainly undervalued by many gardeners. Nothing could be more colourful than the young stems of **Cornus alba** 'Sibirica' (Westonbirt dogwood), brilliantly crimson in the weak winter sunshine. A medium shrub, its stems should be cut down almost to ground level in early spring each year to encourage a thicket of new shoots which are far more colourful than older stems. Include this dogwood in winter groups containing such shrubs as mahonias, **Viburnum tinus** and **Rubus cockburnianus** (whitewashed bramble), a medium shrub whose arching purple stems are covered in brilliant white 'bloom'. Like the cornus, the stems of this bramble are best cut down in early spring each year. All these shrubs thrive in any well-drained fertile soil.

More difficult to place is **Cornus alba** 'Kesselringii', as the purple-black stems need a light background if they are to show up. We suggest a white-variegated evergreen shrub, such as **Prunus laurocerasus** 'Marbled White', might make a suitable background. The stems may also show up well against water so try poolside planting. Again, cut the stems down each year.

Acer palmatum 'Senkaki' (coral-bark

Acer palmatum 'Senkaki', seen here with its bright autumn foliage, has striking coral-red branches which show up really well in winter. It is a large shrub, ideal for woodland gardens (*Denmans, West Sussex*)

maple, see also Coloured foliage, Chapter 5) has strikingly coral-red branches which show up really well in winter, particularly against a dark background of conifers or evergreen shrubs. The foliage is good in spring and autumn. It is a large shrub for the woodland garden or for borders.

DISTINCTIVE HABIT

For winter effect one should not only consider colour but also distinctive habit. For instance, when the leaves have fallen the twisted and curly stems of **Corylus avellana** 'Contorta' (corkscrew hazel) show up really well. In early spring the shoots are draped with yellow catkins. Most people would use this medium shrub as a lawn specimen. It thrives in any well-drained soil and is particularly good on chalk.

PLANTING SCHEME FEATURING COLOURED STEMS

Plant the crimson-stemmed **Cornus alba** 'Sibirica' (Westonbirt dogwood) in winter groups containing such shrubs as mahonias, **Viburnum tinus** and **Rubus cockburnianus** (whitewashed bramble) with white stems.

CHAPTER 7

ROSES

A refreshing trend has swept through the hitherto conservative rose world in recent years – roses are now effectively combined with other plants instead of being grown alone in their own special beds. But companion plants need to be chosen carefully if schemes are to be aesthetically pleasing.

Here we consider some of the roses which associate well with other shrubs – the species and other shrub roses, which can be planted in shrub or mixed borders. They bloom in the summer (some actually start blooming in late spring) and many continue their display into the autumn, when many roses also bear crops of colourful hips (seed capsules). One or two roses are even attractive in winter when their coloured thorns show up well. We also include climbing and pillar roses, and ramblers, for growing on walls, fences, etc.

There are many ideas for combinations of roses and other plants. Any pink or red roses which start flowering in early summer could be planted with philadelphus or mock orange, with its sweetly scented white blossoms.

A charming summer group could be created by planting a purple-leaved cotinus or berberis with red or pink roses. Another stunning combination consists of red or pink roses; **Acanthus mollis latifolius**, a hardy perennial with deeply cut leaves and spikes of purple and white flowers, and a purple-leaved cotinus.

Blue-flowered shrubs associate well with roses of any colour, including **Perovskia atriplicifolia** 'Blue Spire', lavenders, hebes or shrubby veronicas, **Ceanothus** 'Topaz', **Caryopteris** × **clandonensis** 'Heavenly Blue' and **Ceratostigma willmottianum**. Any silver or grey-foliage shrubs (see Chapter 5) would also make pleasing companions, such as santolinas and senecios.

Among summer-flowering hardy perennials (see Chapter 10) that associate well with species and other shrub roses are acanthus, **Artemisia absinthium** 'Lambrook Silver', delphiniums (especially blue or purple cultivars), echinops, eryngiums, blue geraniums, nepeta or catmint, **Salvia nemorosa** 'Lubeca', scabious and **Stachys byzantina** 'Silver Carpet' (ground cover).

Many ornamental grasses combine effectively with these roses, including the green-and-white-striped **Phalaris arundinacea** 'Picta', cream-striped **Miscanthus sinensis** 'Variegatus' and glaucous **Helictotrichon sempervirens**.

Any roses which are in bloom in the autumn or, even better, those which produce

Roses can be grown alone if desired, in the traditional way, although nowadays it is more usual to associate them with other plants (*Private garden, Berkshire*)

ROSES

Above:
A beautiful formal rose garden surrounded by dark green yew hedges. The central bed contains lavender, which associates extremely well with roses of all kinds (*The Rose Garden, Folley Farm, Berkshire*)

Right:
To compare and choose roses it is a good idea to visit a specialist collection, such as the *Royal National Rose Society's Garden, Chiswell Green, Hertfordshire*

colourful hips, may be featured in autumn groups which could include shrubs with seasonal leaf tints and perennials such as **Anemone × hybrida** cultivars, asters or Michaelmas daisies and sedums. Other autumn-flowering shrubs could be included, too, like buddlejas.

A stunning group we can recommend for autumn combines rose species noted for hips, **Cotinus** 'Flame', and a pampas grass, **Cortaderia selloana**.

Winter and spring interest can be maintained around species and other shrub roses by interplanting with **Helleborus orientalis, Iris unguicularis**, snowdrops, muscari and scillas. Do not forget that **Rosa sericea pteracantha**, with large red thorns, could be included in a group of shrubs and plants for winter effect.

Roses are easily grown given a position in full sun and a deep, fertile, well-drained yet moisture-retentive soil, and the species and other shrub roses need virtually no pruning.

144

SPECIES AND THEIR HYBRIDS

Rosa banksiae 'Lutea' (yellow Banksian rose), a strong-growing semi-evergreen climber to at least 7.6m (25ft) in height, produces double pale yellow flowers in late spring and early summer and makes an excellent companion for late spring/early summer-flowering clematis like **C. montana** cultivars, or the blue **C.**

Rosa banksiae 'Lutea' (yellow Banksian rose) is a strong-growing, semi-evergreen climber flowering in late spring and early summer. It needs a warm wall

macropetala 'Maidwell Hall'. This rose needs a warm wall.

Also best against a warm sunny wall is the vigorous climber **R.** 'Mermaid', with shiny evergreen foliage and large, bright yellow flowers with a boss of dark yellow stamens throughout summer. It reaches a height of 7.6m (25ft).

For the shrub border or edge of the woodland garden is **R.** 'Canary Bird', a medium shrub with attractive ferny foliage and masses of single yellow flowers in late spring and early summer. The young growth is purple. **R. chinensis** 'Old Blush' (monthly rose), a small to medium shrub, has a long succession of fragrant pink flowers.

The threepenny-bit rose, **R. elegantula** 'Persetosa', is very attractive with its ferny foliage turning crimson and purple in autumn and small, pale pink flowers from deeper buds in early summer, followed by masses of orange-red hips. A medium shrub, it is excellent for an autumn group.

The extremely vigorous climber **R. filipes** 'Kiftsgate' is usually grown through large mature trees, including evergreen conifers. Here the masses of small, single, scented flowers, produced in early and mid-summer, show up really well. Another good climber which can be grown in the same way is **R. longicuspis**, a semi-evergreen with white flowers which have the fragrance of bananas, followed by red-orange hips. **R.** 'Wedding Day' is a strong climber, capable of attaining 10m (33ft), and so can also be recommended for growing through a large tree. It produces large clusters of highly fragrant creamy flowers which age to pink.

Rosa gallica is the French rose, and there are two kinds we recommend: **R. g. officinalis** (apothecary's rose, red rose of Lancaster), producing semi-double, fragrant, crimson flowers with conspicuous yellow anthers; and 'Versicolor' (syn. 'Rosa

The extremely vigorous climber **Rosa filipes** 'Kiftsgate' is often grown through large mature trees, including evergreen conifers. Here it is seen with honeysuckle and weigela in a cottage-garden setting

Mundi), whose rose-red semi-double blooms are striped with white. Both are small shrubs.

An extremely useful species is **R. glauca** (syn. **R. rubrifolia**), as its grey-purple foliage contrasts so well with many other shrubs and plants. Try planting some clumps of the green-and-white-striped grass, **Phalaris arundinacea** 'Picta', around it. The small single flowers are pink and followed by red hips.

With the current interest in ground-cover roses, the old **Rosa** 'Max Graf' is enjoying renewed popularity. The long trailing stems bear scented rose-pink flowers for a long period in summer.

R. nitida is also a dwarf ground-cover shrub which produces masses of suckers. The stems are covered by fine thorns. The small flowers are rose-red and followed by dark crimson hips, while the foliage turns deep red and purple in autumn. This rose looks superb when used as ground cover with prostrate junipers.

An excellent addition to the shrub border is **R. moyesii** 'Geranium'. This medium shrub has bright red single flowers in profusion, followed by large deep red hips. Try

Rosa moyesii 'Geranium' with **Euphorbia characias wulfenii**, a striking combination. The bright red, single flowers of the rose are followed by large, deep red hips (*Coomblands, Sussex*)

associating it with shrubs noted for autumn leaf colour.

Flowering throughout the summer, **R. ×
odorata** 'Mutabilis' (syn. 'Tipo Ideale') is a small to medium shrub producing a succession of orange to red, fragrant single flowers.

The **R. rugosa** (ramanas rose) cultivars are well worth garden space as they produce several flushes of fragrant flowers during the summer, the blooms being followed by showy hips, like small tomatoes. Most of these compact, very prickly and hardy roses also make very good hedges. Height is about 1.5m (5ft). We recommend 'Blanc Double de Coubert', white, semi-double; 'Frau Dagmar Hastrup', especially good for hedging, light rose-pink, very large dark red hips; 'Pink Grootendorst', very good for hedging, double, bright pink; 'Sarah van Fleet', also recommended for hedging, large semi-double, fragrant, light rose pink; and 'Schneezwerg', with semi-double, fragrant white flowers and orange hips, another good hedger.

The main feature of **R. sericea pteracantha** (syn. **R. omeiensis pteracantha**) is the large, dark red translucent thorns, which show up particularly well during the winter. An ideal shrub for a winter group, where it can be associated with hellebores and winter-flowering shrubs like **Viburnum tinus** cultivars. The latter's evergreen foliage would make a good background for the thorns. This rose is a medium shrub and, in early summer, produces single white flowers followed by red hips.

OTHER SHRUB ROSES

Many more shrub roses, from old-fashioned to modern kinds, are suitable for growing with other shrubs in borders.

OLD-FASHIONED ROSES

The old-fashioned roses are enjoying renewed popularity, particularly because of the increasing interest in the English cottage style of gardening.

These roses are lovely in a riotous cottage-garden border and although they flower only once a year, in early or midsummer, many have the advantage of a rich fragrance. The blooms are generally fully double. The roses make marvellous companions for philadelphus (mock orange), which has white fragrant blossoms in early summer, and some particularly lovely effects can be achieved by growing the pink-flowered cultivars with silver-foliage plants such as **Artemisia absinthium** 'Lambrook Silver'.

We particularly recommend 'Cardinal de Richelieu' (gallica group), velvety, dark purplish crimson, tremendous fragrance, height 1.5m (5ft); 'Celestial' (alba group), semi-double, fragrant, pale pink, grey-green foliage, height 1.2–1.5m (4–5ft); 'Comte de Chambord' (portland group), flat fully double blooms, highly fragrant, deep pink, height 1.2m (4ft); 'Fantin-Latour' (centifolia group), double, flattish fragrant blooms in profusion, palest pink, height 1.8m (6ft); 'Königin von Dänemark' (alba group), quartered double blooms, rich fragrance, bright pink, height 1.5m (5ft); 'Madame Hardy' (damask group), flat double quartered very fragrant blooms, cream-white ageing to pure white, height 1.8m (6ft); and 'Maiden's Blush' (alba group), fully double, strong sweet fragrance, palest pink, height 1.5m (5ft).

BOURBON ROSES

We strongly recommend the comparatively modern but diverse bourbon roses, again because they are highly fragrant and look at home in cottage-garden borders. Flowering starts in early summer and the bushes are repeat-flowering. Popular with the Victorians, bourbon roses are now enjoying renewed popularity with the current interest in Victoriana.

We can thoroughly recommend 'Boule de Neige', fully double, highly fragrant pure white flowers, summer and autumn. fine shiny foliage, height 1.2m (4ft); 'La Reine Victoria', cup-shaped, fragrant, rich lilac-pink blooms, height 1.2m (4ft); 'Madame Isaac Pereire', large fully double, intensely fragrant purple-crimson flowers, height 2.1m (7ft), can be grown as a small climber; 'Madam Pierre Oger', cup-shaped flowers, shaped like a water lily, light silver-pink, superb fragrance, height 1.2m (4ft); 'Souvenir de la Malmaison' (climbing form), flat

'Buff Beauty' is a well-known hybrid musk rose which flowers on and off between early summer and late autumn. The flowers are well scented

'Penelope' is another hybrid musk rose, this time with strongly fragrant flowers. Like other hybrid musks, it is ideal for forming a low hedge

quartered blooms, white and pale pink shades, fragrant, dislikes a wet summer, height 3m (10ft); and 'Zéphirine Drouhin', semi-double carmine-pink flowers with a sweet fragrance, thornless stems, best grown as a climber, height 2.7m (9ft). The latter can be grown intertwined with large-flowered clematis, preferably in purple or blue, for a really stunning effect.

HYBRID MUSK ROSES

This is another comparatively modern group, having been bred in the early part of the twentieth century. We recommend them to the discerning gardener because they flower on and off between early summer and late autumn, and most are fragrant. They grow to a height of 1.2–1.8m (4–6 ft) and have a bushy habit, making them suitable for low hedges if desired.

We recommend the cultivars 'Ballerina', with small, single, pink white-centred blooms carried in large clusters, which is extremely free-flowering and lovely with small silver or grey-foliage shrubs; 'Buff Beauty', producing semi-double, well-scented flowers in apricot yellow, with a vigorous and spreading habit; 'Cornelia', with double, highly scented flowers, copper pink

PLANTING SCHEMES FOR SHRUB ROSES

There are many ideas for combinations of shrub roses and other plants.
• Pink or red roses with white philadelphus.
• Purple-leaved cotinus or berberis with red or pink roses.
• Blue-flowered shrubs with roses of any colour.
• Silver or grey-foliage shrubs with any roses.
• Blue or purple delphiniums with roses in any colour.
• Green-and-white-striped ornamental grasses with any roses.

'Ferdinand Pichard' is an old hybrid perpetual rose and one of the most attractive of the striped cultivars. The double flowers are very freely produced in several flushes and enhance any mixed border

and yellow, vigorous habit; 'Felicia', double deliciously fragrant flowers, salmon-pink and yellow, compact and bushy habit; 'Penelope', semi-double strongly fragrant flowers, pale pink flushed cream; and 'Prosperity', with fully double, strongly fragrant cream-white flowers.

MODERN SHRUB ROSES

Many old roses are well-loved because of their flower shapes and, above all, their fragrance. But unfortunately they bloom only once a year, in the summer, and there is not a very wide range of colours available.

However, as the result of hybridisation between old-fashioned roses and modern kinds there is now a new race which is known as English roses. The flowers have all the charm of the old-fashioned roses but they are recurrent and come in a much wider range of colours. Most are fragrant to a greater or lesser extent, and they look at home in cottage-style or modern borders.

There are now many cultivars of English roses but we particularly recommend 'Claire Rose', cup-shaped flowers turning to flat rosettes of blush pink, ageing white (blooms become spotted in rain), fragrant, height 1.2m (4ft); 'English Garden', flat flowers, apricot-yellow with lighter edges, slight scent, height 90cm (3ft); 'Gertrude Jekyll', rosette-like rich pink flowers, very strong fragrance, height 1.2m (4ft); 'Graham Thomas', cup-shaped flowers, rich pure yellow (there are few yellow old-fashioned roses), strong fragrance, height 1.2m (4ft); 'Heritage', cup-shaped flowers, clear shell pink, strong fragrance, height 1.2m (4ft); 'Mary Rose', large, loose, double, pink fragrant flowers produced continuously

The modern shrub rose 'Constance Spry' produces sprays of very strongly scented flowers, of old-fashioned appearance, in early summer. As it is a tall cultivar it needs supporting and is therefore probably best grown as a climber

small semi-double, cerise-pink fragrant flowers set against grey foliage, height 2.4m (8ft), with an arching habit.

Single-flowered roses have a charm all their own. One of the best is 'Golden Wings', which continuously produces large yellow fragrant flowers with conspicuous mahogany-coloured stamens throughout summer. Height 1.2m (4ft). A beautiful effect is achieved when it is grown with light blue delphiniums.

Also with single blooms is the recurrent-flowering 'Nevada', with cream-white flowers up to 10cm (4in) in diameter. Its height is 1.8–2.4m (6–8ft).

Ideal for very small gardens are the diminutive polyantha roses. 'The Fairy' grows only 60cm (2ft) in height and bears tiny pink flowers from midsummer until late autumn. 'Yesterday' has sprays of semi-double, lilac-pink, sweetly scented blooms on 90cm (3ft) high bushes.

throughout summer, height 1.2m (4ft); 'Pretty Jessica', cup-shaped rich pink flowers, strongly fragrant, height 76cm (2½ft); 'Warwick Castle', flat rosette-shaped bright pink flowers, strongly fragrant, height 76cm (2½ft); 'William Shakespeare', rosette-shaped flowers, dark crimson turning rich purple, fragrant, height 1.2m (4ft); 'Winchester Cathedral', large, loose, double flowers, white and fragrant, height 1.2m (4ft); and 'Yellow Button', flowers rosette-shaped, pale yellow, fruity scent, height 90cm (3ft).

With the English roses possessing so many good qualities it is all too easy to neglect other modern shrub roses. However, many are equally worthy of garden space, such as 'Cerise Bouquet' with sprays of

ROSES TO FILL VERTICAL SPACE

Last but not least we consider the climbing and pillar roses and the ramblers, for training to walls, fences, pergolas, and pillars or tripods in the shrub border (see also section Species and their hybrids, this chapter). Instead of growing these alone, however, consider combining them with other climbing plants, such as the large-flowered clematis, planning for contrasting or harmonising colours. These roses also combine well with the blue-flowered wall shrub **Solanum crispum** 'Glasnevin', or with the blue passion flower, **Passiflora caerulea**.

The modern shrub rose 'Nevada' is recurrent-flowering, producing masses of single cream-white blooms. Single-flowered roses have a charm all their own (*Coomblands, Sussex*)

The climbing rose 'Madame Alfred Carriere' has sweetly fragrant flowers produced in several flushes. It is vigorous, growing to a height of 6m (20ft)

'Felicite et Perpetue' is one of the best-known rambler roses. The small pompon-like flowers have a light fragrance and are produced in large clusters. It blooms once, in midsummer, and grows to 6m (20ft) in height (*Coomblands, Sussex*)

CLIMBING AND PILLAR ROSES

These are tall, stiff-stemmed roses flowering during summer and into autumn. Among our favourites are 'Climbing Madame Caroline Testout', bearing large, globular, fragrant rose-pink flowers, with a second flush in early autumn, its height 6m (20ft); 'Gloire de Dijon', with double, yellow fragrant flowers throughout summer and 'at home' in cottage gardens, height 4.5m (15ft); 'Golden Showers', offering large semi-double, fragrant golden-yellow flowers throughout summer, height 3m (10ft); 'Madame Alfred Carrière', which has large, cup-shaped white flushed pink flowers of sweet fragrance, recurrent-flowering, height 6m (20ft); 'Madame Grégoire Staechelin', with semi-double, glowing pink flowers, very sweet fragrance but only one

PLANTING SCHEME WITH CLIMBING ROSES

Combine climbing, pillar and rambler roses with other climbers such as large-flowered clematis and **Passiflora caerulea** (blue passion flower); also with the blue wall shrub **Solanum crispum** 'Glasnevin'.

Introduced in 1930, climbing rose 'New Dawn' is an outstanding cultivar with very fragrant, well-shaped flowers which are produced in several flushes. It attains a height of about 3m (10ft)

The rambler rose 'Sanders' White', seen here growing with golden meadowsweet, **Filipendula ulmaria** 'Aurea', is well scented and flowers late in the season (*Coomblands, Sussex*)

flush of blooms in summer, its height 6m (20ft); and 'Parkdirektor Riggers', almost single dark crimson flowers in large clusters, repeat flowering, height 3.6m (12ft).

RAMBLERS

These are vigorous summer-flowering climbers with lax stems, and some of the very vigorous kinds are suitable for growing up large mature trees. We recommend 'Alberic Barbier', which has clusters of double cream-white flowers from yellow buds and often produces a second flush of blooms, is ideal for growing into trees and reaches a height of 7.6m (25ft); 'Felicite et Perpetue', with small pompom-like cream-white flowers in large clusters, light fragrance, blooms once in midsummer, height 6m (20ft); 'Rambling Rector', semi-double cream-white flowers, well scented, height 6m (20ft), ideal for training into a small mature tree or large shrub; 'Sanders' White', semi-double pure white flowers, well scented, flowers late in the season, height 5.4m (18ft); and 'Veilchenblau', bearing small fragrant flowers in clusters, purple-violet ageing to lilac, thornless stems, height 4.5m (15ft).

Some roses with lax stems can be grown as ground cover, for example on banks or around larger shrubs. These include 'Bonica', with small light pink flowers, blooming recurrently, height as ground cover 76cm (2½ft); and 'Nozomi', with masses of small, single, pale pink and white blooms, flowering only once in summer, height as ground cover 30cm (12in).

CHAPTER 8

CONIFERS

Conifers are trees and shrubs with either needle-like or scale-like leaves. Most are evergreen although some species are deciduous. Many produce hard, woody, often attractive cones containing the seeds, while others like yews and junipers have fleshy berry-like fruits.

Conifers are extremly diverse in size, shape and foliage colour, making them essential garden plants. In size they range from prostrate shrubs to giant trees, so there are species and cultivars to suit all sizes of garden. Indeed the dwarf conifers have become extremely popular in recent years with the trend towards smaller gardens.

Shapes range from flat mats to mounds, domes, cones and columns, and there are also pendulous and wide-spreading flat-topped shapes. Conifers come in all shades of green, including grey and blue-greens, and there are many with golden or yellow foliage.

THE LARGER CONIFERS

The bigger conifers, like other trees and shrubs, help to form the permanent framework of planting schemes. The more shapely or distinctive ones make fine lawn specimens, or they can be used as focal points to draw the eye to a particular part of the garden.

The larger conifers can also be grown in groups on their own, or mixed with other trees and shrubs. Either way, one has great scope for creating contrast in shape, texture and colour. The permanent 'solid' foliage of the evergreen conifers contrasts superbly with the transient and lighter leaves of deciduous trees and shrubs. For example, conifers with dark green foliage make a marvellous background for shrubs or trees with autumn leaf colour. And some of the bluish or greyish conifers contrast wonderfully with autumnal foliage.

Dark green conifers also make excellent foils for many flowering deciduous trees and shrubs, particularly those with small pale blooms produced in winter. Without a solid background these would never show up.

Large, mature, dark green conifers also make excellent hosts for certain climbing plants: not very dense climbers like ivies, which would end up smothering the trees, but rather subjects such as very tall rambler roses (see Chapter 7). The flowers, especially if white, show up dramatically against the conifer's foliage. Or you might like to try a tall climber noted for autumn leaf colour, like **Vitis coignetiae** whose large leaves turn brilliant crimson and scarlet before they fall.

When using coniferous and broad-leaved evergreens with deciduous trees and shrubs to help build the framework of gardens, aim for approximately one-third evergreen to two-thirds deciduous. This, we feel, is a pleasing balance. Increasing the evergreens at the expense of the deciduous could result in a heavy, sombre effect, remi-

Blue cultivars of Lawson's cypress, **Chamaecyparis lawsoniana**, contrast with so many plants. Here the popular 'Pembury Blue' associates beautifully with variegated hostas (plantain lilies)

niscent of Victorian gardens where evergreens were very much overplanted.

There are many larger conifers from which to choose, but we are certain the following carefully selected collection will appeal to the discerning gardener.

The abies or silver firs are evergreen, mainly cone-shaped trees with short, flat-

---

PLANTING SCHEME FOR CONFERS AND CLIMBERS

Large, mature, dark green conifers make excellent hosts for certain climbing plants such as very tall rambler roses (especially white), or **Vitis coignetiae** with its brilliant autumn leaf colour.

---

tened needle-like leaves with silver bands on the undersides. The upright cones are attractive. Grow these firs in a deep, moisture-retentive soil, avoiding shallow chalky conditions. They are not suitable for areas with industrial pollution.

Making a marvellous lawn specimen, or partner for trees with autumn leaf tints, is **Abies concolor** 'Candicans' (Colorado white fir), a large tree with very conspicuous silver-white or grey foliage. **A. koreana**, a small slow-growing tree with deep green foliage, is noted for its heavy crops of small purplish cones, produced from an early age. A good lawn specimen.

Superb as a lawn specimen or focal point is **Cedrus atlantica** 'Glauca Pendula', a form of the Atlas cedar. This small, evergreen tree with glaucous-blue needles has very long, pendulous branches, which may need to be supported. It grows in any well-drained soil.

Also excellent for creating a focal point is the narrowly conical **Cephalotaxus harringtonia** 'Fastigiata', a medium to large evergreen yew-like shrub with extremely dark green, short, needle-like leaves. It tolerates shade, even complete shade, and is very suitable for chalky soils.

Among the most popular conifers are the numerous cultivars of the Lawson cypress, **Chamaecyparis lawsoniana**. They have flattened sprays of evergreen scale-like foliage and are mainly cone-shaped or columnar. Excellent for mixed groups or as single specimens, they grow in any well-drained soil. A medium to large tree of narrow

---

Chamaecyparis lawsoniana 'Pembury Blue' is a medium tree with brilliant silver-blue foliage, ideal for combining with others chosen for autumn leaf colour. It is seen here with **Hypericum × inodorum** 'Elstead' (foreground) and a **Clerodendrum trichotomum fargesii** (*White Windows, Hampshire*)

Chamaecyparis lawsoniana 'Witzeliana' is a small tree of narrow columnar habit, with brilliant green foliage, and is highly recommended for use as a focal point or lawn specimen.

columnar habit is **C. l.** 'Kilmacurragh', which has deep green foliage and is excellent as an accent plant or focal point. The best blue cultivar, in our opinion, is **C. l.** 'Pembury Blue', a medium cone-shaped tree with brilliant silver-blue foliage which is superb for combining with shrubs chosen for autumn leaf colour, for example. One of the best golden Lawson's is **C. l.** 'Stewartii', a medium to large tree of conical habit. It looks great with 'Pembury Blue'! **C. l.** 'Witzeliana' is a small tree of narrow columnar habit with brilliant green foliage, which

you could use as a lawn specimen or focal point.

Becoming a large shrub or small tree of wide-spreading conical habit is **C. obtusa** 'Tetragona Aurea', with golden-yellow, evergreen, scale-like foliage of moss-like texture. For a striking effect, combine it with an autumn-berrying cotoneaster. It is suitable for any well-drained soil.

A striking focal point or lawn specimen is provided by a form of the Mexican cypress, **Cupressus lusitanica** 'Glauca Pendula', a small spreading evergreen tree with pendulous, glaucous-blue, scale-like foliage. It must be grown in a sheltered position in mild areas only. This conifer was selected by Hillier. Also making a superb focal point is **Cupressus sempervirens** 'Green Pencil', a clone of the Italian cypress chosen by Hillier. Of narrowly columnar habit, it is a medium evergreen tree with deep green, scale-like foliage. Both grow in any well-drained soil.

The maidenhair tree, **Ginkgo biloba**, is generally grown as a lawn specimen as it has distinctive characteristics. Firstly, it is deciduous; secondly, the leaves are of unusual shape, being two-lobed and fan-shaped. They turn clear yellow in autumn. It is a medium-size to large tree of conical habit, thriving in any well-drained soil and tolerating atmospheric pollution. Two forms are also worth considering: 'Fastigiata', of narrowly columnar habit; and 'Tremonia', which forms a narrow cone. Both are medium-size trees.

Juniperus recurva coxii, a variety of the drooping juniper, is a very attractive small evergreen tree for use as a specimen in the lawn or elsewhere. Basically of conical habit, the branchlets are pendulous and the scale-like leaves grey-green. A mature specimen resembles a fountain. This juniper is suited to any well-drained soil, including chalk.

CONIFERS

A specimen of **Picea breweriana**, Brewer's weeping spruce, features in this collection of conifers. It is one of the most beautiful of the weeping trees and here contrasts with dwarf conifers like **Abies concolor** 'Glauca Compacta' (*York Gate, Leeds*)

Like the maidenhair tree, the dawn redwood, **Metasequoia glyptostroboides**, is deciduous but perhaps even more attractive. We recommend the form 'Emerald Feathers', named by Hillier, a medium to large conical tree with lush green feathery foliage turning golden brown in autumn, and red brown bark. Easily grown in any moisture-retentive soil, usually as a lawn specimen.

Several of the piceas or spruces make handsome lawn specimens or focal points. All are evergreen and have sharp, pointed, needle-like foliage. They are easily grown but you should avoid shallow, chalky, or very dry soils and positions exposed to cold winds. **Picea breweriana** (Brewer's weeping spruce) is an incredibly beautiful small to medium-size tree of conical habit, but with spreading branches which carry pendulous 'curtains' of smaller branchlets. The flat leaves are deep blue-green with white undersides.

Picea likiangensis is a medium-size tree of vigorous habit, cone-shaped and with flat blue-green leaves with glaucous undersides. In the spring the young red cones and male flowers are an attraction. **P. omorika** (Serbian spruce) is highly distinctive, resembling a pagoda in outline. It is a medium to large conical tree but the short branches grow downwards and then turn upwards at their tips. The flat, deep green leaves have glaucous undersides. **P. o.** 'Pendula', a medium tree, forms a slender cone shape and has drooping branches.

The golden-yellow form of the oriental spruce, **Picea orientalis** 'Aurea', is a medium cone-shaped tree, but the foliage becomes green as it ages. A useful specimen for a group of conifers or other trees. It

PLANTING SCHEME FOR AUTUMN

The glaucous blue **Picea pungens** 'Hoopsii' contrasts superbly with nyssas, trees which have brilliant autumn foliage.

would look good with **P. pungens** 'Hoopsii', a form of the Colorado spruce with brilliant glaucous-blue foliage. This small to medium conical tree also contrasts superbly with trees or shrubs noted for autumn leaf colour, like the nyssas, for instance. You could also grow it alone as a lawn specimen or focal point (the colour helps to create a sense of distance in a garden), or include it in a heather garden.

The pines are evergreen conifers with needle-like, generally long leaves. They are fussy about their surroundings, being intolerant of atmospheric pollution and, in some instances, needing acid soils. Pines need to be used carefully for they do not associate aesthetically with all plants. In our opinion they look good with white-stemmed birches, rhododendrons and large drifts of heathers. However, like many other conifers, pines can also be used effectively as lawn specimens. Some can help to create a Mediterranean atmosphere in a garden.

We recommend the following pines: **Pinus aristata** (bristlecone pine), large shrub to small tree of dense habit, needles deep green, in bunches of five; **P. montezumae** (Montezuma pine), medium to large tree with a dome-shaped crown, needles blue-grey, in bunches of five, up to 25cm (10in) long, must be grown in a sheltered position such as the edge of woodland; and **P. sylvestris** 'Aurea', a form of the Scots pine with golden-yellow winter foliage. It is a slow-growing small tree of conical habit.

Podocarpus andinus (plum-fruited yew, Chilean yew) is, as you might expect, something like a yew, with flattened needle-like bright green leaves and grey-black damson-like fruits. This large shrub or medium tree is evergreen, of broadly columnar habit and is useful for groups or specimen planting. Any well-drained fertile soil, including chalk, will do.

The golden larch, **Pseudolarix amabilis**, is an attractive deciduous conifer with clusters of bright green needle-like leaves which turn deep yellow in autumn. A medium-size, slow-growing cone-shaped tree, it needs to be grown in lime-free soils.

A tree which stands out particularly well in winter is the golden-leaved form of the Scots pine, **Pinus sylvestris** 'Aurea'. It is a slow-growing small tree of conical habit

It is normally grown as a lawn specimen, as is **Sciadopitys verticillata** (umbrella pine), a slow-growing medium evergreen tree of cone-shaped habit with long, needle-like, dark green leaves arranged in whorls resembling the spokes of an umbrella (hence the common name). This too needs a lime-free soil.

Very distinctive, and therefore suitable for use as a lawn specimen, is **Taxodium ascendens** 'Nutans', a small to medium-size slow-growing tree of broadly columnar habit, with bright green awl-shaped leaves giving a very feathery effect overall. The foliage becomes brown in the autumn. This tree is best with a solid background of dark green conifers or other trees, and must have acid, moisture-retentive soil.

Taxus baccata (common yew) is an excellent evergreen conifer with flattened needle-like leaves, suitable for shade and thriving in any well-drained soil – especially chalk. There are several cultivars we can recommend, these being suited to shrub or mixed borders in association with deciduous shrubs. The yews are also perfectly at home in a woodland garden, where they contribute especially well to the winter scene.

'Adpressa Variegata' is a large shrub whose leaves start dark gold then become yellow-edged; 'Dovastoniana' (Westfelton yew), is a small tree of spreading habit, its branches held horizontally and branchlets pendulous, with very dark green leaves, making an excellent background plant; and 'Dovastonii Aurea', a large shrub with yellow-edged leaves.

The thujas (arbor-vitae) are notable for their aromatic evergreen leaves. They are scale conifers, the foliage being carried in flat sprays like the Lawson cypress, and are suited to any well-drained soil. One of the best golden thujas, at its best in winter, is **T. plicata** 'Aurea', a large broadly columnar tree making a fine lawn specimen.

Tsugas (hemlocks) have short, needle-like, evergreen leaves and are mainly cone-shaped. They thrive in deep, loamy, moisture-retentive yet well-drained soil, but are not suitable for shallow earth over chalk. They take shade and therefore are candidates for woodland gardens. **T. mertensiana** 'Glauca' is a large but slow-growing tree of spire-like habit, with glaucous foliage, which also makes a handsome lawn specimen.

The thujas are notable for their aromatic foliage. One of the best of the golden thujas is **T. plicata** 'Aurea', a large broadly columnar tree making a fine lawn specimen

DWARF CONIFERS

Dwarf conifers have become extremely popular in recent years as gardens have become smaller. They range from prostrate forms and true miniatures to semi-dwarfs and medium-size shrubs up to 3m (10ft) in height. Many are painfully slow-growing and take many years to reach their ultimate size.

But how do we use dwarf conifers in the garden? It has to be said that they must be used with care, as they do not look right in all parts of the garden and certainly do not associate pleasingly with all kinds of plants. They are ideal for creating height and variation in shape and texture on rock gardens. But do not perch them at the top! They look better on the 'lower slopes', just as conifers are found on mountainsides in the wild.

Hillier's collection of dwarf conifers. The dwarfs have become extremely popular in recent years as gardens have become smaller. They can be used in many parts of the plot with other plants, or could even be grown on their own to form a mini pinetum

Prostrate and spreading forms can be allowed to spread over specimen rocks or rock outcrops.

A popular use is to include dwarf conifers in heather gardens. The conifers associate beautifully with these plants; dwarf pines are particularly pleasing, although most types do not look out of place.

Various dwarf conifers make suitable specimens for small lawns, particularly columnar or cone-shaped kinds. They can, of course, be grown on their own if you want to create a mini pinetum. They look good in

PLANTING SCHEMES FOR DWARF CONIFERS

- On rock gardens with alpines.
- In heather gardens.
- On their own in a mini 'pinetum'.

an undulating bed set in a lawn or gravel area.

There are hundreds of dwarf conifers from which to choose, but we are confident the following small selection will appeal to the connoisseur. To avoid repetition of conditions required, characteristics, etc, we refer readers to the section The larger conifers, this chapter.

Abies (silver firs)

We recommend **A. balsamea** 'Hudsonia', dwarf evergreen shrub, slow, bun-shaped, dark green; **A. concolor** 'Compacta', small evergreen shrub, irregular shape, dense, grey-blue; **A. lasiocarpa** 'Compacta', medium evergreen shrub, slow, conical, blue-grey; and **A. nordmanniana** 'Golden spreader', dwarf evergreen shrub, spreads widely, slow, pale yellow. All are suitable for heather gardens (see also The larger conifers, this chapter).

Calocedrus (Incense cedar)

Calocedrus decurrens 'Berrima Gold', small evergreen shrub, introduced by Hillier, columnar, scale-like leaves in flat sprays, dark gold, tinged pink in spring, becoming yellow-green, then bronze in winter. Any well-drained soil.

Cedrus (cedars)

Cedrus libani 'Comte de Dijon', medium evergreen shrub, slow, conical, dense green needles. Looks good with heathers and is ideal as a lawn specimen. (See also The larger conifers, this chapter.)

Several dwarfs are to be found among the abies or silver firs, which are noted for their attractive cones. They need a deep, moisture-retentive soil and detest industrial pollution

One of the best-known of the dwarf abies or silver firs is **A. balsamea** 'Hudsonia' which grows very slowly. It can be confidently recommended for small rock gardens (*Hillier Arboretum, Ampfield, Hampshire*)

Chamaecyparis lawsoniana 'Aurea Densa' slowly makes a compact, conical specimen and can be recommended for the larger rock garden. The golden-yellow foliage is attractive all year round (*Hillier Arboretum, Ampfield, Hampshire*)

Chamaecyparis (false cypress)

Chamaecyparis lawsoniana (Lawson cypress) cultivars (see also The larger conifers, this chapter) include 'Aurea Densa', medium evergreen shrub, slow, conical, compact, golden-yellow, highly recommended for rock gardens; 'Minima Aurea', small evergreen shrub, conical, golden-yellow, ideal for rock gardens; and 'Pygmaea Argentea', small evergreen shrub, rounded habit, slow, deep blue-green foliage tipped cream-white, superb with heathers.

    C. obtusa 'Nana Aurea' (see also The larger conifers, this chapter) is a medium evergreen shrub slowly forming a bush of golden-yellow foliage, ideal for rock gar-

dens. **C. thyoides** 'Purple Heather', a dwarf evergreen shrub for lime-free soils, forms a dense rounded bush, the foliage becoming rich purple in winter. Excellent for the heather garden.

Cryptomeria (Japanese cedar)

There are several dwarf cultivars of **Cryptomeria japonica** and all are evergreen, and best grown in slightly acid, moist but well-drained soil. We recommend 'Elegans Compacta', a medium shrub with plumes of soft foliage, rich purple in winter; and 'Vilmoriniana', a dwarf, globe-shaped shrub, very slow, its foliage awl-shaped and red-purple in winter, which is ideal for the rock or heather garden (it goes well with red or pink winter-flowering heathers).

Juniperus (junipers)

These are evergreen conifers with scale-like adult leaves and needle-like juvenile foliage, liking any well-drained soil and especially suitable for chalk. The numerous dwarf forms include **J. communis** 'Compressa', dwarf shrub, slow, narrow cone shape, grey-green, ideal for small rock gardens (plant in groups for best effect); **J. squamata** 'Blue Star', dwarf shrub, silver-blue awl-shaped leaves; and **J. squamata** 'Chinese Silver', medium to large shrub, silvery blue-green awl-shaped leaves. The latter three add another colour to heather gardens.

Picea (spruces)

There are numerous dwarf spruces which look especially good in heather gardens, and some are also at home on rock gardens (see also The larger conifers, this chapter). We

Juniperus communis 'Compressa' is one of the smallest conifers and painfully slow-growing. It is therefore highly recommended even for the smallest rock garden (*The Morleys, Shropshire*)

recommend **Picea mariana** 'Nana', dwarf evergreen shrub, globe-shaped, grey-green, excellent rock-garden conifer; and **P. pungens** 'Globosa', small evergreen shrub, globular, flat-topped, glaucous blue, brings another colour to the heather garden (try surrounding it with pink heathers).

Pinus (pines)

The dwarf pines are excellent for heather and rock gardens (see also The larger conifers, this chapter). Small forms include **P. parviflora** 'Adcock's dwarf', medium evergreen shrub, compact bush, slow, bunches of short deep blue-green needles at ends of shoots (selected by Graham Adcock, a retired Hillier foreman); **P. strobus** 'Nana', small conical evergreen shrub, form of the Weymouth pine with glaucous green leaves in fives; and **P. sylvestris** 'Beuvronensis', small evergreen shrub, form of the Scots pine, dome-shaped, pairs of grey-green leaves.

Taxus (yew)

Of the dwarf **Taxus baccata** (common yew) cultivars we recommend 'Standishii', a medium evergreen shrub slowly forming a dense, golden column, which is ideal as a small-lawn specimen or focal point (see also The larger conifers, this chapter).

Thuja (arbor-vitae)

Of the dwarf forms, we especially recommend **T. orientalis** 'Aurea Nana', a dwarf evergreen shrub of rounded habit with light yellow-green foliage; **T. orientalis** 'Rosedalis', a small evergreen dome-shaped shrub with soft feathery foliage, bright yellow in spring, light green in summer and purplish brown in winter – this brings a different texture and colour to heather gardens, and is recommended for planting with winter-flowering heathers; and **T. plicata** 'Hillieri' a medium ever-

green shrub raised on the Hillier Nurseries, of rounded shape, slow growth and mossy green foliage (see also The larger conifers, this chapter).

Tsuga (hemlocks)

Dwarf forms of the Eastern hemlock, ideal for rock gardens, include **T. canadensis** 'Nana Gracilis', a small evergreen shrub forming a mound of arching stems; and **T. c.** 'Pendula', a medium evergreen shrub making a mound of pendulous, overlapping branches. The leaves of both have white bands on the undersides (see also The larger conifers, this chapter).

GROUND-COVER CONIFERS

These are mainly prostrate conifers which effectively cover the ground with their spreading stems, forming dense mats of foliage. They are ideal for covering banks, or other areas where one wishes to cut down on cultivation, and there is no doubt they look best when mass planted beause this results in a pleasing textured effect.

Cephalotaxus (plum yews)

Cephalotaxus fortunei 'Prostrata' is a dwarf, evergreen, widely spreading yew-like shrub with dark green foliage, raised on the Hillier Nurseries (see also The larger conifers, this chapter).

Juniperus (junipers)

Some especially effective schemes can be created by planting ground-cover junipers and cotoneasters together, for example in a bold patchwork arrangement; the red cotoneaster berries contrast beautifully with the evergreen foliage of the junipers. We recommend the following: **J. communis** 'Hornibrookii', prostrate shrub, sharply pointed green leaves with silvery undersides; **J. communis** 'Repanda', prostrate

Above:
Juniperus communis 'Repanda' is a prostrate, evergreen, ground-cover juniper. The stems are densely packed, making excellent cover, and the foliage is soft to the touch. It contrasts beautifully with ground-cover cotoneasters (*Hillier Arboretum, Ampfield, Hampshire*)

Right:
Ideal for contrasting with conifers of other shapes is **Juniperus squamata** 'Blue Carpet', a small shrub of spreading habit with striking blue-grey foliage

shrub, soft green foliage; and **J. horizontalis** 'Wiltonii' (syn. 'Blue Rug'), prostrate shrub, glaucous-blue foliage; **J. squamata** 'Blue Carpet', small shrub, spreading habit, blue-grey (see also Dwarf conifers, this chapter).

Juniperus horizontalis 'Douglasii' (foreground), a ground-cover juniper with long spreading branches whose foliage is tinged with purple in autumn and winter, here contrasting beautifully with specimens of **Thuja orientalis** 'Aurea Nana', a dwarf conifer with light yellow-green foliage (*Hillier Arboretum, Ampfield, Hampshire*)

Podocarpus

Ground-cover species include **P. alpinus**, small evergreen shrub, mound-forming spreading habit, blue or grey-green yew-like leaves; and **P. nivalis**, dwarf to medium evergreen, variable in size but usually of low spreading habit, olive green yew-like leaves (see also The larger conifers, this chapter).

Taxus (yew)

The **Taxus baccata** cultivar 'Repens Aurea' is useful for ground cover and brings in a different colour – yellow. The new leaves of this dwarf, spreading shrub are edged with yellow and they later become cream. This also associates well with red-berried ground-cover cotoneasters (see also The larger conifers, this chapter).

CHAPTER 9

CLIMBERS AND WALL SHRUBS

There is a lot of vertical space in a garden and it is sensible, therefore, to make the most of it by growing climbers wherever possible. Also, various shrubs can be grown against walls and fences, including those which are not sufficiently hardy to be grown in more open conditions (these need warm sheltered walls). Such shrubs are commonly referred to as 'wall shrubs'.

TYPES AND THEIR SUPPORTS

There are basically three groups of climbers. One includes the self-clinging plants which attach themselves to supports (walls, fences, tree trunks, etc) by means of aerial roots produced on the stems, as in hedera (ivy); or by adhesive pads on the ends of tendrils, such as those produced by parthenocissus (which includes Virginia creeper).

These climbers need no additional support, although initially they may need a little help such as bamboo canes or wires until they make permanent contact with the wall, fence or treetrunk. Contrary to popular belief, these plants do not damage masonry provided it is sound.

Another group contains climbers which twine their stems around the supports to elevate themselves, a good example being climbing loniceras (honeysuckles). Also within this group are plants with tendrils which curl around supports, such as vitis (grape vines); or with petioles which behave in the same way, as in the case of clematis.

Obviously these climbers, unlike the first group, cannot cling to flat surfaces and therefore need additional means of support. Trellis panels could be attached to walls and fences for the climbers to swarm up: these may be timber or plastic-coated steel panels. They must be fixed about 5cm (2 in) away from the wall or fence with the aid of battens to ensure good air circulation behind the plants, thus avoiding the damp conditions which are conducive to diseases.

Alternatively, horizontal galvanised wires can be fixed to the wall or fence, spaced about 30cm (12in) apart, using metal vine eyes. These also keep the wires away from the wall. Some climbers can also be grown up into trees, which should provide sufficient support, but young plants may need the help of bamboo canes to get them into the tree.

Another group contains climbers which have a somewhat scrambling habit, like the climbing and rambler roses (see Chapter 7) and berberidopsis. These need additional support on walls and fences, as outlined above, and the stems will need tying in with soft garden string. Again, some can be grown up into trees which should provide adequate support.

Other methods of supporting climbers include pergolas and arches (for example, over paths). Generally climbers with aerial roots or adhesive pads are not recommended for these structures – they are better on walls, fences or trees.

Regarding trees as a means of support, you should bear in mind that the tree must be semi-mature or mature before a climber is trained into it, and the climber must be matched to the size of the tree. For instance, do not grow a very tall vigorous climber through a small tree! Small restrained climbers, such as various clematis species and hybrids, can be grown over mature hedges or large shrubs. Climbers may also be grown over tall tree stumps, an option that might appeal in preference to having the stumps removed. They then form attractive features in a garden.

General wall shrubs are grown only against walls and fences. They need no additional support – indeed, they are neither trained nor attached to the wall in any way – they are simply grown *against* it.

Some climbers can also be used as ground cover. To give a few examples, this idea applies to hedera (ivy), parthenocissus (includes Virginia creeper) and some clematis. For instance, cultivars of **Clematis viticella** can be grown over heathers, as they are so light and airy, but generally in this application climbers are used for covering banks or large areas which need to be maintenance-free.

One final point about planting climbers and wall shrubs – do not plant them hard up against walls, fences and trees, as here the soil is inclined to become very dry because rain is deflected. Consequently the plants may not establish, or if they do they may fail to grow well. Instead, position them about 30 cm (12in) from the support and guide the stems to it by means of bamboo canes. Tie the young stems to the canes with soft garden string.

FOR EVERY SEASON

Climbers and wall shrubs can provide colour and interest during every season, so to help you choose plants for colour throughout the year we have grouped our selection into seasons. This is a comprehensive choice of climbers and wall shrubs, although by no means exhaustive – a connoisseur's selection.

SPRING

Useful for growing up small trees or over hedges, large shrubs and tree stumps, is the vigorous semi-evergreen twiner **Akebia quinata** (chocolate vine), with red-purple vanilla-scented flowers in midspring followed, after a hot summer and if several plants are grown together, by purple sausage-shaped fruits. The leaves have five

Spring-flowering **Wisteria sinensis** 'Alba' is a very vigorous climber, capable of reaching 30m (100ft) with suitable support. It would be suitable for growing up a large tree (*Harewood, Buckinghamshire*)

leaflets. It reaches a height of 9m (30ft) or more, is suitable for any well drained soil and tolerant of positions facing north or east.

Various clematis bloom in the spring and they relish cool, shaded soil, but want their heads in the sun. They grow in any well-drained earth and are especially suited to chalky conditions. Clematis can be supported on walls, fences and pergolas, or trained through trees or large shrubs. They cling by means of curling petioles.

Clematis alpina 'Frances Rivis' has blue or violet-blue nodding flowers during mid to late spring. Its height is up to 2.4m (8ft), so it is ideal for growing through small trees or large shrubs, or over low walls. More vigorous are the **C. armandii** cultivars, which grow to 4.5–6m (15–20ft), are evergreen, flower during mid to late spring and need a warm sheltered wall. We recommend 'Apple Blossom' with white, pink-tinted blooms and bronze young foliage, and the pure white 'Snowdrift'.

Clematis chrysocoma produces pink flowers in late spring/early summer, with a further flush in late summer. It is reminiscent of **C. montana** but not as vigorous, attaining a height of at least 2.4m (8ft). It shows up well against a white wall.

There are some excellent cultivars of **C. macropetala**. This is a small restrained grower, reaching about 2.4m (8ft) in height and ideal for growing on low walls or fences, plus large shrubs. It has attractive divided leaves and flowers during late spring and early summer. We recommend 'Maidwell Hall', with deep blue flowers, an excellent companion for early yellow climbing roses like **Rosa banksiae** 'Lutea'; and 'Markham's Pink', deep rose-pink. **Clematis** 'White Swan' with pure white flowers, is similar to **macropetala** cultivars and is also worth growing.

The cultivars of **C. montana** are

PLANTING SCHEME FOR CLEMATIS

Some clematis such as **C. alpina** 'Francis Rivis', **C. macropetala** cultivars, **C. viticella** cultivars, **C. tibetana vernayi** (**C. orientalis**), **C. tangutica** and large-flowered garden clematis can be trained through trees or large shrubs.

---

extremely vigorous and can be grown through large trees or up high walls, and over outbuildings and large pergolas. Their height is 6–9m (20–30ft) and they flower in late spring. We recommend the cultivars 'Alexander', with fragrant cream-white flowers; 'Elizabeth', in soft pink, with a slight scent; and 'Tetrarose', with lilac-rose flowers set against bronze leaves, which is beautiful against a white wall. We also recommend the variety **C. montana wilsonii** with small, white, scented blooms in early summer. A superb effect can be achieved by growing it through an evergreen tree or conifer.

Forsythia suspensa makes a good wall shrub, with its arching stems laden in early to mid spring with nodding, bright yellow flowers. This large shrub is extremely hardy and thrives in any well-drained soil. For interest later in the year a **Clematis viticella** cultivar could be grown over a mature specimen (see Summer, this chapter).

There are no finer climbers for pergolas or house walls than wisterias, which produce their long pendulous trusses of pea-shaped flowers in late spring and early summer. They can also be grown up large trees. Wisterias have a twining habit of growth and are suitable for any fertile well-drained soil, but chalky ones should be improved as much as possible. **Wisteria**

There are several clones of **Abutilon ×
suntense**, a wall shrub which produces masses of
saucer-shaped flowers in summer, set against
felted leaves. Only suited to mild areas (*Old
Rectory Cottage, Tidmarsh, Berkshire*)

floribunda 'Rosea', a cultivar of the Japanese wisteria, has long trusses of light rose
flowers marked with purple and grows up to
9m (30ft). Much more vigorous, capable of
reaching 30m (100ft) with suitable support,
is **W. sinensis** (Chinese wisteria), with
scented mauve flowers in late spring. We
also recommend the equally vigorous
cultivar 'Alba', with white scented blooms.

SUMMER

Abutilons are mainly conservatory plants
but some can be grown outdoors in mild
areas. They are treated as wall shrubs and
positioned against warm, sheltered, south-
facing walls or solid fences. Any well-
drained soil is suitable. Abutilons bloom for
a long period in summer, producing either
bell or saucer-shaped pendulous flowers,
and can be effectively grown with other
exotic-looking wall shrubs such as the
yellow-flowered fremontodendron.

We especially recommend clones of
**Abutilon × suntense (A. ochsenii × A.
vitifolium**), which produce masses of

saucer-shaped flowers set against distinctive lobed leaves covered in grey 'felt'. 'Jermyns', raised on the Hillier Nurseries, is a medium to large shrub with white flowers. We suggest you also try **A. vitifolium** cultivars, large shrubs with similar flowers and foliage. With pure white blooms is 'Tennant's White', while 'Veronica Tennant' has mauve flowers.

Actinidia kolomikta (kolomikta vine) is a vigorous twining climber to 4.5–6m (15–20ft) in height, suitable for growing on high south or west-facing walls. It is grown for its large leaves with unusual variegation – the top half is white and pink, the lower half green. It produces its best colour in full sun. Suitable for any well-drained fertile soil, a pleasing effect is achieved when it is grown with pink climbing roses.

The twining climber **Aristolochia macrophylla** (syn. **A. durior**, **A. sipho**) (Dutchman's pipe) is an unusual-looking subject whose tubular yellow and brown flowers are bent like a siphon. They appear in early summer, set against kidney or heart-shaped leaves. It grows to a height of 9m (30ft) given a suitable support, such as walls, fences, pergolas and trees, and thrives in any well-drained fertile soil in sun or partial shade.

Two evergreen climbers which need similar conditions are **Asteranthera ovata** and **Berberidopsis corallina** (coral plant). They need humus-rich, acid or neutral, moisture-retentive soil. The former must have partial shade and the latter full shade. The asteranthera is self-clinging by means of aerial roots and produces tubular, two-lipped, red, white-throated flowers in early summer. Capable of attaining 6m (20ft) in height, it can be grown up a tree in a woodland garden, or up a north-facing wall. It must have shelter and is recommended only for milder areas.

Berberidopsis is only moderately hardy and needs sheltered conditions. It can grow to a similar height and produces pendulous crimson flowers during late summer, set against thick, leathery, spine-edged leaves. Best grown on a shady wall or fence, it also makes an excellent background for a peat garden.

Also evergreen is **Bignonia capreolata** (cross vine), a tendril climber with clusters of exotic-looking, tubular, orange-red flowers in early summer. It is vigorous, attaining a height of 9m (30ft) or more and thriving in any fertile well-drained soil, but is only recommended for milder areas. It can be grown up high walls or trees and contrasts well with any blue ceanothus still flowering in early summer.

Equally exotic-looking, and associating well with the blue passion flower, **Passiflora caerulea**, are the campsis, shrubs with climbing stems thriving in full sun and any well-drained soil. Grow them on high walls or over outbuildings. Trumpet-shaped flowers are produced in late summer and early autumn, hence the common name, trumpet vine. **C. radicans**, with bright orange and dark red flowers, is the one normally grown, but we also recommend the cultivar 'Flava' ('Yellow Trumpet') with deep yellow blooms. Both attain a height of around 12m (40ft) and support themselves by means of aerial roots. **C. × tagliabuana** (**C. grandiflora** × **C. radicans**) 'Madame Galen' has salmon-red flowers in late summer and needs some additional support such as trellis. This climber's height is 9m (30ft).

Large white philadelphus-like flowers, each with a boss of golden stamens, are produced in midsummer by **Carpenteria californica**, a medium-size evergreen shrub which needs to be grown on a sunny, sheltered, south or west-facing wall. It thrives in any moisture-retentive yet well-drained soil. We also recommend the

The climbing shrub **Campsis × tagliabuana** 'Madame Galen' produces its exotic-looking flowers in late summer. They associate well with those of the blue passion flower

Ideal for growing through a tree is the 7.5m (25ft) tall **C. rehderiana**, with pinnate foliage which makes a good background for the pendulous, bell-shaped, pale yellow flowers produced in late summer and autumn. They have the fragrance of cowslips.

Clematis texensis is rather tender and has semi-woody stems, to about 3.6m (12ft) in height. The stems may partially die back in winter, when the plant should be well protected. It is recommended for a warm, sheltered wall. We suggest the cultivars 'Duchess of Albany', with nodding, tubular bright pink flowers from mid summer to early autumn; and 'Gravetye Beauty', whose ruby-red flowers, produced in late summer and early autumn, are bell-shaped to start with but star-shaped when fully open.

Clematis viticella cultivars are extremely versatile. They are slender climbers to about 3.6m (12ft) in height and very suitable for growing through medium-size to large shrubs, or over hedges. Also, an unusual effect is achieved if they are planted between winter-flowering heathers and allowed to trail over them. They provide colour when the heathers are out of flower. There are numerous cultivars, including 'Alba Luxurians' whose white flowers, flushed with mauve, show up well against dark green shrub or heather foliage; and 'Kermesina', with crimson flowers.

The large-flowered garden clematis are extremely popular summer-flowering climbers and some charming effects can be achieved when they are planted with climbing roses, either over walls or fences or on pergolas, arbours or arches. They can also be grown into small trees or large shrubs. For instance, try the bright blue 'Ascotiensis' or Wedgwood-blue 'H. F. Young' with red or pink roses. 'Carnaby', with raspberry-red flowers and suitable for shade, 'Niobe' with deep red flowers and the

cultivar 'Bodnant', with larger flowers than the species.

Summer-flowering clematis that we recommend (see also Spring section, this chapter) include **C. flammula**, a vigorous grower to 5m (16ft) and suitable for swarming over old hedges or walls, with masses of small, white, fragrant flowers from late summer to mid autumn. **C. florida** can attain a similar height but we recommend the cultivars 'Alba Plena', with white double flowers, and 'Sieboldii' whose white flowers have a cluster of blue-purple petal-like stamens in the centre.

Fremontodendron 'California Glory' is a large evergreen wall shrub which produces its exotic-looking flowers throughout summer.
Recommended only for mild areas and needing a very sunny wall

raspberry-pink 'Lincoln Star' would look best with white roses. 'Countess of Love-lace' has double and single pale lilac flowers which look lovely beside yellow roses, and the large cream-white blooms of 'Henryi' go well with a red rose. 'Yellow Queen', with large cream-yellow flowers, would look good with a blue-flowered climber such as **Solanum crispum** 'Glasnevin'. These large-flowered clematis attain 2.4–3.6m (8–12ft) in height.

Combining beautifully with mauve-flowered abutilons or blue ceanothus are the fremontodendrons (fremontias), large evergreen shrubs with bold, showy, saucer-shaped, bright yellow flowers throughout summer, usually starting in late spring. **F. californicum** is the species normally

grown, and we also recommend **F.** 'California Glory'. These shrubs are hardier than many people suppose but should be grown on a sunny, south-facing wall. They thrive in any well-drained soil and are especially suitable for chalk.

Hederas or ivies are extremely versatile evergreen climbers, attaching themselves to walls or fences by means of aerial roots. They can also be used as ground cover, for example on banks, in woodland gardens or between shrubs. Marvellous textured effects are produced when ivies are mass planted, and this applies especially to many of the small-leaved kinds. If you want ground cover then buy plants grown specially for the purpose – not caned specimens intended for use as climbers, as these will not lie flat when planted. It is not recommended that ivies are grown up trees or other plants, nor up pergolas, arches, etc, as they can densely clothe their host with heavy foliage. Ivies can succeed in sun, partial shade or full shade and in any soil, provided it is well-drained and moisture-retentive.

On walls the tall ivies look good with climbers noted for autumn leaf colour, such as parthenocissus and vitis. Try a large-leaved ivy, such as **Hedera algeriensis** 'Margino-maculata' or **H. colchica** 'Sulphur Heart', with the large-leaved **Vitis coignetiae**, whose foliage turns brilliant scarlet and crimson in autumn.

Of the large-leaved ivies we can recommend **Hedera algeriensis** 'Margino-maculata', a cultivar of the Algerian ivy whose leaves are heavily variegated cream-white and which reaches a height of about

Large-flowered garden clematis like 'Ville de Lyon' are popular summer-flowering climbers which associate well with climbing roses. This cultivar flowers in the period midsummer to midautumn

178

Large-leaved variegated ivy contrasting dramatically with a pyracantha, which makes an excellent wall shrub. These two could be grown on a shady wall if desired (*Coates Manor, Sussex*)

6m (20ft); and **H. colchica** 'Sulphur Heart' (syn. 'Paddy's Pride'), which has leaves splashed with yellow in the centre and grows to a height of 4.5m (15ft).

Hedera helix (common ivy) cultivars are the small-leaved ivies with variable lobed leaves, either plain green or variegated. There are many to choose from but we particularly recommend 'Adam', with white-edged leaves, height about 1.2m (4ft) as a

climber; 'Bird's Foot', bearing very small, plain green, deeply divided leaves and creating excellent texture when boldly planted as ground cover or overflowing from a patio tub, a slow compact grower; 'Buttercup', which has deep yellow leaves giving their best colour in sun, and attains a height of 1.8m (6ft); 'Glacier', with silver-grey, white-edged leaves, height 3m (10ft); 'Green Ripple' has sharply lobed leaves with a long central lobe, colour plain green, creating excellent texture when mass planted as ground cover and reaching 1.2m (4ft) in height as a climber; 'Ivalace', with curled and crimped, shiny plain green foliage, creating attractive ground cover and attaining a height of 90cm (3ft) as a climber; and 'Little Diamond' which has grey-mottled, cream-edged leaves and forms a dwarf

PLANTING SCHEME FOR IVIES

Tall ivies, such as the large-leaved **Hedera algeriensis** 'Margino-maculata', can be combined effectively with climbers noted for autumn leaf colour, for example **Vitis coignetiae**.

Hedera helix 'Buttercup', with yellow leaves, contrasting well with a grey santolina. This ivy colours best in sun and will grow 1.8m (6ft) up a wall (*Cloudesley Road, London*)

A superb study in foliage shape, colour and texture: the variegated **Hedera helix** 'Glacier', a popular small-leaved ivy, with a silver-leaved pulmonaria, ferns and hostas. Ideal for a shady spot (*White Windows, Hampshire*)

The climbing hydrangea, **Hydrangea petiolaris**, is a vigorous self-supporting climber for high walls, attaching itself by means of aerial roots. The flowers are produced in early summer

bush, recommended only for ground cover.

The climbing hydrangea, **Hydrangea petiolaris**, is a vigorous self-supporting climber for high walls, attaching itself by means of aerial roots. It produces flat heads of green-white flowers, with white sterile florets around the edges, in early summer. It can attain a height of 18–25m (60–80ft) and will grow in sun or partial shade, or on a north-facing wall. It tolerates atmospheric pollution and will succeed in moisture-retentive yet well-drained soil.

Somewhat similar are pileostegia and schizophragma, both with aerial roots. **Pileostegia viburnoides** needs the same conditions as the hydrangea. It is evergreen, though, with 15cm (6in)-long leathery leaves, and panicles of cream-white flowers in late summer and autumn. Its eventual height is 6m (20ft), but it's a slow grower. The schizophragmas have large flat heads of cream-white flowers, up to 30cm (12in) in diameter, each surrounded by large cream sterile florets, in midsummer. Best flowering is achieved in full sun, but any well-drained soil is suitable. **S. hydrangeoides** is recommended, together with **S. integrifolium** which has very conspicuous sterile florets; both grow up to 12m (40ft) in height.

The jasmines are favourite summer-flowering climbers of twining habit for walls, fences, pergolas and arbours, with usually-fragrant starry flowers. **J. officinale** is the common white jasmine, with highly fragrant white flowers from early summer to early autumn. It makes a superb companion for red or pink climbing roses and attains a height of up to 12m (40ft). **J. × stephanense** has light pink, scented blooms during early and mid summer, is vigorous and capable of reaching 7.5m (25ft) in height. **J. humile** 'Revolutum' is a medium evergreen shrub best grown against a sunny wall, with bright yellow,

---

PLANTING SCHEME FOR JASMINE

Jasminum officinale (common white jasmine) makes a superb companion for red or pink climbing roses.

Lonicera periclymenum 'Graham Thomas', a cultivar of the woodbine, produces an abundance of fragrant flowers in summer. It can be grown over many types of support, including large shrubs

slightly scented flowers produced throughout summer. The jasmines thrive in any fertile well-drained soil and tolerate atmospheric pollution.

Equally popular summer-flowering twining climbers, often with fragrant flowers, are the loniceras or honeysuckles. These look best when growing through trees or large shrubs or over high hedges, but are suitable for walls, fences, pergolas and arbours too, where they make good companions for climbing roses. Honeysuckles grow in any well-drained soil and generally flower best with their heads in the sun. We recommend **Lonicera × americana**, a vigorous hydrid up to 9m (30ft) in height with fragrant flowers during early and mid summer, which start white and change to deep yellow flushed with purple; **L. caprifolium** (perfoliate honeysuckle), up to 6m 20ft) in height with fragrant cream-white flowers in early and mid summer, and perfoliate upper leaves; **L. periclymenum** 'Graham Thomas', a cultivar of the woodbine with an abundance of fragrant cream-white flowers which age to yellow, its height 7m (23ft); **L. periclymenum** 'Serotina' (late Dutch honeysuckle), bearing highly fragrant red-purple flowers in mid summer to mid autumn and growing to 7m (23ft) in height; and **L. tragophylla**, with large clusters of bright, golden-yellow flowers in early and mid summer, needing virtually full shade, and ideally grown through a tree in a woodland garden; its height is 4.5–6m (15–20ft).

One almost needs a stately home to show off **Magnolia grandiflora** to advantage. There is no doubt that it looks best against an old wall, although any high, sunny wall will do. This large evergreen shrub has big, shiny, thick leaves which have red-brown tomentum below, and in summer and autumn huge cream, fragrant, bowl-shaped flowers almost 30cm (12in) across. It takes many years to start flowering but will grow in any deep, fertile, well-drained soil including chalk.

Forms we recommend include 'Charles Dickens', with large pink bud scales enclosing the young leaves, like pink candles; 'Exmouth', noted for its very large blooms which are produced comparatively early in life; 'Goliath', which also blooms when quite young, but has smaller leaves which lack the brown tomentum below; and 'Undulata', also with very large flowers, and wavy-edged leaves which are green below.

Magnolia delavayi is also a large evergreen shrub best grown against a wall, and it thrives in partial shade or full sun. Any deep, fertile, well-drained soil is suitable, including chalk. It has large blue-green leaves with glaucous undersides and in late summer and early autumn produces cream-white, bowl-shaped flowers with a slight scent, up to 20cm (8in) in diameter.

The blue passion flower, **Passiflora caerulea**, is a vigorous climber to a height of 9m (30ft) which clings by means of tendrils. It needs plenty of sun and shelter but thrives in any well-drained fertile soil. Although the hardiest passion flower, it is not recommended for areas with severe winters. In mild climates the boldly lobed foliage is evergreen.

The flowers consist of white tepals (outer petal-like segments), and a ring of filaments (corona) which have blue tips, white centres and purple bases. There is also a white-flowered cultivar which we recommend, called 'Constance Elliott'. These exotic-looking blooms are produced in summer and autumn and associate well with other flamboyant climbers like campsis with their orange, red or yellow trumpet-shaped flowers.

There are several climbing rubus but we recommend **R. henryi bambusarum**, an evergreen which can climb to a height of 6m (20ft). Pink flowers are produced in summer and show up well against the shiny deep green foliage, each leaf consisting of three leaflets with white tomentum on the undersides. The flowers are followed by black fruits. This climber, which will thrive in any well-drained soil, is grown for both its flowers and attractive foliage.

The solanums are vigorous wall shrubs with potato-like flowers and need a sunny, sheltered position, although they thrive in any well-drained soil. They are not recommended for areas with very severe winters. **Solanum crispum** 'Glasnevin', which makes such a good companion for climbing roses, especially red or pink cultivars, is a semi-evergreen shrub to a height of about 6m (20ft), with clusters of purplish-blue flowers with yellow centres in summer and autumn. **S. jasminoides** is more tender, a vigorous semi-evergreen shrub reaching 6m (20ft), which twines its stems around supports. The flowers, carried in clusters during summer and autumn, are slate-blue and each has a yellow centre. We also recommend the white-flowered cultivar 'Album'.

Quite unusual is the bluebell creeper, **Sollya heterophylla**, an evergreen twining plant to a height of at least 1.8m (6ft) and producing pendulous clusters of bell-shaped medium blue flowers in summer and autumn. Unfortunately it can only be grown outdoors, against a sunny sheltered wall, in the mildest areas; elsewhere it must be grown in a cool conservatory. It will thrive in any well-drained soil.

Needing the same conditions is **Tecomaria capensis** (syn. **Bignonia capensis**,

Summer and autumn-flowering **Solanum crispum** 'Glasnevin' is a vigorous wall shrub recommended for areas where winters are not too severe. It makes a good companion for fremontodendron (seen here) or climbing roses

Tecoma capensis), the Cape honeysuckle, an evergreen twiner which grows vigorously to a height of 1.8–3m (6–10ft). Scarlet trumpet-shaped flowers are produced during late summer and show up well against the pinnate foliage. We stress that this can be grown outdoors only in very mild climates; otherwise it must be accommodated in a conservatory.

Trachelospermum jasminoides, an evergreen twining climber with very fragrant white flowers in summer, is reminiscent of jasmine. Going up to 9m (30ft) in height, it needs a sunny sheltered wall but cannot be recommended for very cold areas.

In the latter, grow it in a cool conservatory. For the same conditions is **Dregea sinensis** (syn. **Wattakaka sinensis**) with slender 3m (10ft)-high stems which carry umbels of fragrant white red-spotted flowers in summer. The leaves have grey tomentum on the undersides.

AUTUMN

The most important climbers for autumn leaf colour are the parthenocissus and vitis.

Some parthenocissus can climb to the top of the tallest houses and support themselves either with adhesive pads on the ends of tendrils, or with twining tendrils. The former cling tightly to walls, while the latter can be allowed to grow over hedges, or through trees and large shrubs. They are ideal for shady or semi-shady (north or east-facing) walls and thrive in any well-drained soil. The autumn leaf colour of parthenocissus contrasts beautifully with the ever-green foliage of tall ivies, particularly the large-leaved kinds. All parthenocissus can also be grown as ground cover, especially on large banks where they resemble molten lava in the autumn!

We recommend **Parthenocissus henryana**, which clings by means of adhesive pads. The leaves are composed of three to five velvety leaflets, which are dark green or bronze with white or pink veins in summer, but in autumn turn brilliant red. It climbs to a height of 9m (30ft) and is best grown on a wall. Also best on a wall is **P. quinquefolia**, the Virginia creeper, which can attain a height of 15m (50ft) or more. It is self-clinging, using adhesive pads. Leaves composed of five leaflets turn to shades of glowing orange and scarlet in autumn. **P. tricuspidata** 'Veitchii' is a form of the Boston ivy, a self-clinging climber with adhesive pads which can reach a height of 21m (70ft) and is best grown on a wall. The lobed leaves turn dark reddish purple in the autumn.

Vitis use twining tendrils to support themselves. The ornamental vines can be grown on walls and fences, through large trees, or over a large old hedge, and are suited to any well-drained soil. Like parthenocissus, they also associate pleasingly with large-leaved ivies, contrasting beautifully with the evergreen foliage when their own leaves take on brilliant autumn tints. For instance, **Vitis coignetiae** makes a superb companion for **Hedera algeriensis** 'Margino-maculata'. This vine has large rounded leaves, about 30cm (12in) in diameter, which turn crimson and scarlet in autumn. Its height is up to 15m (50ft). **V. vinifera** 'Purpurea' is the Teinturier grape, with lobed leaves which are red when they first open then change to dark purple, growing to a height of 7m (23ft). A very pleasing effect is achieved when this climber is combined with red climbing roses.

Trachelospermum jasminoides is an evergreen twining climber with very fragrant jasmine-like flowers in summer, but it cannot be recommended for very cold areas

A vigorous twining, fruiting climber for autumn, **Celastrus orbiculatus**, the staff vine, can attain a height of 14m (46ft). In autumn the leaves turn yellow, but male and female plants, or a hermaphrodite plant, are needed for seed capsules to be produced. When the capsules split open they reveal yellow interiors and conspicuous red seeds. Suited to any soil and partial or full shade, this vine can be grown up walls and fences, over large shrubs and tall hedges or through trees.

Several clematis (see also Spring, this chapter) flower in the autumn, including **C.** × **jouiniana** 'Cote d'Azure', a sub-shrubby

Parthenocissus quinquefolia or Virginia creeper is a vigorous self-clinging climber which produces superb autumn leaf colour. Ideal for shady or semi-shady walls (*Coates Manor, Sussex*)

Garrya elliptica 'James Roof' is a large evergreen winter-flowering shrub generally grown against a sunny sheltered wall. The winter jasmine, with yellow flowers, is an effective companion

climber with small azure-blue flowers, attaining a height of up to 3.6m (12ft). It is useful for low walls or for covering tree stumps, and would also look good with any red climbing rose which has an autumn flush of blooms.

C. tibetana vernayi (syn. **orientalis**) and **C. tangutica** should, in our opinion, be in every garden. The first, the orange-peel clematis, has pendulous, bell-shaped flowers composed of thick yellow sepals in late summer and early autumn, set against divided greyish foliage, its height 3–3.6m (10–12ft). **C. tangutica** produces pendulous, lantern-shaped, deep yellow flowers in autumn, followed by attractive silvery seed heads. The divided blue-green foliage is also attractive, and it grows to 4.5–6m (15–20ft) in height. Both are useful for growing over low walls or fences, pergolas, shrubs or hedges, and for use as ground cover on banks.

WINTER

One can have clematis in flower during every season. **C. cirrhosa balearica**, the fern-leaved clematis, produces light yellow blooms up to 5cm (2in) in diameter during the dark days, when the attractive divided

foliage becomes flushed with bronze. It reaches 1.8–3m (6–10ft) in height (see also Spring, this chapter).

Two plants which are suitable for growing side by side, when they contrast beautifully in form and colour, are **Garrya elliptica** 'James Roof' and the winter jasmine, **Jasminum nudiflorum**. The garrya is a large evergreen shrub with long grey-green catkins in mid and late winter. Grow it on a sunny, sheltered wall and in any soil. The jasmine is a medium shrub with masses of starry, bright yellow flowers produced during the period from late autumn to late winter. It also contrasts well with green-leaved ivies, and tolerates more shade than the garrya (it can even be grown on a north-facing wall).

PLANTING SCHEME FOR WINTER

Suitable for growing side by side, when they contrast beautifully in form and colour, are **Garrya elliptica** 'James Roof' with grey-green catkins and the yellow-flowered winter jasmine, **Jasminum nudiflorum**.

189

CHAPTER 10

PERENNIALS AND BULBS

Hardy perennials, both herbaceous and evergreen, are as important as shrubs and can be grown effectively on their own in traditional hedge-backed herbaceous borders, or in groups of informal island beds set in grass or gravel.

However, many gardeners today grow most of their plants in mixed borders, the framework of these being formed by shrubs. Among the shrubs can be planted hardy perennials, and other plants such as hardy bulbs, in bold groups and drifts.

The perennials and bulbs should be chosen carefully to ensure they combine effectively with the shrubs – not all do so by any means, especially the more highly bred kinds. That is the basis on which we have selected the following hardy perennials and bulbs – they all combine beautifully with their woody neighbours.

As the majority of perennials and bulbs are comparatively small plants they should, for impact, be planted in large groups or drifts of each subject. Average spacing of perennials is four to five plants per square metre (square yard), but slim, non-spreading perennials like crocosmias can be planted at seven per square metre, while large or very spreading kinds such as bergenias, the largest hostas and **Macleaya cordata** would be better at three plants per square metre. Bulbs, of course, are planted a matter of centimetres (inches) apart: from about 8cm (3in) for small or miniature bulbs, to 15–20cm (6–8in) for larger bulbs like lilies.

PERENNIALS TO ASSOCIATE WITH SHRUBS

Hardy perennials can provide colour and interest all the year round, even in winter. One should consider not only their flowers, but also the foliage, for many perennials have bold, colourful or architectural leaves which contrast effectively with many shrubs.

Generally speaking the species and less highly bred perennials associate best with shrubs, but highly bred plants, such as the modern delphinium hybrids, can be effectively combined with shrubs which have also been extensively moulded by plant breeders, such as hybrid shrub roses.

SPRING

Bergenia

These are evergreen perennials with large, rounded, glossy leaves which can be effectively used as ground cover around many shrubs, including those relishing partial shade. Bergenias also associate well with some other ground-cover plants, such as prostrate junipers – excellent contrasts in foliage texture. They are suitable for any well-drained soil, but the winter leaf colour is more pronounced in full sun and poor soils. Racemes of pink, red or white flowers are produced in early or mid spring. Cultivars worth growing are 'Ballawley', with red flowers and winter foliage, its height up to 60cm (24in); 'Evening Glow', bearing crimson-purple flowers, its winter foliage copper-coloured and height 30cm

Many gardeners today grow most of their plants in mixed borders, which include shrubs, hardy perennials, bulbs and the like. Perennials and bulbs should be chosen carefully so that they combine effectively with the shrubs (*Coldham, Kent*)

(12in); **B.** × **schmidtii**, with pink flowers, early, and 30cm (12in) in height; and 'Silver Light', offering white, flushed pink flowers, its height 30cm (12in).

Brunnera

Also good ground cover with its rough-textured heart-shaped leaves, ideally grown in partial shade with moisture-retentive soil, is **Brunnera macrophylla** (Siberian bugloss), with tiny, bright blue flowers like those of forget-me-nots (myosotis) in early spring. It grows to a height of 60cm (24in) and is very useful for a woodland garden. There is also a variegated form called 'Dawson's White'.

Dicentra (Dutchman's breeches)

These perennials produce pendulous heart-shaped flowers and attractive ferny foliage. They make pleasing ground cover and are best grown in partial shade with moisture-retentive soil, rich in humus. They associate well with camellias and other woodland shrubs. We recommend 'Baccharal' with purple flowers and grey-green foliage, its height 30cm (12in), and 'Stuart Boothman' with carmine flowers, height 45cm (18in).

Epimedium (barrenwort)

Dainty ground-cover perennials, for partial shade and moisture-retentive soil rich in humus. Ideal for woodland gardens, they produce delicate racemes of small, pendulous, cup-shaped flowers. The young foliage is often bronze. We recommend **E. perralderianum**, yellow, bronze young foliage, height 25cm (10in); **E.** × **rubrum**, crimson, good autumn leaf tints, height 25cm (10in); and **E.** × **youngianum** 'Niveum', white, young foliage bronze, height 15cm (6in).

Euphorbia (spurge)

The flowers of spurges are surrounded by

colourful bracts which last for a long period. There are many from which to choose, but for spring we recommend **E. griffithii** 'Fireglow', a 76cm (2½ft)-high perennial with brilliant orange-red bracts. It associates well with silver or grey-foliage plants, including the weeping silver pear, **Pyrus salicifolia** 'Pendula'. **E. characias wulfenii** is a 1.2m (4ft)-tall architectural plant with large heads of green-yellow bracts in spring and summer, and glaucous evergreen foliage, a marvellous companion for phormiums. Any well-drained soil suits euphorbias.

Geranium (crane's bill)

Excellent ground-cover plants which flower for a long period. Some can be grown in partial shade, including the white-flowered **G. macrorrhizum** 'Album' and the pale pink **G. m.** 'Ingwersen's Variety', both with aromatic foliage, and can be planted around woodland shrubs. Their height is 30cm (12in) and any well-drained soil is suitable.

Helleborus

Distinctive, often evergreen perennials with cup-shaped flowers, best grown in partial shade and in any well-drained yet moisture-retentive soil. They are ideal for combining with late winter and early spring-flowering shrubs. **Helleborus orientalis** (Lenten rose), for instance, can be effectively planted around hamamelis or witch hazel, camellias, early rhododendrons and other woodland shrubs. It has flowers in shades of crimson and purple, plus white, is evergreen and attains a height of 45cm (18in). **H. atrorubens** (difficult to obtain) is similar and has red-purple flowers. **H. foetidus**, the stinking hellebore, produces large heads of green flowers edged with red and deeply divided evergreen foliage, and reaches 60cm (24in) in height. **H. argutifolius** (syn. **H. lividus corsicus**)

Helleborus orientalis, the Lenten rose, is a late winter to early spring-flowering evergreen perennial which associates effectively with many shrubs such as witch hazels, camellias and rhododendrons

sports large clusters of yellow-green flowers, has handsome glaucous evergreen foliage and grows to the same height. Try these last two with the rose-purple **Rhododendron mucronulatum**.

Incarvillea

Flowering in late spring and early summer, **Incarvillea delavayi** has trumpet-shaped, rose-pink flowers on 60cm (24in) stems and is suitable for the front of a mixed border, growing in any fertile well-drained soil and associating well with silver or grey-leaved shrubs.

Pachysandra

For evergreen ground cover in shade (including deep shade) **Pachysandra terminalis** takes some beating, but it needs to be planted in large drifts to provide a pleasing textured effect. It has clusters of diamond-shaped leaves, silver-variegated in the cultivar 'Variegata'. It is 30cm (12in) in height and suited to any well-drained soil.

Polygonatum (Solomon's seal)

The Solomon's seals are highly distinctive plants which look most at home in woodland gardens, among shrubs like rhododendrons, camellias, enkianthus and other woodlanders. From the arching stems of **Polygonatum × hybridum** hang rows of white, green-tipped tubular flowers, which appear in late spring. This 1.2m (4ft)-high plant needs cool conditions with dappled shade, and moisture-retentive yet well-drained soil.

Pulmonaria (lungwort)

The lungworts flourish in partial shade and moisture-retentive soil and produce heads of tubular flowers. The most favoured colour is blue, as in the deep blue **Pulmonaria angustifolia** 'Azurea', which associates pleasingly with primroses, **Primula vulgaris**. Such a combination could make a delightful carpet around woodland shrubs. Also worth growing are **P. rubra** 'Bowles' Red' with red flowers, and the bright rose-pink **P. saccharata** 'Pink Dawn'. **P. saccharata** cultivars have white-spotted leaves. All attain 25cm (10in) in height.

Smilacina (false spikenard)

Feathery spikes of white flowers are produced by **Smilacina racemosa**, set against attractive oval leaves. This distinctive perennial, height up to 90cm (3ft), relishes partial shade and moisture-retentive, acid to neutral soil, well supplied with humus. It shows up well against a background of rhododendron or camellia foliage.

Tiarella (foam flower)

Tiarella cordifolia makes good ground cover for shade, and is excellent for carpeting a woodland floor. It has evergreen lobed foliage and spikes of tiny, white starry flowers in late spring. Height is 20cm (8in), and it needs moist soil yet good drainage.

Trollius (globe flower)

Revelling in moist soil, and taking partial shade, trollius have showy, globe-shaped flowers in shades of yellow or orange. They are beautiful with moisture-loving primulas and irises beside a woodland stream, with spring-flowering shrubs. We recommend 'Golden Queen', bright orange; 'Goldquelle', buttercup-yellow; and 'Orange Princess', orange-yellow. Height is 60cm (24in).

There are many summer-flowering hardy perennials but numerous others are grown mainly for their attractive foliage. Therefore, for easy reference, we have split our choice into two sections – Summer plants for flowers and Summer plants for foliage.

SUMMER PLANTS FOR FLOWERS

Agapanthus (African lily)

Associating beautifully with red or pink shrub roses are **Agapanthus** Headbourne Hybrids, with heads of tubular flowers in shades of blue during late summer/early autumn. The strap-shaped foliage is handsome. Height is up to 1.2m (4ft) and any well-drained soil is suitable.

Part of a mixed border in summer, featuring buddlejas and hemerocallis or day lilies – a dramatic contrast in colour, shape and texture (*Overbecks, Devon, National Trust*)

Alchemilla (Lady's mantle)

Alchemilla mollis, with clouds of green-yellow flowers set against soft, hairy leaves, seems to associate well with any shrub. It grows in any well-drained soil and reaches 30cm (12in) in height.

Anchusa

Useful for combining with red or pink shrub roses is **Anchusa azurea** 'Loddon Royalist', with spikes of deep blue flowers. Height is about 90cm (3ft) and any well-drained soil will do.

Astilbe

The astilbes are distinctive perennials with feathery plumes of red, pink or white flowers. They look superb at the water's edge, or in a border with moist soil, in association with primulas, moisture loving irises and hostas. They prefer dappled shade. We recommend the **A.** × **arendsii** cultivars 'Bressingham Beauty', which is pink and 90cm (3ft) tall; 'Fanal', deep red, 76cm (2½ft); 'Fire', salmon-red, 60cm (24in); and 'Irrlicht', white, 60cm (24in). Also, **A. chinensis** 'Pumila', lilac-rose, late summer/autumn, 30cm (12in); and **A. tacquetii** 'Superba', rose-lilac, 1.2m (4ft).

Campanula (bell flower)

Campanulas associate well with various shrubs, including shrub and species roses. Of diverse habit, they all have bell-shaped flowers, mainly in shades of blue. We recommend **C. alliariifolia** 'Ivory Bells', colour as name, suitable for shade, height 45cm (18in); **C. glomerata** 'Superba', violet-blue, up to 76cm (2½ft)' **C. lactiflora**

'Loddon Anna', lilac-pink, up to 1.5m (5ft); and **C. persicifolia** 'Telham Beauty', light blue, height 90cm (3ft).

Crocosmias or montbretias are hardy perennials which flower in mid or late summer and are especially recommended for cottage-garden borders. This dazzling cultivar is 'Lucifer'

Clematis

Making a lovely companion for shrub roses is the herbaceous clematis, **C. heracleifolia** 'Wyevale', with fragrant, tubular, deep blue flowers. It grows to a height of 90–120cm (3–4 ft) on any well-drained soil and is good on chalk.

Crambe

Crambe cordifolia is one of the largest perennials for the back of a border. Branching sprays of tiny white flowers are carried in summer above large lobed leaves. When in flower it is up to 1.8m (6ft) tall. Any soil with good drainage is suitable.

Crocosmia (montbretia)

From clumps of broad, grassy foliage spikes of brightly coloured funnel-shaped flowers arise in mid or late summer. Crocosmias grow from corms and thrive in any well-drained soil, and are especially recommended for a cottage-garden border, with old-fashioned roses, silver-foliage plants and the like. We recommend the hybrids 'Citronella', lemon-yellow, 60cm (24in) high; 'Emily McKenzie', dark orange and mahogany, 60cm (24in); and 'Lucifer', rich red, 90cm (3ft).

Delphinium

The **D. elatum** hybrids, with their tall, stately spikes of flowers in shades of blue, purple, pink, white and cream, contrast beautifully with shrub roses, both in shape and colour. For instance, try blue delphiniums with red roses. Average height is 1.8m (6ft); any fertile, well-drained soil is suitable.

Dianthus (border pinks)

The most famous of all border pinks, 'Doris', is excellent for planting in front of shrub roses, particularly small-growing kinds. Also combine it with silver or grey-foliage shrubs like senecios or santolinas. It produces clear pink flowers throughout summer and grows to a height of 15–25cm (6–10in). It is suitable for any well-drained soil and good on chalk.

Diascia

Diascia rigescens is of trailing habit but has upright stems of salmon-pink flowers over a long period. Height is 22cm (9in). It makes an excellent companion for silver-foliage shrubs on any well-drained soil. It is slightly tender.

Dierama (wand flower)

Dierama pulcherrimum is an excellent waterside perennial with arching stems of pink, purple or white funnel-shaped flowers and evergreen grassy foliage, to a height of 1.5m (5ft). It needs shelter and moisture-retentive soil, and associates well with willows, **Osmunda regalis** and other waterside plants.

Digitalis (foxgloves)

The foxgloves are ideal for planting among woodland or other shrubs, relishing partial shade and moisture-retentive soil, although they succeed in dry conditions. We recommend **D. grandiflora** (syn. **D. ambigua**) with spikes of tubular cream-yellow flowers to a height of 76cm (2½ft), which show up well against dark rhododendron or camellia foliage.

Echinops (globe thistle)

Echinops humilis 'Taplow Blue' is a thistle-like plant with globular heads of bright blue flowers, growing to 1.2m (4ft) in height. Its divided grey-green foliage is attractive and it combines well with **Philadelphus coronarius** 'Aureus', **Elaeagnus pungens** 'Maculata', and purple-leaved shrubs like cotinus cultivars or berberis. Any well-drained soil is suitable.

Eryngium (sea holly)

These perennials have the same uses as echinops. We recommend **Eryngium alpinum**, with large conical purple-blue flower heads surrounded by feathery blue bracts, height 76cm (2½ft); and **E. tripartitum**, with small, conical, steel-blue flower heads on branching stems, height 90–120cm (3–4 ft). Both are suited to any well-drained soil.

Gentiana (gentian)

Gentiana asclepiadea (willow gentian) is a 90cm (3ft)-tall perennial with narrow, willow-like leaves and, in late summer and autumn, deep blue trumpet-shaped flowers on arching stems. It needs partial shade and a moisture-retentive soil: try it with white hydrangeas.

Geranium (crane's bill)

Making good ground cover in shade is **G. endressii** 'A. T. Johnson', with silver-pink flowers and attaining 45cm (18in) in height. **G.** 'Johnson's Blue', of similar height, bears

Hemerocallis 'Golden Chimes' (foreground) and **Achillea filipendulina** 'Gold Plate', two hardy summer-flowering perennials which should be in every mixed border, as they associate beautifully with many shrubs (*Royal Horticultural Society's Garden, Wisley, Surrey*)

bright blue flowers all summer and **G. wallichianum** 'Buxton's Variety' produces dark blue flowers during summer and early autumn, its height only 30cm (12in). Geraniums are among the essential perennials and associate well with many shrubs, including shrub roses (eg blue geraniums with yellow roses) and yellow shrubby potentillas (see also Spring perennials, this chapter).

Hemerocallis (day lily)

Like geraniums, day lilies are also essential companions for shrubs, with their clumps of broad, grassy, contrasting foliage and long succession of lily-like flowers, each of which lasts only one day, in a wide range of colours.

Day lilies are particularly useful for planting among rhododendrons and azaleas, taking over when their display has finished. We also like yellow day lilies with purple-foliage shrubs.

There are numerous cultivars from which to choose, many of which originated in the USA. Some of our favourites include 'Golden Chimes', with deep yellow flowers, 60cm (24in) high; 'Pink Damask', dark pink, 76cm (2½ft); and 'Stafford', dark crimson, up to 90cm (3ft). Any well-drained yet moist soil is suitable, together with full sun or partial shade.

Iris

The sword-like leaves of irises contrast well with broad-leaved shrubs, but it is primarily for the flowers that most kinds are grown. **Iris laevigata** is a waterside species, enjoying moist or wet soil and sun or partial shade. It even grows in shallow water. Large, deep blue flowers are produced during early and mid summer by this 60–90cm

(2–3ft) plant, which is lovely with willows and other waterside specimens. Flowering at the same time is the light blue border iris, **I. pallida dalmatica** (Dalmatian iris), its height 76cm (2½ft), which combines beautifully with border paeonias and philadelphus. The **I. sibirica** (Siberian flag) cultivars can be planted in borders or by water and flower during early and mid summer. We recommend 'Caesar', dark violet-purple; 'Perry's Blue', sky blue; and 'Snow Queen', white, all growing to 90cm (3ft).

Lamium (dead nettle)

The carpeting **Lamium maculatum** cultivars make good ground cover in partial shade, such as woodland gardens. We recommend 'White Nancy', with white flowers and semi-evergreen silver-white foliage. Any well-drained yet moist soil is suitable.

Ligularia

Very distinctive is **Ligularia dentata** 'Desdemona', with large heart-shaped leaves and big orange daisy-like flowers carried on purple stems during mid and late summer. It is best grown by water or in a moist border, and is suitable for partial shade. This plant reaches a height of 1.2m (4ft).

Lysimachia (loosestrife)

Effectively grown with any broad-leaved shrubs which like moisture-retentive soil in sun or partial shade is **Lysimachia clethroides**, with long curved spikes of white flowers from mid summer to early autumn, its height up to 90cm (3ft). It looks

Part of a mixed border in summer. Some temporary tender plants have been included here, such as cannas or Indian shot (bottom left) (*Overbecks, Devon, National Trust*)

good with a background of dark evergreen shrubs.

Macleaya (plume poppy)

These are handsome perennials in all respects, growing in any well-drained soil. **M. cordata** produces spikes of white flowers and large, rounded, lobed grey-green leaves. **M. microcarpa** 'Coral Plume' has bold feathery spikes of pink-buff flowers and similar foliage. Both grow to around 1.8m (6ft). Allow entire plants to be seen, and aim for a background of dark evergreens.

Meconopsis (blue poppy)

Meconopsis betonicifolia, with sumptuous blue poppy flowers in late spring and early summer, is a plant for the woodland garden, ideally grown in association with rhododendrons, candelabra primulas, hostas and ferns. It needs moist, humus-rich, acid soil and partial shade. Height is 90–120cm (3–4ft).

Monarda (bergamot)

Aromatic perennials with whorls of tubular, hooded flowers throughout summer, scarlet in 'Cambridge Scarlet' and rose-pink in 'Croftway Pink'. Both attain 60–90cm (2–3ft) in height. Any moisture-retentive soil is suitable, and bergamots combine beautifully with old-fashioned roses and/or silver-foliage shrubs in a cottage-garden border.

Nepeta (catmint)

The aromatic catmints associate particularly well with shrub and species roses, making ideal companions for old roses in a cottage-garden border. **Nepeta** 'Six Hills Giant' has grey foliage and lavender-blue flowers, and grows to a height of 60cm (2ft); while **N.** 'Souvenir d'Andre Chaudon', with deep lavender-blue tubular flowers and grey green foliage, is shorter at 30cm (12in). Any well-drained soil is suitable.

Oenothera (evening primrose)

As it needs extremely well-drained soil and plenty of sun, **Oenothera tetragona** 'Fireworks' is an ideal candidate for the garden devoted to Mediterranean climate plants, where you can combine it with ceanothus, hebes, cistus, and so on. It produces a long succession of bright yellow, cup-shaped flowers from red buds and grows 30cm (12in) tall.

Osteospermum (Cape marigold)

Also requiring the above conditions are the carpeting evergreen osteospermums, with showy daisy flowers in summer. They are ideal for associating with small silver-foliage plants but are not recommended for the coldest areas. We suggest **O. barberiae** (syn. **O. jucundum, Dimorphotheca barberiae**), offering masses of pink flowers, its height 30cm (12in); and **O. ecklonis**, with white, blue-centred flowers, 45cm (18in) in height.

Paeonia (peony)

Very showy perennials with large bowl or globe-shaped blooms in late spring or early summer, associating beautifully with border irises, old roses and philadelphus, and especially at home in old-fashioned cottage-garden borders. Peonies relish deep, fertile, well-drained soil and will take partial shade.

Cultivars we recommend are 'Bowl of Beauty', bearing red-pink and white semi-double flowers, 90cm (3ft) in height; **P. officinalis** 'Rosea Plena', deep pink double, 60cm (2ft); **P. officinalis** 'Rubra Plena', crimson-red double, 60cm (2ft); **P. peregrina** 'Sunshine', single vermilion flushed salmon-rose, late spring, 90cm (3ft); 'Duchesse de Nemours', double white, fragrant, 70cm (28in); 'Felix Crousse', double crimson, fragrant, 76cm (2½ft); and 'Sarah Bernhardt', double pink, fragrant, 90cm (3ft).

Penstemon

Producing a mass of bright red tubular flowers throughout summer, **Penstemon** 'Garnet' makes a superb companion for silver, grey or purple-foliage shrubs and is 60–76cm (2–2½ft) in height. **P. heteropyllus** 'Blue Gem' has funnel-shaped, azure-blue flowers and attains only about 35cm (14in) in height. Any well-drained fertile soil is suitable.

Persicaria (knotweed)

Persicaria bistorta 'Superba' (syn. **Polygonum bistorta** 'Superbum') produces its soft pink conical flower heads from mid summer to early autumn and contrasts well with many shrubs. Height is 60–76cm (2–2½ft) and it grows in any well-drained soil, tolerating partial shade.

Potentilla (cinquefoil)

Very showy free-flowering perennials with saucer-shaped blooms which look particularly at home in cottage-garden borders, mixing well with silver or grey-foliage plants and old-fashioned roses. We recommend **P. atrosanguinea** 'Gibson's Scarlet', brilliant red, 45cm (18in); **P. nepalensis** 'Miss Wilmott', pink with red centre, 30–45cm (12–18in)'; 'William Rollison', semi-double, orange-red, 45cm (18in); and 'Yellow Queen', semi-double, bright yellow, 60cm (24in). Any well-drained soil is suitable.

Salvia (sage)

The spikes of violet-blue flowers produced by **Salvia nemorosa** 'Lubeca' contrast well with many shrubs, including shrub roses. This sage is a dwarf plant 45cm (18in) in height and grows in any well-drained soil.

Sisyrinchium (satin flower)

With semi-evergreen iris-like foliage, **Sisyrinchium striatum** produces spikes of pale yellow flowers in summer to a height of 45–60cm (18–24in). A pleasing companion for blue-flowered dwarf or small ceanothus, it is suited to any well-drained soil and tolerates partial shade.

Verbascum (mullein)

The mulleins produce bold spikes of flowers and are highly recommended for cottage-garden borders, where they contrast well with old roses and other shrubs. Among the hybrids, 'Gainsborough' has light yellow flowers all summer and grows 60–120cm (2–4ft) tall; the 90cm (3ft)-high 'Mont Blanc' is white with grey, felty foliage; and 'Pink Domino' has rose-pink flowers, its height 1.2m (4ft). Any well-drained soil is suitable.

Zantedeschia (arum lily)

The arum lily, **Z. aethiopica**, with white spathes from mid to late summer and attractive arrow-shaped foliage, looks well with evergreen shrubs such as **Fatsia japonica** and ivies, say in a cool courtyard with partial shade; or it can be grown by the waterside. Outdoor cultivation is recommended only in mild areas, growing the hardier cultivar 'Crowborough'. Height is up to 90cm (3ft) and any moisture-retentive soil will do.

SUMMER PLANTS FOR FOLIAGE

Acanthus (bear's breeches)

Bear's breeches are indeed distinctive, with their deeply cut foliage which contrasts with so many shrubs, such as purple-leaved cotinus, phormiums, yuccas and shrub roses. A further attraction is the bold spikes of funnel-shaped flowers produced in summer. **A. mollis latifolius** has bright green foliage and produces rose-purple and white flowers in late summer, growing to a height of 1.2m (4ft), and **A. spinosus** is similar but with very deep green, shiny spine-tipped foliage. Any well-drained soil is suitable.

PERENNIALS AND BULBS

Ajuga (bugle)

Excellent ground cover among shrubs is provided by **Ajuga reptans** 'Burgundy Glow', whose semi-evergreen purple leaves are bordered with cream and pink, eventually turning red. Of prostrate habit, with spikes of blue flowers in spring, it is ideal for partial shade and any moisture-retentive soil. A pleasing scheme consists of small purple-leaved berberis growing through a carpet of this ajuga.

Artemisia (wormwood)

One of the best silver-leaved perennials for associating with shrubs is **Artemisia absinthium** 'Lambrook Silver' with finely divided evergreen aromatic leaves. Its height is 76cm (2½ft) and it needs sheltered conditions and well-drained soil. This plant associates with many shrubs – try it with shrub roses, purple and golden-leaved shrubs, etc. An ideal plant, too, for the hot dry area with Mediterranean-climate specimens.

Carex (sedge)

Some of the carex have colourful grassy foliage, including **C. morrowii** 'Evergold'. This has bright gold, variegated evergreen leaves and can be used as ground cover around various shrubs, such as purple-leaved berberis and blue-flowered caryopteris. It is only 20cm (8in) tall. Not recommended for very cold areas, but it succeeds in any moisture-retentive soil.

Gunnera

Many people find **Gunnera manicatea** highly amusing, looking as it does like a giant rhubarb maybe 2.4m (8ft) high and with a similar spread, but it is certainly an impressive waterside plant for the large garden. The massive 1.5m (5ft)-wide leaves are carried on thick, prickly stalks. In the autumn the dead leaves should be folded over the plant's crown, which is then covered with a heap of bracken or leaves to protect it from hard frosts. The plant needs mosit soil and shelter. Grow it with weeping willows, coloured-stemmed dogwoods and other waterside plants.

Heuchera (coral bells)

Becoming very popular is **Heuchera** 'Palace Purple' with dark purple heart-shaped leaves the year round and, in summer, sprays of tiny white flowers. Height is 45cm (18in). Associates well with many shrubs, including red shrub roses.

Hosta (plantain lily)

The hostas mainly have large, bold foliage which comes in all shades of green, plus 'blue', gold and variegated, forming superb ground cover in moist soil and partial shade or sun. They can be used effectively around woodland shrubs like rhododendrons, kalmias, camellias, pieris, enkianthus, etc, in combination with candelabra primulas, meconopsis, ferns and other woodlanders. Hostas are excellent for underplanting Japanese maples, contrasting superbly with hydrangeas and many other shrubs, and can also provide shade at soil level for lilies, with which they contrast beautifully. They also associate well with paving and architecture.

Hostas produce spikes of lilac or white, lily-like flowers in summer. Unfortunately, it is essential to place slug pellets around

---

PLANTING SCHEMES FEATURING SUMMER FOLIAGE

Hostas (plantain lilies), with their large, bold foliage, make effective ground cover around woodland shrubs such as rhododendrons and camellias, and among Japanese maples, hydrangeas and many other shrubs.

An effective group in a mixed border: the blue-leaved **Hosta** 'Halcyon', the yellow-leaved bamboo **Pleioblastus viridistriatus**, and white-flowered **Viburnum plicatum** 'Mariesii' (*Savill Gardens, The Great Park, Windsor, Berkshire*)

fragrant mauve flowers, height 30cm (12in); **H.** 'Hyacinthina', grey-green foliage and lilac flowers, height about 45cm (18in); **H.** 'Royal Standard', light green foliage and slightly fragrant white flowers, height 60cm (24in); **H. sieboldiana elegans**, deeply ribbed blue-grey foliage which contrasts beautifully with red or pink primulas or astilbes, flowers light lilac, height 60cm (24in); **H.** 'Thomas Hogg', dark green cream-edged leaves, deep lilac flowers, height 30cm (12in); and **H. undulata**, leaves wavy with a white band in the centre, flowers pale violet, height 45cm (18in). Heights refer to the foliage.

Iris

We have already discussed these under summer flowers, but not **I. pallida** 'Variegata', one of the best variegated-foliage perennials. The sword-like leaves are glaucous and striped with cream, making this an excellent companion for many plants, including kniphofias and yuccas. Blue flowers are produced in late spring/early summer. Any well-drained soil is suitable.

Kniphofia (red-hot poker)

These are very distinctive clump-forming perennials with grassy foliage and, in summer, bold spikes of tubular flowers. They combine well with many shrubs and other plants which also enjoy very well-drained soil and plenty of sun, such as yuccas and ornamental grasses. They also look good in areas devoted to Mediterranean-climate plants, in gravel areas and in association with paving (for example in patios).

There are numerous species and hybrids, including **K.** 'Atlanta', glaucous foliage, yellow and red pokers, height 90cm (3ft); **K.** 'Candlelight', clear yellow pokers, height about 45cm (18in); **K. caulescens**, glaucous foliage, light red pokers, height 1.2m (4ft);

hostas to prevent damage from slugs and snails. From the countless species, hybrids and cultivars available we especially recommend **H. fortunei** 'Albopicta', with variegated pale green and cream-yellow foliage and lilac flowers, its height 45–60cm (18–24in); **H. fortunei** 'Aurea', yellow in spring/early summer, lilac flowers, height about 45cm (18in); **H.** 'Frances Williams', glaucous and beige variegated foliage, mauve flowers, height up to 60cm (24in); **H.** 'Halcyon', blue foliage, lovely with pink or red primulas or astilbes, lilac-blue flowers, height 30cm (12in); **H.** 'Honeybells', green foliage and

If desired, hardy herbaceous perennials can be grown in the traditional way – in their own special border – but this will be largely devoid of interest in the winter (*Jenkyn Place, Hampshire*)

K. galpinii, orange pokers, 90cm (3ft); **K. 'Little Maid'**, pale yellow and ivory pokers, height 60cm (24in), lovely with **Iris pallida 'Variegata'**; and **K. uvaria**, orange-scarlet and yellow pokers, height 1.2m (4ft).

Ophiopogon **(lilyturf)**

These perennials have evergreen grassy foliage which makes excellent low ground cover around shrubs. The foliage of **O.** **planiscapus** 'Nigrescens' is of very unusual colour – it is black-purple and contrasts well with many shrubs, including pink-flowered kinds. Lilyturf is excellent for partial shade and any well-drained soil.

Rheum **(rhubarb)**

The ornamental rhubarbs are so distinctive that they are usually grown alone as lawn specimens or focal points. **R. palmatum** 'Bowles' Crimson' is the one usually recommended, with large, lobes, palmate leaves which are deep red when they first emerge, and 1.8m (6ft)-high panicles of deep red flowers in summer. It needs a deep,

flowers in early or midsummer, height 1.2m (4ft); **R. pinnata**, large pinnate leaves, pink flowers in mid to late summer, height 76cm (2½ft); and **R. pinnata** 'Superba', with bronze leaves and clear pink flowers in mid to late summer, height 76cm (2½ft).

Ruta (rue)

Ruta graveolens 'Jackman's Blue' is one of the most useful foliage perennials. The deeply cut, evergreen foliage is grey-blue and this contrasts well with shrubs of any colour, including old-fashioned pink shrub roses and **Philadelphus coronarius** 'Aureus'. Yellow flowers are produced in midsummer and height is 60cm (2ft). The plant looks most at home in a cottage-garden border but is suited to any style of garden, where it should be grown in sun or partial shade and any well-drained soil.

Stachys

Stachys byzantina (syn. **S. lanata**, **S. olympica**) 'Silver Carpet' (lamb's ears) is one of the best evergreen, mat-forming ground-cover perennials for combining with shrubs. The woolly, grey, oval leaves associate with anything but some particularly pleasing effects are achieved when the plant is used among pink shrub roses, or other pink-flowered shrubs. It is non-flowering, attains a height of 15cm (6in), and needs a very well-drained soil .

fertile, moisture-retentive yet well-drained soil, and sun or partial shade.

Rodgersia

These bold-leaved perennials have various uses but demand moisture-retentive soil. A sheltered site is needed to prevent wind from damaging the leaves, and the plants will be happy in sun or partial shade. They are excellent for pool or streamside in conjunction with coloured-stemmed dogwoods and willows, **Osmunda regalis**, bog irises and other moisture-loving plants. We recommend the species **R. aesculifolia**, with large horse-chestnut-like leaves and white

Tellima (fringecups)

Tellima grandiflora 'Purpurea' is valued for its semi-evergreen, red-purple leaves, which offset the spikes of pink bell-shaped flowers produced in late spring. Height is up to 60cm (2ft). This plant is excellent for ground cover in partially shaded, cool conditions with moisture-retentive soil, and ideal for ground cover around rhododendrons and other woodland shrubs. Use it with 'blue' hostas and red astilbes.

AUTUMN

Anemone

The **Anemone × hybrida** cultivars, with their cup-shaped flowers in pink shades, like 'Bressingham Glow', 45cm (18in), and 'Queen Charlotte', 60cm (2ft); and in white, such as 'White Queen', up to 1.2m (4ft), are excellent for including in groups of shrubs noted for autumn leaf tints and berries. They generally start flowering in late summer but go on into mid autumn. They will succeed in any well-drained soil, including chalk.

Aster

These perennials with daisy-like flowers are also recommended for groups of shrubs with good autumn leaf tints and colourful berries, especially the **A. amellus** cultivars like 'Brilliant' with bright pink flowers, reaching a height of 60cm (2ft); and the violet-blue 'King George', 76cm (2½ft). Also recommended is **A. frikartii** with blue, orange-centred flowers, height 76cm (2½ft). Any fertile well-drained soil is suitable for asters.

Kirengeshoma

Cream-yellow, funnel-shaped flowers are produced by **Kirengeshoma palmata**, set against bright green lobed leaves. This 90cm (3ft)-tall plant relishes partial shade and moisture-retentive soil, and is quite superb for the woodland garden, contrasting with Japanese maples and other shrubs with autumnal leaf tints. Plant it in bold groups.

Liriope (lilyturf)

Liriope muscari has evergreen, grassy foliage and spikes of violet-purple flowers. Best mass planted to create ground cover among shrubs, it grows to a height of 30cm (12in) in any well-drained soil.

Schizostylis (Kaffir lily)

Schizostylis coccinea has grassy foliage and star-shaped scarlet flowers, and reaches a height of about 60cm (2ft). There are several cultivars, such as the deep red 'Major', clear pink 'Mrs Hegarty' and 'Sunrise', and light pink 'Viscountess Byng'. It needs a moisture-retentive soil and sheltered site, and looks superb with silver-foliage shrubs.

Sedum (ice plant)

With their flat heads of flowers which attract butterflies, the ice plants contrast beautifully with shrubs noted for autumn leaf colour, flowers or berries. 'Autumn Joy' comes in salmon-pink and attains 60cm (2ft) in height; 'Ruby Glow' is about half this height with ruby-red flowers; and **S. spectabile** 'Brilliant' is a magenta-rose shade and 45cm (18in) in height. Any well-drained soil is suitable.

WINTER

Iris

Surprisingly, perhaps, the few perennials that flower in winter are mainly irises. No shrub border or woodland garden should be without **I. foetidissima**, the gladwyn or stinking iris. This species is excellent for growing under trees and large shrubs, and tolerates shade and dry or moist soil. It produces bold clumps of evergreen grassy foliage and the purple or yellow summer flowers are followed by far more attractive seed pods, which open to expose numerous bright scarlet pips. It grows to 90cm (3ft).

Needing hot arid conditions to flower well is **I. unguicularis** (syn. **I. stylosa**), the Algerian iris, with lavender-blue flowers set among evergreen grassy foliage. Its height is 20cm (8in) and it is suited to the hot, dry, Mediterranean-climate garden, gravel area or patio border.

BULBS TO ASSOCIATE WITH SHRUBS

Snowdrops, hellebores and miniature hardy cyclamen making a superb spring display under trees (*Old Rectory Cottage, Berkshire*)

As with perennials, there are bulbs (and we are including corms and tubers here, too) for every season, but the majority provide their display in spring. The species and less highly bred bulbs associate best with shrubs, and they should be planted in very bold, informal drifts or groups between shrubs for best effect. Small bulbs can even be planted right under shrubs to make maximum use of the ground, provided they obtain sufficient sun. They can even be allowed to poke through low ground-cover shrubs such as heathers – crocuses are particularly effective in this respect.

There is concern today about buying bulbs which have been dug from the wild. We advise you to ascertain from bulb specialists that they are completely satisfied that all bulbs offered have been garden or nursery grown. If grown by the specialists themselves, so much the better.

SPRING

Anemone (windflower)

A 10cm (4in)-high carpet of **Anemone blanda** covering a woodland floor is a beautiful sight in early spring. The daisy-shaped flowers are white, pink or blue. There are named cultivars such as 'Atrocaerulea', deep blue; 'Radar', deep red-carmine with a white centre; and 'White Splendour', pure white. Grow them in well-drained soil in sun or partial shade, and plant them 5cm (2in) deep. **A. nemorosa** is the wood anemone, which forms 15cm (6in)-high carpets of white, star-shaped flowers and whose cultivars include the lavender-blue 'Robinsoniana' and white 'Vestal'. Anemones are essentially woodland plants for cool shady conditions.

207

Chionodoxa (glory of the snow)

Chionodoxa sardensis will form a stunning blue carpet around such spring-flowering shrubs as forsythia, kerria and magnolias. The starry flowers have white centres. The plants are up to 15cm (6in) tall and grow in any well-drained soil, where you should plant the bulbs 8cm (3in) deep.

C. luciliae has medium-blue starry flowers with white centres and needs the same conditions.

Crocus

There are numerous crocuses for growing through low shrubs such as heathers, for naturalising in short grass under trees, and for drifting among shrubs. They need plenty of sun and to be planted 8cm (3in) deep in well-drained soil. **Crocus chrysanthus** cultivars come in various colours, height 8cm (3in); **C. ancyrensis** is deep yellow, height 5cm (2in); **C. sieberi** has pale mauve blooms, height 8cm (3in); and **C. thomasinianus** sports lilac flowers and naturalises vigorously, its height 8cm (3in).

Cyclamen

Ideal for carpeting the ground beneath shrubs are the hardy cyclamen, which revel in dry soil and shade. **C. coum** has pink, carmine or white flowers and handsome rounded, dark green, silver-marbled leaves, and is up to 15cm (6in) tall. Somewhat similar is **C. repandum**, which produces fragrant deep pink flowers with twisted petals.

Erythronium dens-canis, the dog's-tooth violet, is a spring-flowering tuberous perennial, essentially a woodland plant enjoying partial shade and humus-rich moist soil

Both should be planted just beneath the soil surface. Do ensure cyclamen tubers are garden or nursery raised and not collected from the wild.

Erythronium

Nodding flowers with reflexed petals endear the erythroniums to most gardeners. They are essentially woodland plants, enjoying partial shade and humus-rich moisture-retentive soil, although they can also be drifted among shrubs in a border or naturalised in grass under deciduous trees. Plant them 10–15cm (4–6in) deep. We can recommend **E. dens-canis** (dog's tooth violet), with pink-purple flowers and brown or grey-blotched leaves, plus its cultivars,

208

height 15cm (6in); **E.** 'Pagoda', pale yellow, height about 30cm (12in); and **E. revolutum** 'White Beauty', white flowers and grey-mottled leaves, height up to 30cm (12in).

Fritillaria (fritillary)

The fritillaries are diverse in habit but all have bell-shaped flowers. The 60–90cm (2–3ft)-high **F. imperialis** (crown imperial), with clusters of orange flowers (or yellow in cultivar 'Lutea'), is especially suitable for planting among larger shrubs such as rhododendrons and azaleas and will take partial shade. The 30cm (12in)-high **F. meleagris** (snake's head fritillary) can be naturalised in short grass, say around a specimen tree, and has white flowers heavily chequered with purple. Normally supplied mixed but there are several cultivars, including the white 'Alba'. **F. pontica** carries green, purple-tipped flowers on 45cm (18in)-high stems and **F. verticillata** is slightly taller with cream, green-marked blooms. The latter needs a moist humus-rich soil, but the others grow in any well-drained earth, although **F. meleagris** also enjoys moist conditions. Plant fritillaries up to 15cm (6in) deep; or 20cm (8in) for the crown imperial.

Galanthus (snowdrop)

Snowdrops herald the spring with their white, pendulous flowers and indeed may start flowering in late winter. Plant them in woodland gardens or shrub borders – they associate with most shrubs and look lovely planted among hellebores such as **H. orientalis**. **G. nivalis** is the common snowdrop, which has several cultivars including the double 'Flore Plena', and 'S. Arnott' with larger flowers. There are numerous other species. All grow about 15cm (6in) high. Plant them 8cm (3in) deep immediately after flowering in any moisture

retentive yet well-drained soil, and in partial shade.

Leucojum (snowflake)

Leucojums are similar to, and have the same uses and cultural needs as, snowdrops. The white flowers are more bell-shaped, though. **L. aestivum** 'Gravetye Giant' attains about 60cm (2ft) in height and is recommended for the shrub border, but the best choice for growing under shrubs is **L. vernum** as it attains only 20cm (8in) in height. Plant them 8–10cm (3–4in) deep. Make sure you do not buy bulbs collected from the wild.

Muscari (grape hyacinth)

Grape hyacinths are marvellous for massing under or around spring-flowering shrubs such as yellow forsythias and the white, flushed purple **Magnolia × soulangeana**, which they complement by producing a long succession of blue, poker-shaped blooms. There are numerous species like **M. azureum**, with dense spikes of pale blue flowers, its height 10–15cm (4–6in); and **M. latifolium**, producing very dark violet flowers, height 25cm (10in). Plant them all 8cm (3in) deep in any well-drained soil.

Narcissus (daffodil)

Miniature narcissus look lovely drifted among shrubs in a woodland garden or shrub border, or they can be naturalised in short grass, say under deciduous trees. **N. bulbocodium** (hoop petticoat) has rush-like leaves, golden-yellow widely trumpet-shaped flowers and attains only 15cm (6in) in height. For maximum flowering grow it in full sun and dry soil. **N. lobularis**, with flowers in two shades of yellow, grows 12cm (5in) high and needs time to become established.

Needing moisture-retentive soil and flourishing in partial shade is **N. cyclamineus**, with deep golden-yellow flowers each composed of a long trumpet and swept-back petals, whose height is 15–20cm (6–8in). Try planting it with **Primula denticulata**, the lilac drumstick primrose. Its taller cultivars – height 20–38cm (8–15in) – are admirable for drifting among shrubs in the border, perhaps in combination with bergenias, and include the yellow 'February Gold', 'Peeping Tom' and 'March Sunshine'; cream and yellow 'Jack Snipe'; and the light creamy-white 'February Silver'. Plant these narcissus 8–10cm (3–4in) deep.

Ornithogalum (star of Bethlehem)

These bulbs mainly have starry, white flowers which show up well against a background of evergreen ground cover, such as that provided by small-leaved ivies, or when emerging through clumps of bergenia. **O.**

The tulips, like **Tulipa batalinii**, are bulbs for hot arid areas as they like a summer baking. Plant them in the Mediterranean-climate garden, in patio borders or in gravel areas

balansae has green-striped flowers, height 10–15cm (4–6in); **O. narbonense** sends up 30cm (12in) spikes of flowers; and **O. nutans** carries pendulous bell-shaped flowers on stems up to 45cm (18in) high. Plant ornithogalums 8cm (3in) deep in any well-drained soil. **O. nutans** is best grown in partial shade.

Scilla (squill)

The scillas, with their starry or bell-shaped bright blue flowers, like **S. bifolia** and **S. siberica**, make an underplanting of striking contrast for golden forsythia, pale yellow **Corylopsis pauciflora** or **Corylus avellana** 'Contorta' with its yellow catkins. Plant squills 8cm (3in) deep in any well-drained yet moisture-retentive soil; they will take partial shade.

Tulipa (tulip)

The tulips are for hot, dry areas as the bulbs like a summer baking, so plant them in the garden for Mediterranean-climate plants, in patio borders, or in gravel areas. Especially recommended for alkaline soils, they look particularly lovely with silver or grey-leaved shrubs. There are many species, including **T. aucheriana**, with star-shaped pink flowers, growing 20cm (8in) high; **T. batalinii**, cream-yellow, 15cm (6in); **T. clusiana** (lady tulip), white, flushed red, up to 30cm (12in); **T. fosteriana** cultivars such as 'White Emperor', 45cm (18in), excellent for shrub borders; **T. kaufmanniana** (water-lily tulip), white, flushed red and yellow, 15–20cm (6–8in); **T. marjolettii**, light yellow marked with rose-red, 45cm (18in); **T. praestans**, pure red, 30–45cm (12–

The species tulip **Tulipa marjolettii** planted with the hardy perennial **Brunnera macrophylla**, which has blue forget-me-not-like flowers. An unusual spring bedding scheme, but the idea could be used in a mixed border, too
(Royal Botanic Gardens, Kew)

18in); **T. pulchella**, cup-shaped violet-red, 10–15cm (4–6in); and **T. tarda**, star-shaped white flowers each with a bright yellow centre, 15cm (6in). Lily-flowered tulips are excellent for shrub borders. Plant tulips 15cm (6in) deep.

SUMMER

Allium (ornamental onion)

At last the alliums are gaining the popularity they deserve, and hence many more are becoming available. Their dense, rounded umbels of flowers, rising from clumps of narrow foliage, last for a long period in the summer. Alliums are best grown with shrubs which need plenty of sun and very good drainage: they are ideal for the Mediterranean-climate garden, patio borders and gravel areas, perhaps in association with silver-foliage shrubs.

We recommend the following species: **A. aflatunense**, offering purple flowers in large heads, height 76cm (2½ft), a striking companion for yellow-foliage shrubs; **A. atropurpureum**, dark purple flowers in late spring, height up to 90cm (3ft); **A. caeruleum**, blue star-shaped flowers in a large rounded umbel, height about 60cm (2ft); **A. cernuum**, umbels of pink nodding flowers, height up to 45cm (18in), a lovely companion for tall bearded irises; **A. karataviense**, grown more for its broad, metallic, grey-purple leaves than the extra-large heads of lilac flowers, height up to 20cm (8in); **A. moly**, one of the most popular species, with many heads of yellow star-shaped flowers, height about 25cm (10in); **A. neapolitanum grandiflorum**, with scented white blooms in loose heads during late spring, height 60cm (2ft); **A. rosenbachianum album**, green-white flowers in large globular heads, height up to 76cm (2½ft); **A. sphaerocephalon**, dense umbels of pink-purple flowers, height 60cm

(2ft), a lovely companion for philadelphus; and **A. unifolium**, heads of purple-pink star-shaped flowers in late spring, height 30cm (12in). Plant allium bulbs 8–10cm (3–4in) deep.

Camassia (quamash)

These are very useful early-summer-flowering bulbs, with racemes of mainly blue, starry flowers. Some stunning effects can be achieved by planting them among yellow-leaved shrubs. **Camassia cusickii** has pale lavender-blue flowers and grows up to 90cm (3ft) in height, and of similar stature is **C. leichtlinii** with pure blue or white flowers. Plant the bulbs 8–10cm (3-4in) deep; quamash are easily grown in any moisture-retentive soil and tolerate partial shade.

Crinum

Crinum × powellii is ideal for growing with silver-foliage shrubs. Large trumpet-shaped pink flowers are produced from mid summer to early autumn. Height is 45cm (18in), and you should plant the large bulbs 25–30cm (10–12in) deep. Choose a sunny position with well-drained soil.

Lilium (lily)

There is a huge range of lilies from which to choose, both species and hybrids, some being suited to acid soils while others will grow in alkaline conditions. Lilies are ideal bulbs for woodland gardens, mixed or shrub borders, where they should be planted in bold groups or drifts, say between rhododendrons, azaleas and kalmias, but among other shrubs, too. Lilies can also be grown with roses and in containers.

Lilies like sun but should have their bulbs in cool, shaded conditions, which could be provided by the shrubs, or by growing smaller perennials like primulas, hellebores, and ferns among the lilies. Plant them

The summer-flowering bulb **Crinum × powellii** is best grown in a warm sunny spot with well-drained soil. Ideal for associating with silver-foliage shrubs

in well-drained yet moisture-retentive soil rich in humus, setting the bulbs in 20cm (8in)-deep holes so that they are covered with about 10cm (4in) of soil.

Most of the following are easy and reliable. The beautiful **Lilium candidum** (Madonna lily), with pure white bell-shaped flowers on 90cm–1.5m (3–5ft) stems, likes alkaline soils but must be planted shallowly with the tips of the bulbs only just below the soil surface. It is very difficult to establish and resents disturbance. The Harlequin hybrids freely produce nodding Turk's-cap flowers in many colours on 90–150cm (3–5ft) stems, and grow in any well-drained soil. **L. henryi** has pendulous, tangerine-orange flowers with swept-back petals on 1.2–2.1m (4–7ft)-high stems and does not mind alkaline soils.

With purple Turk's-cap flowers is the popular **L. martagon**, which can be grown in alkaline soils and whose height is 90–180cm (3–6ft). Make sure you do not buy wild-collected bulbs. The lime-tolerant 'Sterling Star' is a beautiful Asiatic hybrid lily producing upward-facing white flowers with dark spots, on stems up to 90cm (3ft) high. **L. × testaceum** is a **candidum**

PLANTING SCHEME FEATURING LILIES

Lilies are ideal for woodland gardens, for mixed or shrub borders, and drifted between rhododendrons, azaleas, kalmias and other shrubs.

hybrid with pendulous, salmon-orange flowers. Lime tolerant, it grows 1.2–1.5m (4–5ft) in height. Most people love the tiger lily, **L. lancifolium** (syn. **L. tigrinum**), but the best form to grow is **L. l. splendens**. The Turk's-cap flowers are bright orange and liberally covered with dark purple spots. Its height is 1.5–1.8m (5–6ft) and it is best grown in acid soils.

Other lilies well worth growing include lime-tolerant **L. regale** (regal lily), with white and pink-purple funnel-shaped flowers, height up to 1.8m (6ft); **L. speciosum rubrum**, with carmine flowers late in the season, height up to 1.5m (5ft), for lime-free soils; and the hybrids 'Pink Perfection' and 'Golden Splendour', both lime tolerant.

AUTUMN

Colchicum (autumn crocus)

The colchicums are ideal candidates for the shrub border as their large leaves, which are produced in the spring, take up a lot of ground. In autumn big flowers, often goblet-shaped, bloom and look lovely under or around shrubs with colourful autumn leaves or berries.

Species we recommend are **C. agrippinum**, bright purple-pink, height 10–15cm (4–6in); **C. autumnale**, with purple, pink or white flowers, height 10–15cm (4–6in), plus cultivars like 'Album', white; 'Albo-plenum', double-white; and 'Roseum Plenum', amethyst-violet; **C. byzantinum**, light purple-pink, height 15–20cm (6–8in); **C. cilicicum**, light pink to dark rose-purple, height 15–20cm (6–8in); and **C. speciosum**, light to dark pink-purple, height 15–20cm (6–8in), plus the white cultivar 'Album'. Plant the corms 8–10cm (3–4in) deep.

Crocus

Numerous crocuses flower in the autumn

> **PLANTING SCHEME FEATURING AUTUMN CROCUS**
>
> **Crocus goulimyi**, in light lilac with a white throat, looks lovely naturalised around a specimen acer noted for its autumn leaf colour.

(see also Spring bulbs section, this chapter), including **C. goulimyi**, displaying light lilac flowers with white throats, height 10cm (4in), lovely naturalised around a specimen acer with autumn leaf colour; **C. medius**, deep purple, height 10cm (4in); **C. sativus** (saffron crocus), purple, height 10cm (4in), which needs hot summers to succeed fully; and **C. speciosus**, light purple-blue, very easy, height 12.5–15cm (5–6in), plus the white, blue-veined 'Artabir' and dark violet-blue 'Oxonian'.

Cyclamen

Several miniature cyclamen flower in the autumn (see also Spring bulbs, this chapter), including **C. hederifolium** (syn. **C. neapolitanum**), with light or dark pink flowers and ivy-shaped leaves marbled with silver-green; **C. hederifolium album** (syn. **C. neapolitanum album**), with pure white flowers and similar foliage; and **C. purpurascens** (syn. **C. europaeum**), bearing scented pink or red-purple flowers and silver-marbled leaves. All attain 10cm (4in) in height. Make sure you do not buy wild-collected tubers.

Galanthus (snowdrop)

It comes as a surprise to some people to learn that one can have snowdrops in flower during autumn (see also Spring bulbs, this chapter). **Galanthus reginae-olgae** has green-tipped flowers and the leaves have a grey central stripe. It is 10–20cm (4–8in) high.

Ideal for carpeting the ground beneath shrubs are the hardy cyclamen, like autumn-flowering **Cyclamen hederifolium** (syn. **C. neapolitanum**), which revel in dry soil and shade

Nerine

Nerine bowdenii needs a very warm, sunny, sheltered border and well-drained soil. Ideal for the garden devoted to Mediterranean-climate plants, patio bed or gravel area, it looks lovely planted with silver or grey-foliage shrubs. Heads of pink flowers with wavy reflexed petals are carried on 45–60cm (18–24in)-high stems. Plant the bulbs 10cm (4in) deep.

WINTER

Eranthis (winter aconite)

Eranthis hyemalis starts flowering in late winter, or earlier if the weather is mild, producing bright yellow, bowl-shaped flowers

each surrounded by a collar of bright green, leafy bracts. The tubers should be planted 2.5cm (1in) deep in moisture-retentive yet well-drained, humus-rich soil, in sun or partial shade; moisture during the growing season is particularly important. Winter aconite grows 10cm (4in) high and is ideal for use under shrubs. Try planting it under **Hamamelis mollis**, which has yellow, spidery winter flowers, perhaps mixing it with the common snowdrop, **Galanthus nivalis**, whose flowers immediately follow those of eranthis.

PLANTING SCHEME WITH WINTER BULBS

Try planting a mixture of winter aconite (eranthis) and common snowdrop (**Galanthus nivalis**) under **Hamamelis mollis** (witch hazel).

CHAPTER 11

GRASSES AND FERNS

Hardy, ornamental, perennial grasses and ferns can introduce different shapes and textures to planting schemes. For that reason alone we strongly recommend the liberal use of these foliage plants among shrubs and other hardy perennials. We include bamboos here, as they form part of the grass family even though most have woody stems, unlike other perennial grasses.

The grasses and bamboos produce long, narrow leaves which contrast well with those of shrubs and other plants, whose foliage is of different shapes, such as rounded and palmate.

The ferns' leaves are known as fronds and are often feathery, creating a marvellous textured contrast with numerous shrubs, especially those having simple smooth leaves, for example many rhododendrons.

ORNAMENTAL GRASSES

These may be evergreen, semi-evergreen or herbaceous plants forming clumps, tufts or carpets of foliage. They do flower, although most are grown primarily for their attractive leaves. Their flowering heights have been given in the following descriptions. Grow them in shrub or mixed borders, in the vicinity of patios (they contrast well with architecture) and in gravel areas.

Unless otherwise stated, ornamental grasses will thrive in any well-drained soil and are best sited in a sunny spot.

For the shrub or mixed border, tall grasses are often demanded. These include the slightly tender **Arundo donax** 'Macrophylla', with glaucous foliage, and the cream-variegated **A. d.** 'Variegata', which grow to around 2.4m (8ft). They are suited to moist soil also.

Cortaderia selloana (pampas grass) is

Below left:
Ornamental grasses may be grown on their own or they can be used to introduce different shapes and textures to more general planting schemes (*Royal Horticultural Society's Garden, Wisley, Surrey*)

Below:
Architectural plants, those with bold or otherwise distinctive foliage, are becoming very popular today, especially in modern gardens. They include bamboos and ornamental grasses (*Architectural Plants, Sussex*)

Pampas grass or cortaderia is one of the most popular tall grasses and is recommended for specimen planting in a lawn, and for including in groups of shrubs with autumn leaf colour (*York Gate, Leeds*)

The massive **Miscanthus sacchariflorus**, or Amur silver grass, can be planted at the back of a border where it would contrast beautifully with purple-leaved shrubs

one of the most popular tall grasses and is grown as much for its 2.4m (8ft)-high silvery plumes of flowers in late summer and autumn as for its arching, evergreen foliage. It is a marvellous grass for planting as a lawn specimen, and for including in groups of shrubs with autumn leaf colour. Try also the cultivars 'Gold band', with golden-yellow variegated foliage, height when in flower 1.5m (5ft); 'Pumila', a compact form at only 1.2–1.5m (4–5ft) high; 'Rendatleri', with pink-tinted flowers, 1.8–3m (6–10ft) high; and 'Sunningdale Silver', sporting cream-white flowers, 1.8m (6ft) high.

For moist or wet soil, say by a pool, is **Glyceria maxima** 'Variegata', with cream-and-green-striped leaves, height at least 1.5m (5ft).

The massive **Miscanthus sacchari-florus** (Amur silver grass) can be planted at the back of a border where its grey-green leaves on 2.4m (8ft)-tall stems contrast beautifully with purple-leaved shrubs. There are some excellent **Miscanthus sinensis** cultivars, including 'Gracillimus' with narrow, arching green leaves, height 1.5–1.8m (5–6ft); 'Silver Feather', bearing silvery flowers, 1.8m (6ft); 'Variegatus', with cream-and-green-striped leaves, 1.5–1.8m (5–6ft); and 'Zebrinus', whose leaves are marked with transverse yellow bands, height 1.5–1.8m (5–6ft).

The evergreen stipas have very narrow foliage but are grown mainly for their flowers. **Stipa calamagrostis** (syn. **Achnatherum calamagrostis**) has blue-green leaves and arching, feathery plumes of flowers to a height of 90cm (3ft). The narrow-leaved **S. gigantea** (golden oats)

Festuca glauca, blue fescue, is a dwarf grass, seen here in a grey and silver planting scheme, but it also associates well with many other plants including shrubs and shrub roses (*White Windows, Hampshire*)

produces panicles of silvery flowers up to 2.4m (8ft) in height during summer, and **S. pennata** (feather grass) has silvery buff plumes of flowers to a height of nearly 90cm (3ft).

Among smaller ornamental grasses are several with needle-thin, glaucous evergreen foliage, which contrast beautifully with purple or yellow-leaved shrubs, with shrub roses and indeed with any pink or red-flowered shrub. **Festuca glauca** (blue fescue) forms dense tufts 25cm (10in) high, while **Helictrotrichon sempervirens** (blue oat grass) is somewhat larger, attaining 90cm (3ft) when in flower.

There are several good small variegated grasses, including **Hakonechloa macra**

A colourful group in a mixed border, including the blue oat grass, **Helictotrichon sempervirens**, and the yellow-leaved dogwood, **Cornus alba** 'Aurea', a medium-size shrub (*Royal Horticultural Society's Garden, Wisley, Surrey*)

'Albo-aurea' whose arching leaves are striped yellow and cream and flushed with bronze, height about 90cm (3ft) when in flower. **Milium effusum** 'Aureum' (Bowles' golden grass) is recommended for the woodland garden as it enjoys partial shade. The evergreen leaves are golden-yellow and it reaches a height of up to 90cm (3ft) when in flower.

Molinia caerulea 'Variegata' (variegated purple moor grass) forms dense

The yellow-and-cream-striped **Hakonechloa macra** 'Albo-aurea' is a small grass which can be grown with many other plants such as shrubs (*Royal Horticultural Society's Garden, Wisley, Surrey*)

clumps of cream-edged leaves and slender panicles of purple-tinted flowers, to a height of 45cm (18in).

Although rampant, **Phalaris arundinacea** 'Picta' (gardener's garters) is one of the most beautiful of all variegated grasses, with very light white-and-green-striped leaves. Actually it makes excellent ground cover around large shrubs, and when in flower is about 90cm (3ft) in height. A superb effect is created when this grass is

---

PLANTING SCHEME WITH ORNAMENTAL GRASS

A superb effect is created when the green-and-white striped grass, **Phalaris arundinacea** 'Picta', is associated with purple-leaved shrubs such as **Corylus maxima** 'Purpurea', **Cotinus coggygria** 'Velvet Cloak' or C. 'Grace'.

---

associated with purple-leaved shrubs like **Corylus maxima** 'Purpurea', some berberis cultivars, **Cotinus coggygria** 'Velvet Cloak', C. 'Grace', and **Sambucus nigra** 'Guincho Purple' ('Purpurea').

BAMBOOS

These evergreens can be used in the same way as other grasses. Also, some of the tall ones make excellent lawn specimens or focal points. A bamboo walk or tunnel is an idea for larger gardens – tall bamboos are planted on each side of a path to form screens – and clumps of bamboos can also be planted on the edge of woodland to provide a contrast in foliage shape.

Although flowers are occasionally produced these are not particularly attractive, and flowered stems (but usually not entire

The Chilean bamboo, **Chusquea culeou**, here contrasting beautifully with a red-leaved photinia and a golden-variegated elaeagnus (*Hillier Arboretum, Ampfield, Hampshire*)

plants) die after blooming. The stems of bamboos are correctly known as canes and can be highly attractive.

Unless otherwise stated, bamboos relish moisture-retentive yet well-drained soil in a sheltered position, and they take sun or shade.

Thamnocalamus spathaceus (syn. **Arundinaria murieliae, Sinarundinaria mureliae**) makes a superb lawn specimen with its clumps of non-rampant, yellow green canes. Its height is 3.6m (12ft). **Sinarundinaria nitida** (syn. **Arundinaria nitida**) is excellent for the shrub border, producing dense clumps of arching, purple-flushed canes clothed with narrow foliage. It also looks good in light woodland with rhododendrons and camellias, and grows to a height of 4.5m (15ft). Quite colourful for a bamboo is the deep-yellow-and-dark-green-striped **Pleioblastus viridistriatus** (syn. **Arundinaria viridistriata, A. auricoma**), which has thin, purple-green canes. It is 1.5m (5ft) in height and spreads slowly. A dramatic but beautiful effect is created by planting this species with blue or grey hostas.

Making an excellent lawn specimen is **Chusquea culeou** (Chilean bamboo), which forms dense clumps of solid, dark green canes, well clothed with dainty narrow foliage. It reaches 4.5m (15ft) in height and is slow-growing. Another good lawn specimen is **Phyllostachys nigra** 'Boryana', a cultivar of the black bamboo, with abundant arching green canes which eventually turn yellow and marked with purple. This bamboo is up to 4m (13ft) tall. Another phyllostachys worth growing is **P.**

Thamnocalamus spathaceus is a graceful bamboo which forms non-rampant clumps of yellow-green canes. It can be included in a bamboo 'walk' or used as a focal point or lawn specimen (*Stream Cottage, Sussex*)

The golden bamboo, **Phyllostachys aurea**, with a purple-leaved berberis; quite a contrast in colour, shape and texture (*Stream Cottage, Sussex*)

aurea (golden bamboo), whose canes start off bright green then change to creamy yellow. They form large clumps and grow up to 3.6m (12ft) high.

Two dwarf bamboos which make good ground cover are **Sasa veitchii** (syn. **S. albomarginata**, which forms thickets of purple canes up to 1.2m (4ft) in height and whose long, broad leaves take on light straw-coloured margins in autumn; and **Shibataea kumasasa**, with zig-zag canes 50–76cm (20–30in) high and broad lanceolate leaves, which thrives in moist soil.

FERNS

Most ferns can be planted under or around shrubs. They require partial shade and almost all need moisture-retentive soil. In the woodland garden, or indeed in the mixed border, they can be effectively combined with flowering and foliage perennials such as candelabra and other moisture-loving primulas, meconopsis, polygonatums, lilies and hostas.

One of the daintiest hardy ferns is **Adiantum pedatum** (northern maidenhair fern), which is best grown in acid to neutral soil. It has long, semi-evergreen, deeply divided medium green fronds on dark brown or black stems and its height is up to 45cm (18in).

Most ferns can be planted under or around shrubs. They require partial shade, almost all need moisture-retentive soil, and they can be combined with many other perennials which like the same conditions (*Gardener's Cottage, Sussex*)

Tolerating a position in full sun is **Asplenium trichomanes** (maidenhair spleenwort), with semi-evergreen fronds consisting of rounded, bright green leaflets. It grows up to 15cm (6in) high and makes pleasing ground cover.

Athyrium filix-femina (lady fern) forms tufts of deeply divided, pale green fronds to a height of 60–120cm (2–4ft) and is excellent for woodland planting.

The blechnums prefer acid to neutral soil. Making good ground cover is **B. penna-**

PLANTING SCHEMES WHICH INCLUDE FERNS

Most ferns which need partial shade and moist soil can be planted under or around shrubs needing similar conditions, combining them with flowering and foliage perennials such as candelabra and other moisture-loving primulas, meconopsis, polygonatums, lilies and hostas.

marina with evergreen or semi-evergreen deep green fronds, 15–30cm (6–12in) tall. **B. spicant** (hard fern) is evergreen, the lance-shaped fronds being deep green and leathery. It reaches 30cm (12in) or more.

The tallish dryopteris ferns look good in groups in the woodland garden or mixed border, with other woodland-type plants. **D. dilatata** (broad buckler fern) can reach a height of 90cm (3ft) and has broad, medium green fronds, while of similar height is **D. filix-mas** (male fern) with broad, lance-shaped, medium green fronds carried in shuttlecock formation. Both are semi-evergreen or herbaceous and have deeply divided fronds. For similar use, and preferring very moist or wet soil, is **Matteuccia struthiopteris** (ostrich-feather fern) which has very deeply divided, lance-shaped, bright green fronds also held in shuttlecock formation, and also 90cm (3ft) tall. It is excellent with moisture-loving primulas.

As it needs wet soil, a suitable fern for poolside planting, in association with astilbes, **Dierama pulcherrimum**, moisture-loving irises and other waterside plants is **Onoclea sensibilis** (sensitive fern), with triangular, very deeply divided pale green fronds to a height of 45cm (18in). Also for the poolside is **Osmunda regalis** (royal fern), with bright green, deeply divided oblong fronds which turn golden-brown in autumn. It attains a height of up to 1.8m (6ft).

Rather different from most hardy ferns is the evergreen **Phyllitis scolopendrium** (hart's-tongue fern), with long, tongue-shaped, bright green fronds. The leaves of the cultivar 'Crispum' have frilled edges. Height is up to 45cm (18in) and it thrives in alkaline soils. as does the evergreen **Polypodium vulgare** (common polypody), with lance-shaped, fishbone-like, medium green fronds to a height of 30cm (12in). Both make pleasing ground cover and a lovely effect is achieved if snowdrops are allowed to grow between and through them.

Some bold ferns are found among the polystichums, such as **P. aculeatum** (hard shield fern) with semi-evergreen wide, lance-shaped, shiny dark green fronds to a height of 60cm (2ft). Very feathery in appearance is **P. setiferum** 'Plumosodivisilobum' (soft shield fern), whose evergreen fronds are extremely finely divided and reach a height of 45cm (18in). It makes a beautiful foil for candelabra primulas and lilies.

The tallish male fern, **Dryopteris filix-mas**, looks good in groups in a woodland garden or mixed border with other woodland-type plants

A classic combination for a moist spot in partial shade – **Primula japonica** with the ostrich-feather fern, **Matteuccia struthiopteris** (*Savill Gardens, The Great Park, Windsor, Berkshire*)

CHAPTER 12

ALPINES AND
PEAT-GARDEN PLANTS

There is a great deal of interest in alpines or rock-garden plants but the way in which they are grown has changed considerably over the last few decades.

Few people now contemplate constructing part of a mountainside on a steep bank! Due to gardens being reduced considerably in size, and invariably flat, and the high cost of rock, many people now build either small flat rock gardens or scree beds. The latter are simply very well-drained, slightly raised beds surfaced with broken rock, mimicking a drift of broken rock at the base of a cliff face. The scree bed associates particularly well with modern architecture and indeed, in this situation, is possibly a better proposition than a flat rock garden. A rock garden or scree bed should be sited in an open sunny position, as most alpines require these conditions.

A peat garden is also a raised bed, but this time filled with an acid, peaty, moisture-retentive soil for growing small lime-hating plants. It should be sited in partial shade (dappled shade cast by trees is ideal) as the plants do not like too much sun, and again it blends well into a modern garden. A peat bed provides one with the opportunity of growing some real gems. There is, however, concern today over the use of peat in gardens and the effect its extraction is having on peat bogs. Indeed, we have played down its use throughout this book and recommended alternatives, but so far there is no tried and tested alternative if you want to create a traditional peat garden. However, try to make sure you buy peat extracted by licensed producers.

BUILDING A ROCK GARDEN AND SCREE BED

To build a flat rock garden, form several small outcrops by slightly sinking rocks into the soil. The outcrops should have planting spaces or beds between them, and the rock used should be indigenous to the locality. Ideally, the area for the rock garden should first be contoured or shaped to make it undulate gently, which is more interesting than a perfectly flat site.

For each outcrop, start off with a keystone (large well-shaped piece of rock) and then place more rocks on each side, so that they appear to be part of the keystone.

Many people these days build small, flat, rock gardens for growing alpines, which are more in keeping with today's small plots (*Private garden, Surrey*)

ALPINES AND PEAT-GARDEN PLANTS

Try to create the impression that each outcrop is a single, large piece of stone. Big pieces of rock – say up to 25kg (½cwt) – are aesthetically more pleasing than small bits, and their strata lines should all run in the same direction.

The site should be very well drained. If the garden soil is inclined to lie wet, remove about 30cm (12in) of the topsoil and replace it with a 15cm (6in) layer of hardcore topped with a 30cm layer of gritty well-drained compost: 7 parts loam, 3 parts peat and 2 parts coarse horticultural sand or grit (parts by volume). If drainage is good, simply dig the site to a spade's depth and mix grit and peat into the soil.

After planting a rock garden, cover the soil with a thin layer of stone chippings or pea shingle to create an attractive appearance, prevent annual weeds from growing, and keep the soil moist in dry weather.

A scree bed can be any shape and size. Depth depends on your soil drainage: if good, the bed can be 30cm (12in) deep, but if poor make the bed double this depth.

There is a choice of materials for building up the sides of the bed: natural stone, using it to create a dry-stone wall; bricks, or ornamental concrete walling blocks, bonded with mortar (incorporate drainage holes in the base); or timber railway sleepers.

A layer of rubble or hardcore should be placed in the base to ensure good drainage: 10cm (4in) if your soil is well drained, 15cm (6in) or more if drainage is poor. Cover this with a thin layer of coarse leafmould, then fill the bed with a well-drained compost consisting of 10 parts stone chippings or pea shingle, 1 part coarse horticultural sand, 1 part loam and 1 part peat (parts by volume). After planting, the scree bed is covered with a thin layer of broken rock or stone chippings.

A CHOICE OF ALPINES

Apart from the alpines and other dwarf plants recommended below, miniature bulbs can also be planted on a rock garden. Plenty have been described in Chapter 10. Dwarf conifers can be recommended too, and a good selection will be found in Chapter 8.

As a general rule, plant trailing alpines and prostrate shrubs or conifers so that they cascade over rocks, and hummock-forming kinds in the level beds between rocks.

The beauty of alpines is that many plants can be grown in a restricted space. Small raised beds, which today are a popular method of growing, can hold quite a large collection of plants (*Private garden, Surrey*)

ALPINES AND PEAT-GARDEN PLANTS

SPRING

Excellent for a scree bed is **Convolvulus cneorum**, a small evergreen shrub with silvery foliage, and white and pink funnel-shaped flowers. The small cytisus (brooms) are excellent rock-garden or scree-bed shrubs, for example **C. procumbens**, of prostrate habit with yellow flowers; **C. purpureus**, a dwarf shrub with lilac-purple flowers; the white variety **C. p. albus**; and the dark purple cultivar **C. p.** 'Atropurpureus'.

Particularly recommended for scree beds are the small daphnes, like **D. cneorum**, a prostrate evergreen shrub with very fragrant rose-pink flowers; and the dwarf evergreen shrubs **D. napolitana**, of similar colour and fragrance; **D. × mantensiana** 'Manten', rose-purple; **D. retusa**, dark rose-purple and very fragrant; and **D. tangutica**, with beautifully scented, white and purple flowers.

Needing very good drainage and therefore especially suited to the scree bed is **Euryops acraeus**, a dwarf evergreen shrub with bright yellow, daisy-like flowers set against silver-grey foliage.

Requiring moister soil, ideally acid to neutral, but lime tolerant, is **Fabiana imbricata** 'Prostrata'. This small shrub forms a mound of evergreen foliage studded with tiny white flowers tinged with mauve.

Like the related brooms, **Genista lydia** will thrive in very sunny, well-drained conditions. A dwarf shrub of somewhat pendulous habit, ideal for growing over a rock, it

Dionysias are small, compact, cushion-forming alpines and are very popular with alpine enthusiasts, who grow them in pans in alpine houses (cold greenhouses). This is **D. bryoides**

Genista lydia is a dwarf shrub of somewhat pendulous habit, ideal for growing over a rock. This fantastic flower display occurs during late spring and early summer

Saxifrages are popular, usually compact alpines for rock gardens and for growing in sinks or raised alpine beds. There is a huge range from which to choose, most of them flowering in the spring, like **Saxifraga oppositifolia** 'Splendens' shown here

SUMMER

There is no need for the rock garden or scree to be dull and uninteresting in summer, as there are so many suitable plants which provide a colourful display during that season. An example is the carpeting acaenas, which are evergreen perennials with attractive foliage and coloured burrs (prickly fruits). The yellow-green burrs of **A. buchananii** are set against ferny grey-green foliage, while **A. microphylla** has scarlet-red burrs and bronze foliage. For a striking effect try combining the latter with another carpeting perennial, **Lysimachia nummularia** 'Aurea' (creeping Jenny), which has yellow foliage.

Armerias or thrift are essential rock or scree perennials and we particularly recommend **A. maritima** 'Vindictive', which forms cushions of evergreen grassy foliage studded with rounded heads of dark pink flowers. Height is 10cm (4in).

Campanulas or bell flowers are also essential perennials for providing summer colour on rock gardens. **C. cochlearifolia** (syn. **C. pusilla**) is a creeping species about 10cm (4in) in height with pale blue flowers from early summer to early autumn. **C. portenschlagiana** is also creeping, and produces pale violet-blue bells throughout summer, set against evergreen foliage. It is very vigorous, so not recommended for small rock gardens. Its height is 10cm (4in).

produces masses of golden-yellow flowers in late spring and early summer.

Although recommended for the rock garden, **Polygala chamaebuxus** needs a cool position with acid, humus-rich, moisture-retentive soil (if a suitable spot cannot be found, consider growing it in a peat bed). It is a dwarf evergreen shrub forming a mat of growth and bearing cream, pea-shaped flowers tipped with yellow. The variety **P. c. grandiflora** has purple and yellow flowers.

With yellow strawberry-like blooms set against hairy, trifoliate leaves is **Waldsteinia ternata**, a carpeting perennial about 10cm (4in) high which is particularly recommended for a scree bed.

SUMMER PLANTING SCHEME FOR ROCK GARDEN

For a striking effect try combining the carpeting bronze-leaved **Acaena microphylla**, which has scarlet-red prickly fruits, with another carpeting perennial, **Lysimachia nummularia** 'Aurea' (creeping Jenny), which has yellow foliage.

Genuine or imitation stone sinks provide a means of growing small compact alpines. In these one can create mini rock gardens, and they make perfect features for patios (*Royal Horticultural Society's Garden, Wisley, Surrey*)

The alpine dianthus (pinks) are excellent for the scree bed as they like very good drainage. **D. deltoides** (maiden pink) has masses of pink flowers in summer and grows 15cm (6in) high. **D.** 'La Bourbille' is bright pink and attains only 8cm (3in) in height. Double, dark rose-pink flowers are a feature of **D.** 'Excelsior', while **D.** 'Mrs Sinkins' has double white flowers. Both attain 15–25cm (6–10in) in height. Dianthus have evergreen, greyish foliage.

Producing its small, white, yellow-centred rose-like flowers in early summer is the evergreen carpeting perennial **Dryas octopetala** (mountain avens). The blooms are followed by feathery seed heads and are set against dark green foliage shaped like that of oak. The plant is only 8cm (3in) tall.

The foliage of many saxifrages is very attractive throughout the year. **Saxifraga exarata**, shown here, is certainly handsome even when not in flower. It produces white blooms during early or midsummer

Helianthemum hybrids, or rock roses, seen here growing in paving, are also highly recommended for rock and scree gardens. They flower profusely during summer (*Barnsley House, Gloucestershire*)

Dwarf willows, such as **Salix × boydii**, are often grown on rock gardens. This is a slow-growing dwarf shrub which gives a mature atmosphere to the display

Hebes or shrubby veronicas are ideal scree plants as swift drainage is essential for their well-being. Of the many small species try **H. pimeleoides** 'Glaucocaerulea', a prostrate evergreen shrub with tiny, grey-blue leaves and light lavender-coloured flowers. It makes a pleasing companion for acaenas, as both come from New Zealand.

Helianthemums or rock roses are ideal dwarf carpeting shrubs for the scree, or for trailing over rocks on the rock garden, and produce masses of small rose-like flowers. The evergreen hybrids include the copper-coloured 'Coppernob', raised on the Hillier Nurseries; plus 'Wisley Pink', 'Wisley Primrose' and 'Wisley White', colours as names. Also try the species **H. oelandicum alpestre**, with yellow flowers set against grey-green foliage, and the cushion-like **H. lunulatum** which is studded with yellow flowers. Both are dwarf evergreen shrubs.

The alpine St John's wort, **Hypericum olympicum** 'Grandiflorum', is a mound-shaped perennial 15–30cm (6–12in) high producing masses of bright yellow, cup-shaped flowers in summer and making an excellent companion for blue campanulas.

Moltkia petraea, a little-known dwarf semi-evergreen sub-shrub, is well worth growing on the rock garden for its violet-blue, tubular flowers which start to appear in early summer. It needs acid to neutral soil.

For its size, **Oenothera missouriensis** (evening primrose) produces remarkably large, light yellow, bowl-shaped flowers. This is a mat-forming, trailing perennial about 10cm (4in) high, ideal for growing over a rock, perhaps in association with blue campanulas. Several penstemons, with tubular flowers in early summer, are suitable for the rock garden, including the scarlet **P. newberryi**, which is a dwarf evergreen shrub, and **P. fruticosus scouleri** 'Albus', a dwarf plant with white blooms.

The thymes revel in hot dry conditions so are ideal carpeting plants for the scree or rock garden. **Thymus drucei** cultivars, like 'Pink Chintz', are especially recommended

The prostrate evergreen shrub **Pimelea prostrata** is something different for the rock garden or scree, producing scented white flowers set against small grey-green leaves. It needs acid to neutral soil. The evergreen, mat-forming perennial **Persicaria affinis** 'Donald Lowndes' (syn. **Polygonum affine** 'Donald Lowndes') is useful for providing autumn colour on the rock garden, producing short spikes of rose-red flowers from early summer to mid autumn. It is about 15cm (6in) high.

Dwarf willows such as **Salix × boydii** are often grown on rock gardens. This is a slow-growing dwarf shrub with oval, hairy, grey leaves carried on gnarled branches, giving a mature atmosphere to the planting. Another dwarf shrub that can be recommended for the rock garden is **Spiraea japonica** 'Alpina', which forms a neat mound studded with tiny rose-pink flower heads in summer.

The thymes revel in hot dry conditions and so are ideal carpeting plants for the scree, but they can also be recommended for rock gardens. **Thymus drucei** cultivars are evergreen perennials about 2.5cm (1in) high and include 'Coccineus', with deep crimson flowers, and the pink-flowered 'Pink Chintz'. **T.** 'Porlock' forms a dense evergreen hummock about 8cm (3in) high which is studded with pink flowers in late spring and early summer. **T. × citriodorus** 'Silver Queen' is a spreading, evergreen shrub about 10cm (4in) high with silvery-white variegated leaves.

BUILDING A PEAT GARDEN

A peat garden can be built on acid or alkaline soil but is filled with acid compost in which to grow lime-hating plants. It can be any size and shape and quite informal in outline. If your soil is acid the minimum depth of the bed can be 30cm (12in), but if it is alkaline increase the minimum depth to 45cm (18in).

Use peat blocks to build up the bed. They are approximately the size of bricks and are supplied dry. Before use they must be soaked thoroughly in water for at least a day. The blocks are laid like bricks in a bonded or staggered formation, and it is a good idea to tilt the walls slightly inwards for stability. During laying, the joints are filled with compost and can be planted with rosette-forming or trailing plants such as ramondas and lithospermum.

An 8cm (3in)-deep layer of rough peat should be placed in the bottom of the bed before adding the compost, which can be made up of 4 parts sphagnum peat (must be moist), 1 part loam (fibrous and acid) and 1 part coarse sand (must be lime-free) – parts by volume.

After planting the bed, topdress with a layer of sphagnum peat. This mulch should be topped up in spring each year. The compost must be kept moist, so it should be watered as necessary in dry weather. It is important to water the peat blocks as well in dry weather, to prevent them from drying out which will cause them to shrink.

A CHOICE OF PLANTS FOR THE PEAT GARDEN

Small lime-hating plants of restrained habit are grown in a peat garden, and a collection can provide colour and interest during spring, summer and autumn.

SPRING

The compact form of the bog rosemary, **Andromeda polifolia** 'Compacta', is a dwarf to small evergreen shrub which produces masses of bright pink, urn-shaped flowers on bushy plants set against dark green foliage.

The evergreen cassiopes are essential peat-garden plants with their profuse, white, bell-shaped flowers. Best-known is **C. lycopodioides**, a prostrate shrub forming a mat of branches covered in scale-like, deep green leaves. **C.** 'Muirhead' is a dwarf shrub of bushy habit with similar foliage and pendulous blooms.

Hepatica nobilis, a choice semi-evergreen perennial about 8cm (3in) high, bears cup-shaped flowers in blue, pink, red or purple shades, plus white, set against rounded, lobed leaves. Double forms are also available.

Kalmia polifolia, a dwarf evergreen shrub, is a gem for the peat garden, producing saucer-shaped, bright rose-purple flowers in midspring. Even more desirable is the rare **Kalmiopsis leacheana**, a dwarf evergreen shrub with pink blooms similar to kalmia, produced from early spring onwards.

In a peat garden or bed sited in partial shade one can grow a collection of choice, lime-hating plants, such as rhododendrons and pieris. However, in a small garden one would go for dwarf plants (*Hillier Arboretum, Ampfield, Hampshire*)

Shady peat bed planted with such desirable woodland plants as erythroniums, anemones and trilliums (*Private garden, Surrey*)

Suitable for planting in the walls if desired is the trailing, prostrate evergreen shrub **Lithospermum diffusum** 'Heavenly Blue' (syn. **Lithodora diffusa** 'Heavenly Blue'), with beautiful funnel-shaped, dark true-blue flowers. It needs as much sun as you can give it in order to bloom well. If necessary, plant it on the rock garden but ensure moist, acid soil.

Menziesia ciliicalyx purpurea, a small slow-growing shrub, bears clusters of pendulous, urn-shaped, rose-purple flowers in late spring and early summer. Rather heath-like in habit, and indeed in the same family, is **Phyllodoce aleutica**, a dwarf evergreen shrub with creamy or light yellow flowers in late spring and early summer. A hybrid between **Phyllodoce** and **Rhodothamnus**, × **Phyllothamnus erectus** produces clusters of bell-shaped, rose-pink flowers in midspring. It is a dwarf evergreen shrub.

It is even possible to grow pieris in a peat bed these days, with the recent introduction of dwarf cultivars. The non-flowering **Pieris japonica** 'Little Heath' is grown for its foliage. This small evergreen shrub has deep green leaves edged white, copper-coloured when young.

Now for a really choice primula – **P. whitei** from the Petiolares section, plus its cultivar 'Arduaine'. This is like an ice-blue common primrose and can be planted in the joints of the peat-block walls if desired. Also for horizontal wall planting, if desired, is **Ramonda myconi**, a rosette-forming evergreen perennial with attractive crinkled, deep green leaves and heads of flat blue flowers. Its height is 8cm (3in). **Shortia uniflora** 'Grandiflora' is a very desirable small evergreen perennial, about 8cm (3in) high, producing cup-shaped, fringed white and pink flowers set against round, shiny leathery leaves.

Dwarf rhododendrons are regarded as almost essential plants for the peat garden. There are many species and hybrids from which to choose; here is our selection. All are evergreen.

Species rhododendrons

R. campylogynum 'Crushed Strawberry', dwarf shrub raised on the Hillier Nurseries, strawberry pink flowers, late spring.

R. forrestii repens, prostrate shrub, scarlet bell-shaped flowers, midspring.

R. hanceanum 'Nanum', dwarf shrub, slow, cream, midspring.

R. impeditum, dwarf shrub, purple-blue, midspring.

R. moupinense, small shrub, deep pink, early spring.

R. polycladum 'Scintillans' (syn. **R. scintillans**), small shrub, blue flowers, midspring.

R. roxieanum oreonastes, small shrub, bell-shaped flowers, cream flushed rose, midspring.

R. williamsianum, small shrub, pale pink bell-shaped flowers, midspring.

Hybrid rhododendrons

'Blue Diamond', small shrub, lavender-blue, mid spring.

'Blue Tit', dwarf to small shrub, lavender-blue, late spring.

Dwarf rhododendrons are regarded as almost essential plants for the peat garden. There are many species and hybrids to choose from, including some delightful blue-flowered kinds like the late spring-flowering 'Blue Tit' (*Savill Gardens, The Great Park, Windsor, Berkshire*)

'Cilpinense', small shrub, bell-shaped white flushed pink flowers, early spring.

'Cowslip', small shrub, bell-shaped cream/pale yellow flowers, late spring.

'Curlew', dwarf shrub, light yellow, bell-shaped flowers, late spring.

'Doncaster', small shrub, crimson-scarlet, late spring.

'Dora Amateis' small shrub, pure white, late spring.

'Elisabeth Hobbie', dwarf shrub, bell-shaped scarlet flowers, mid spring.

'Elizabeth', dwarf shrub, deep red, midspring.

'Elizabeth Lockhart', small shrub, bell-shaped dark red blooms, midspring.

'Fabia', small shrub, scarlet, orange within, late spring.

'Gartendirektor Glockner', small shrub, bell-shaped rose-red flowers.

The dwarf hybrid rhododendron 'Fabia' is an excellent choice for the peat garden. The spectacular flowers are produced during late spring

Rhododendron 'Praecox' is a small semi-evergreen hybrid which flowers during late winter and early spring. It is highly recommended for the peat garden

'Golden Torch', small shrub, cream-yellow, late spring.

'Intrifast', dwarf shrub, violet-blue, late spring.

'Moerheim', dwarf shrub, violet-blue.

'Pink Drift', dwarf shrub, lavender-rose, late spring.

'Praecox', small shrub, semi-evergreen, rose-purple, late winter/early spring.

'Princess Anne', dwarf shrub, light yellow, late spring.

'Ptarmigan', dwarf shrub, white, early to mid spring.

'Racil, small shrub, pale pink, midspring.

'Remo', small shrub, bright yellow, midspring.

'Saint Tudy', small shrub, bell-shaped blue flowers, mid to late spring.

'Scarlet Wonder', dwarf shrub, ruby red, late spring.

'Surrey Heath', dwarf shrub, rose-pink.

'Temple Belle', small shrub, bell-shaped rose-pink blooms, mid to late spring.

'W. F. H.', small shrub, scarlet, late spring.

SUMMER

To keep up the display through summer, plant generous groups of the following peat-garden plants. Some of them are related to rhododendrons, like **Arctostaphylos uva-ursi** (red bearberry), a prostrate evergreen shrub with tiny white, pink tinted, urn-shaped flowers set against bright green oval leaves and with red berries in autumn. There are many gaultherias (also rhododendron relations), but for the peat garden we need compact restrained kinds. They are evergreen and produce small, urn-shaped white flowers followed by conspicuous berries. **G. cuneata** has white berries, **G. hookeri** produces blue berries and **G. miqueliana** with blue-grey foliage bears edible white or pink berries. All are dwarf shrubs.

A choice hardy gesneriad, **Mitraria coccinea**, will revel in the sheltered peat garden and produce tubular, brilliant orange-red flowers set against shiny evergreen foliage. It is a dwarf shrub of spreading habit.

Equally choice is **Ourisia coccinea**, an evergreen perennial throwing upright stems carrying tubular scarlet flowers. It is 15–30cm (6–12in) high.

With tubular crimson flowers is **Philesia magellanica**, a dwarf evergreen suckering shrub recommended only for mild areas with a moist climate.

× **Phylliopsis hillieri** 'Pinocchio', a hybrid of phyllodoce and kalmiopsis which occurred on the Hillier Nurseries, is a very unusual dwarf evergreen shrub with tiny, shiny leaves making a good background for the racemes of small, deep pink, bell-shaped flowers. It starts blooming in spring but continues into summer.

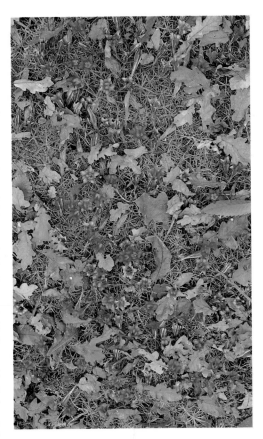

What better for autumn colour in the peat garden than a carpet of **Gentiana sino-ornata**. This is the most popular of all gentians and has true-blue flowers

AUTUMN

What better for autumn colour than carpets of true-blue gentians? Species of these herbaceous perennials that will revel in the peat garden, contrasting beautifully with autumnal leaf tints and berries of any nearby shrubby plants, include **Gentiana farreri** with upward-facing trumpet-shaped flowers in Cambridge blue, each with a white throat, height 10cm (4in); **G. × macaulayi**, with dark blue trumpets, height 15cm (6in); and **G. sino-ornata**, the most popular of all, with the most brilliant true-blue trumpet-shaped flowers striped with greeny yellow and dark blue, height 15cm (6in).

AUTUMN PLANTING SCHEME FOR PEAT GARDEN

In a peat garden, the true-blue flowers of gentians such as **Gentiana farreri**, **G. × macaulayi** and **G. sino-ornata** will contrast beautifully with the autumn leaf tints and berries of any nearby shrubby plants.

CHAPTER 13

CONSERVATORY PLANTS

The 1980s saw a boom in conservatories. Not since the Victorian period had so many been installed in private homes, and there is no reason to believe this trend will not continue into the 1990s.

The conservatory creates another habitat for plants but it is not necessary to provide a great deal of heat to enjoy a wealth of interesting and colourful exotics. If a cool conservatory is maintained – that is, with a minimum temperature of 7°C (45°F) – an extremely wide range of tender shrubs and climbers can be grown. Some are on the borderline of hardiness, including many of the fascinating shrubs from Australia and New Zealand, being just a bit too tender to be grown out of doors in Britain. The cool conservatory provides the perfect home for them.

HOW TO GROW THE PLANTS

Basically there are two ways of growing shrubs and climbers in a conservatory. The most ambitious is to plant them in raised soil beds, where the plants grow that much better than those in tubs because their roots are less restricted.

The beds can be made to any shape desired and can be built around the edge of the conservatory as well as in the middle, if space permits. However, do not build beds hard up against conservatory or house walls as this can result in problems from damp. Leave a gap between beds and walls.

Beds can be built up with various materials on the concrete floor of the conservatory, for instance bricks, ornamental concrete walling blocks, natural stone or logs. Raised beds should be about 45cm (18in) deep and can be filled with best-quality topsoil such as a light to medium loam, or with a soil-based potting compost (the most expensive choice).

When planting has been completed the beds can be mulched with pulverised bark to create an attractive finish. A 5cm (2in)-deep layer will be sufficient.

The alternative to soil beds, and certainly the most usual method with amateur gardeners, is to grow shrubs and climbers in tubs. These can be anything from 30 to 45cm (12 to 18in) upwards in diameter and depth, and should be filled with soil-based potting compost for most subjects, with drainage material in the bottom.

Tubs are available in various materials, designs and sizes. Popular, and appropri-

These days, when we are seeing a conservatory boom, it is usual to use the conservatory as an extra room – a 'garden room' – as well as a place providing suitable conditions for tender plants (*Strawberry House, Sussex*)

ate for conservatories, are the square wooden containers reminiscent of Versailles tubs used to grow citrus fruits. Alternatively, choose from the wide range of terracotta pots in classical or modern styles. There are also self-watering tubs available.

Young shrubs and climbers should not be planted immediately in large tubs because they will have too great a volume of soil around their roots, which is then liable to remain wet, much to the distaste of the plants whose roots may rot. Instead, pot them on annually, or at least before the present container becomes packed with roots. One can safely move a plant into a pot two sizes larger than its previous container. The best time to pot on is in late winter or early spring, just before the plants start into growth.

When plants are in their final containers they can be topdressed annually in the spring by scraping away 2.5–5cm (1–2in) of the old compost from the surface and replacing it with fresh. Every few years it is a good idea to repot, which means the plant is removed from its container, has its soilball reduced in size, generally including some root pruning, and is then replaced in the same container but with a fresh supply of compost.

Climbers can be trained to the back wall of the conservatory and up into the roof area. They will need to be supported: for instance, horizontal galvanised wires spaced 30–45cm (12–18in) apart could be fixed to the wall and up into the roof. They should be stretched quite tightly and fixed by means of vine eyes.

Alternatively, fix trellis panels to the wall. Trellis panels come in timber and plastic-coated steel, and should be held about 5cm (2in) away from the wall by means of buffers of some kind, such as old cotton reels. This ensures air circulation behind the plants and also allows them to twine more easily.

Shrubs and climbers will benefit from being fed regularly during the growing season, say from mid spring to early autumn. Use a well-balanced liquid fertiliser about once a fortnight, applied according to the manufacturer's instructions. But do not feed newly potted plants until they are well-established in their new containers, which generally takes eight weeks or so.

A CHOICE OF PLANTS FOR THE CONSERVATORY

SPRING

One of the first shrubs to flower in the spring – indeed, it generally starts in late winter – is **Acacia baileyana** (cootamundra wattle), with clusters of small, globular, fluffy yellow flowers against a background of finely divided blue-grey foliage. It is a large evergreen shrub which may need pruning back. **A. dealbata** (silver wattle) is similar, also a large shrub but with evergreen, ferny, silver-green foliage.

Jasminum mesnyi (syn. **J. primulinum**) (primrose jasmine) is a semi-evergreen climber producing semi-double,

There is a wide range of tender shrubs, climbers and perennials that can be grown in a conservatory, some providing colour from their flowers, others being essentially foliage plants (*Cokes Barn, Sussex*)

The semi-evergreen climber **Jasminum mesnyi**, or primrose jasmine, starts flowering from early spring onwards. It attains a height of up to 3m (10ft)

The abutilons have a very long flowering period in the summer. The pendulous bell-shaped flowers come in various colours; this is a well-known hybrid named 'Ashford Red'

bright yellow flowers from early spring onwards. It grows up to 3m (10ft) in height.

The leptospermums bring a touch of the southern hemisphere to northern latitudes. These evergreen shrubs, which prefer acid to neutral soil, flower profusely, bearing small blooms rather like tiny single roses. **Leptospermum lanigerum** (syn. **L. pubescens**) is a small shrub with attractive silvery foliage which becomes bronzy in autumn. The flowers are white. Suitable as a wall shrub in mild areas. **L. scoparium** (manuka, New Zealand tea tree) cultivars are best known, including 'Red Damask' with double, dark red flowers, and the pink 'Keatleyi' with red young foliage and shoots. Both are medium-size shrubs.

SUMMER

The abutilons certainly justify valuable conservatory space, as they have a very long flowering period. They display pendulous bell-shaped flowers, pinky red in the hybrid 'Ashford Red' and orange and red in 'Kentish Belle'. Both are medium shrubs and suitable for a warm wall outdoors in mild areas.

Bougainvilleas are among the most popular climbers for cool conservatories and their common name, paper flower, has been given on account of the brightly coloured, papery bracts which surround the insignificant flowers. **B. glabra** is evergreen or semi-evergreen and sports red-purple bracts. It reaches a height of 5m (15ft). Also usually evergreen is **B. spectabilis**, with red-purple bracts in large trusses, height 7m (22ft). There are numerous hybrids with bracts in various colours like shades of red, pink, orange and yellow, plus white. Their height is approximately 5m (15ft).

Bouvardia × domestica is a small evergreen shrub with a very long flowering period. The tubular blooms are carried in large clusters at the tips of the stems and

PLANTING SCHEME FOR THE SUMMER CONSERVATORY

Cassia obtusa (**Senna** × **floribunda**), a shrub with deep yellow flowers and attactive pinnate foliage, contrasts beautifully with the evergeen shrub **Brunfelsia pauciflora** which has blue-purple, saucer-shaped flowers.

Bougainvilleas or paper flowers are among the most popular summer-flowering climbers for cool conservatories. There are numerous hybrids whose flower bracts come in various colours

may be red, pink or white. Popular is the cultivar 'President Cleveland', whose blooms are brilliant red.

A shrub which deserves a place in every conservatory for its easy-going nature and long succession of blue-purple, saucer-shaped flowers, is **Brunfelsia pauciflora** (syn. **B. calycina**). This is a small evergreen shrub of spreading habit. The cultivar 'Macrantha' is similar.

Contrasting beautifully with the brunfelsia, if it is still in flower, is **Cassia obtusa** (syn. **Senna** × **floribunda**) which has attractive pinnate foliage and clusters of large, deep yellow flowers in late summer and autumn. It is a medium-size shrub.

The cestrums are useful shrubs for growing on the back wall and produce clusters of long, tubular flowers. **C. aurantiacum** sports orange-yellow flowers, while those of **C.** 'Newellii' are orange-red. Both are medium-size evergreen shrubs which can also be grown against a warm wall in mild areas.

Citrus fruits are the original conservatory plants – indeed they were grown from the late fifteenth century in orangeries, the forerunners of today's conservatories. Citrus are excellent trees or shrubs for the cool conservatory, where it is mainly oranges and lemons that are grown. We especially recommend 'Meyer's Lemon', a large semi-evergreen shrub with very fragrant white flowers followed by extra-large fruits. The

deep green foliage is attractive, too. If desired, plants can be placed outdoors for the summer.

The almost-hardy scrambling climber, **Clianthus puniceus** (parrot's bill), produces clusters of bright red, parrot-beak-like flowers set against semi-evergreen pinnate foliage. It grows to a height of 3.6m (12ft). There are also some attractive cultivars, including 'Flamingo' with pink flowers and the pure white 'White Heron'. The form **albus** also has white flowers.

There are comparatively few conifers suitable for conservatory cultivation, but one of the most beautiful is **Cupressus cashmeriana** (Kashmir cypress). Almost certainly it will eventually outgrow the conservatory, as it makes a small to medium-size tree, and sadly we sometimes come across specimens with their tops cut out. However, it is well worth giving it a home for

The stems of the shrub **Erythrina crista-galli**, or coral tree, die down in the winter in cool climates. The spectacular flowers are produced during summer

flowers produced from early to late summer, and large leaves with downy undersides.

Erythrina crista-galli (coral tree) is a fascinating shrub whose stems die down in the winter in cool climates, when they should be pruned out. The stems are spiny and carry leaves composed of three oval leaflets, and racemes of large, waxy, crimson pea-like flowers (it's in the pea family). It can reach a height of up to 3m (10ft), but generally less when pot-grown in a cool climate. It needs plenty of sun to flower well and can be placed outdoors in summer if desired.

The flamboyant **Hibiscus rosa-sinensis** cultivars will give a colourful, exotic touch to the cool conservatory yet are easily grown. They are evergreen, neatly rounded medium shrubs, which produce a long succession of flared trumpet-shaped flowers. The species itself is bright crimson, but usually cultivars are grown like 'The President' in bright pink and the variegated 'Cooperi' with crimson blooms. There are also cultivars available with yellow and salmon-coloured flowers.

A favourite climber for the cool conservatory is **Hoya carnosa** (wax plant), with pendulous clusters of small, white, waxy star-shaped flowers which age to pink. They are fragrant. The plant is evergreen, with thick fleshy leaves, and attains a height of about 4.5m (15ft) or sometimes more, although it is a slow grower. It is best planted in a peat-based potting compost, as it likes plenty of humus in the soil.

Another favourite climber is **Jasminum polyanthum**, whose big clusters of white flowers tinted with pink create a heady fragrance in the conservatory throughout the summer. This is an evergreen twining climber with pinnate foliage, which is capable of attaining a height of at least 3m (10ft).

a few years. Unfortunately this cypress is suitable for outdoor cultivation only in the mildest areas. The conifer is basically cone-shaped, but the upright branches carry 'curtains' of pendulous branchlets which create a very graceful weeping effect. The evergreen foliage, carried in flat sprays, is blue-grey in colour.

The large-growing daturas are cultivated for their huge, pendulous, trumpet-shaped flowers, but they certainly take up quite a bit of space. They can, however, be restrained in large pots or tubs and cut back hard in early spring. Making large shrubs are **D. sanguinea**, with orange-red flowers in early sumer set against a background of big leaves covered in hairs; and **D. suaveolens** (angel's trumpet), with white fragrant

The flamboyant **Hibiscus rosa-sinensis** cultivars will give a colourful, exotic touch to the cool conservatory in summer, yet are easily grown. They are evergreen shrubs of medium size

A favourite evergreen climber for the cool conservatory is **Hoya carnosa** or wax plant, with fragrant flowers over a long period in summer. It attains a height of about 4.5m (15ft) but is a slow grower

Jovellana violacea is an unusual small evergreen shrub producing bell-shaped, two-lipped light violet flowers, marked with purple inside, set against neat oval foliage. It is very closely allied to calceolaria.

Lantana camara is worth every inch of space in a cool conservatory, as it seems never to be out of flower. The main blooming period is spring to autumn and it bears heads of small tubular flowers with five lobes, which are yellow when they first open but then change to red. It is a small evergreen shrub of round or spreading habit which needs very good light if it is to flower well. There are numerous colour forms of lantana available, which are well worth looking out for.

It is possibly safe to say that **Lapageria** rosea is the most popular conservatory climber today. In fact, demand very often exceeds supply. It is little wonder the Chilean bellflower (it is the national flower of Chile) is so popular, for it sports the most flamboyant flowers. They are bell-shaped, pendulous, about 8cm (3in) in length, of waxy texture and pinky red in colour, and continue to be produced well into the autumn. The oval, leathery evergreen leaves are deep green. Able to attain a height of 4.5m (15ft), lapageria must have acid or lime-free soil. Use soilless potting compost if pot-grown, otherwise work plenty of leafmould into the soil bed before planting.

Although most mandevillas are tropical climbers, **M. laxa** (syn. **M. suaveolens**)

249

(Chilean jasmine) is suited to the cool conservatory and may even be grown on a warm wall in mild areas. This twining climber has white flowers, in shape something like those of vinca (periwinkle). They are scented and carried in clusters on the slender stems. Heart-shaped leaves help to make this a most attractive climber overall, which can reach a height of 4.5m (15ft) and may be semi-evergreen or deciduous.

Metrosideros excelsa (New Zealand Christmas tree or rata) is becoming better

The evergreen shrub **Nerium oleander**, popularly known as oleander, flowers over a long period in summer and continues into autumn. The flowers come in numerous colours

known with the increased interest in New Zealand plants. It is a large evergreen shrub with conspicuous bottle-brush, bright crimson flowers, consisting mainly of stamens. It has oval deep green leaves covered with white felt below.

Holidays in the Mediterranean possibly account for the popularity of **Nerium ole-**

ander (oleander). Many conservatory owners now possess one and it is certainly worth the space, for this medium evergreen shrub flowers over a long period, continuing its display well into the autumn. The flat, five-lobed flowers are carried in clusters and may be pink, red, purple-red, yellow or orange, plus white. There are double-flowered cultivars, too. Plenty of sun is needed for optimum flowering, and indeed the plant would benefit from a spell out of doors during the summer. It has dark green, leathery lanceolate leaves.

The passion flowers are vigorous evergreen or semi-evergreen climbers, attaching themselves to supports by means of tendrils, and are recommended only for the larger conservatory. Each flower has a conspicuous central corona or ring of filaments (anther stalks). **Passiflora quadrangularis** (giant granadilla) has flowers in a combination of white, purple and blue, and these are followed by edible, oval, yellow fruits. Height is up to 7.6m (25ft). **P. racemosa** (red passion flower) has brilliant scarlet, pendulous flowers and grows up to 4.5m (15ft) high. Both of these are evergreen.

A very popular evergreen scrambling climber for the cool conservatory is **Plumbago auriculata** (syn. **P. capensis**) (Cape leadwort), which produces clusters of beautiful pure mid-blue flowers throughout summer. The display may well continue into late autumn or early winter. Its height can vary from 3 to 6m (10 to 20ft).

Rhodochiton atrosanguineum (syn. **R. volubile**) is an evergreen climber with rather unusual, pendulous, tubular flowers having bell-like calyces. The tubular part is very dark purple and the calyx red-purple. It grows to a height of 3m (10ft).

One of the essential conservatory shrubs is **Tibouchina urvilleana** (syn. **T. semidecandra**) (glory bush). This large ever-

Passiflora quandrangularis, the giant granadilla, is a vigorous evergreen climber to 7.6m (25ft) in height and is better suited to the larger conservatory. The exotic-looking flowers are produced during summer and are followed by edible yellow fruits

green shrub has the most beautiful green, velvety foliage, with conspicuous veins, and in summer through to late autumn or early winter it produces a succession of saucer-shaped, blue-purple flowers with a satiny texture. It really imparts an atmosphere of tropical rainforest, yet is easily grown in the cool conservatory. It is best planted in a neutral or acid compost and needs plenty of sun to flower well. Although eventually a tall shrub to 3m (10ft), it can be cut back in the spring if one needs to reduce its height.

If you have sufficient space, **Sparmannia africana** is well worth considering for its big, evergreen, lobed leaves and clusters of white flowers which start to appear in late spring and continue to be produced throughout summer. Each flower has a conspicuous cluster of yellow and red stamens. It is a large shrub but can be cut back after flowering, which will not only reduce its height (ultimately 3.5 to 4.5m (12 to 15ft)), but also result in a more compact and bushy plant.

CONSERVATORY PLANTS

WINTER

We have already seen (Plants for summer, this chapter) that many conservatory plants continue flowering well into autumn, so that season is taken care of as far as colour is concerned. But what can we expect in winter? There is no shortage of shrubs that flower during that season in a cool conservatory, but we have picked out two which we recommend highly.

One of these is **Correa × harrisii**, a small evergreen shrub which can in fact be grown outdoors in the very mildest areas. It pro-

Although we have considered only woody plants in this chapter, it is worth bearing in mind that there are several tender perennials suited to the cool conservatory, such as arum lilies or zantedeschias. The one shown here is **Z. aethiopica** 'Green Goddess' which produces green and white spathes in the summer (*Royal Horticultural Society's Garden, Wisley, Surrey*)

duces an abundance of 2.5cm (1in)-long, tubular, rose-scarlet flowers during late winter, set against narrow oval leaves with hairy undersides. Out of doors it will flower in the spring. This shrub is ideally suited to the small conservatory and is well worth looking out for. It should be grown in acid to neutral soil or compost.

A rather unusual shrub, but one which is well worth seeking, is **Luculia gratissima**. It is a semi-evergreen of medium size and during the winter, under glass, it produces big terminal panicles of tubular, five-lobed, fragrant pink flowers. The oval leaves grow up to 20cm (8in) in length and have conspicuous veins. If you want to reduce height, prune back flowered stems after blooming.

THE BIGGER THE BETTER

This, then, is a comparatively small but choice selection from the huge range of conservatory plants available today. We have just touched the tip of the iceberg with Australian and New Zealand plants, for example. Our advice is to buy the largest conservatory you can possibly afford and accommodate, as you will fill it with plants very quickly.

Remember that during the summer some plants can be transferred outdoors so that they get a good dose of sunshine (this has been indicated where appropriate, such as with oleanders, citrus fruits and erythrina). An ideal place to park them is on a paved area or patio immediately outside the conservatory. This means that you will not have far to move what may be heavy plants, and there will be less likelihood of forgetting to water them, as can happen if they are out of sight in some distant part of the garden. Besides the plants will probably be at their best in summer and will need to be prominently placed in order to be enjoyed to the full.

CHAPTER 14

PATIOS AND CONTAINERS

The patio is an essential feature of most gardens today and is the ideal place for growing plants in ornamental containers of various kinds, such as tubs and large pots. Container growing has probably never been more popular than it is today.

For many people, however, filling containers and patio beds with seasonal bedding plants is too time-consuming and so we have come up with a list of permanent plants. They are primarily recommended for growing in containers but are also suitable for planting in any beds or borders in or around the patio.

Containers in classical styles are a good choice for use in period settings. They are available in imitation stone and terracotta (*Spindthrift, Buckinghamshire*)

ORNAMENTAL CONTAINERS

These are really the same as those recommended for conservatory shrubs and climbers (see Chapter 13), but additionally there is a wide range of ornamental concrete or reconstituted-stone tubs in various styles, plus a variety of frost-proof terracotta containers. Again, use large tubs or pots – anything from 30 to 45cm (12 to 18in) and upwards in diameter and depth. These will hold large single specimens of shrubs, trees, climbers, etc, or several smaller plants, such as hardy perennials, could be planted in them.

Composts, planting and general care of plants in containers is the same as outlined in Chapter 13. Containers must never be allowed to dry out and in hot weather may need watering twice a day. During frosty periods insulate containers with straw.

Alpines and miniature bulbs are, of course, ideally suited to growing in containers on patios and in this instance they are generally planted either in genuine old stone sinks, or imitations of them. Concrete or reconstituted-stone troughs of arious kinds also make good containers for mini rock gardens.

CREATING PLEASING EFFECTS

Dotting containers haphazardly around the patio is rarely pleasing aesthetically and instead you should group several together. Of course, there is no limit to ossible combinations of shrubs, trees, perennials, conifers, roses, bulbs, etc. One idea is to create seasonal groups of plants; for instance, using shrubs as a background for other plants like bulbs, perennials and roses.

Here are a few examples. For spring, a group could consist of a forsythia and an evergreen pieris to form the background, while in front could be tubs of bulbs like blue muscari and perennials such as bergenias and hellebores.

A summer group could create a Mediterrean atmosphere. How about tubs of cistus, hebes and yuccas (the latter is in fact pleasing all the year round) to form the framework, with further tubs of eryngiums and allium species?

You might like a bold-foliage group for summer, such as **Fatsia japonica** forming the background, with tubs of phormiums, hostas and ornamental grasses providing foreground interest.

For autumn how about an **Acer palmatum** cultivar to provide striking leaf olour, surrounded by tubs of **Nerine bowdenii** and schizostylis?

A winter group could have several evergreen shrubs like mahonias and a **Vibur-**

There are numerous permanent plants suitable for growing in containers, including shrubs and hardy perennials. They can be grouped together to create pleasing contrasts in colour, shape and texture (*Turnpike Cottage, Dorset*)

num tinus cultivar to form the framework, and around these could be grouped tubs of hellebores and **Erica carnea** (syn. **E. herbacea**) cultivars.

As we said earlier, ideas are limitless. Now it's up to you!

Apart from grouping tubs, you may wish to have individual plants as focal points or specimens. For instance, well-shaped shrubs like conical conifers or trimmed hollies (ilex) could be set at the corners of a patio, on either side of a flight of steps (at the bottom), or on either side of a front door. In the last two instances, use identical pairs of plants and containers. The plants in the following select lists are those we especially recommend for growing in ornamental tubs and, of course, in patio beds and borders, too. All are fully described in the previous chapters, so we have simply given bald lists here.

GROUP OF CONTAINERS FOR SUMMER COLOUR

A summer group of planted containers could create a Mediterranean atmosphere. Try grouping together tubs of cistus, hebes and yuccas to form the framework, and include further tubs of eryngiums and allium species.

GROUP OF CONTAINERS FOR WINTER COLOUR

There is no need for the winter patio to be devoid of colour. A group for the darker months might comprise several evergreen shrubs like mahonias and a **Viburnum tinus** cultivar to form the framework, and around these could be positioned tubs of hellebores and **Erica carnea** (syn. **E. herbacea**) cultivars.

A hardy sedum growing in a stone container, an ideal home for these sun-loving, drought-tolerant plants. The container is surrounded by an ornamental ivy, itself an excellent container plant (*Herterton House, Northumberland*)

TREES

Small to medium-size trees in containers are useful for providing dappled shade on the patio, as well as giving height to plant groups. There are a number that do not mind this restricted form of cultivation:

Acer davidii, Acer griseum, Crataegus prunifolia, Ficus carica, Gleditsia triacanthos 'Sunburst', **Ligustrum lucidum** 'Excelsum Superbum', **Ligustrum lucidum** 'Latifolium', **Malus floribunda, Malus** 'Golden Hornet', **Malus** 'Hillieri', **Malus** 'John Downie', **Malus** 'Royal Beauty', **Malus trilobata, Malus tschonoksii, Meliosma veitchiorum, Morus nigra, Prunus** 'Aruanogawa', **Prunus** 'Spire', **Prunus** 'Pink Perfection', **Prunus serrula, Prunus subhirtella** 'Autumnalis Rosea', **Prunus subhirtella** 'Pendula Rubra', **Pyrus calleryana** 'Chanticleer', **Pyrus salicifolia** 'Pendula', **Robinia × slavinii** 'Hillieri', **Robinia pseudoacacia** 'Frisia', **Robinia pseudoacacia** 'Rozynskyana', **Sorbus aucuparia** 'Fastigiata', **Sorbus** 'Joseph Rock', **Sorbus scalaris, Sorbus vilmorinii**, and **Trachycarpus fortunei.**

Corydline australis, the cabbage tree, and its purple form, shown here, makes an excellent container plant but is not too hardy. In areas subject to hard winters it should be moved into a frost-free conservatory over winter (*Martley and District Horticultural Society's Garden, Chelsea Flower Show, 1990*)

SHRUBS

Many kinds of shrubs can be grown in containers where they make useful additions to groups, helping to form a permanent framework or acting as a background for other plants.

FOR SPRING FLOWERS
Azaleas (evergreen hybrids), **Berberis** 'Goldilocks', **Camellia** cultivars, **Choisya ternata, Coronilla glauca, Daphne** ×
burkwoodii, Forsythia cultivars, **Kalmia latifolia, Magnolia stellata** 'Waterlily', **Mahonia trifoliolata glauca, Pieris** species and cultivars, **Prunus laurocerasus** 'Otto Luyken', **Rhododendron** hybrids, **Rhododendron yakushimanum**, and **Rosemarinus officinalis** cultivars.

Hydrangeas are excellent shrubs for containers, but make sure they have partial shade and are well supplied with water during the growing season (*Coates Manor, Sussex*)

FOR SUMMER FLOWERS

Abelia × **grandiflora**, **Callistemon citrinus** 'Splendens', **Callistemon salignus**, **Cistus** species and cultivars, **Fuchsia magellanica** 'Versicolor', **Grevillea rosmarinifolia**, **Grevillea juniparina sulphurea**, **Hebe** (any species or cultivars), **Hydrangea macrophylla** cultivars, **Hydrangea serrata** cultivars, **Lavandula stoechas**, **Ligustrum quihoui**, **Potentilla** species and cultivars, and **Zauschneria californica**.

FOR AUTUMN FLOWERS

Mahonia species and cultivars (flowering continues into winter).

FOR WINTER FLOWERS

Erica carnea (syn. **E. herbacea**), **Erica** × **darleyensis**, **Viburnum tinus**, and **Hamamelis mollis** 'Pallida'.

FOR DISTINCTIVE FOLIAGE

Acer shirasawanum 'Aureum' (syn. **japonicum** 'Aureum'), **Acer palmatus** cultivars (purple-leaved), **Aucuba japonica** 'Crotonifolia', **Ballota pseudodictamnus**, **Cotinus** 'Grace', **Cotinus coggygria** 'Velvet Cloak', **Eleagnus pungens** 'Maculata', **Euonymus fortunei** 'Emerald 'n' Gold' and other cultivars, **Fatsia japonica**, **Helichrysum italicum serotinum**, **Ilex** × **altaclerensis** 'Camelliifolia', **Ilex** × **altaclerensis** 'Golden King', **Ilex aquifolium** 'Golden Milkboy', **Ilex aquifolium** 'Silver Milkmaid', **Ligustrum japonicum** 'Rotundifolium', **Nandina domestica**, **Perovskia atriplicifolia** 'Blue Spire', **Phormium** species and cultivars, **Pieris formosa forrestii** and forms, **Pittosporum tenuifolium** 'Irene Paterson', **Pittosporum tenuifolium** 'Purpureum', **Prunus laurocerasus** 'Marbled White', **Sambucus racemosa** 'Tenuifolia', **Viburnum davidii**, **Yucca** species and cultivars.

FOR AUTUMN LEAF COLOUR

Acer japonicum cultivars, **Acer palmatum** cultivars, **Cotinus** 'Flame', and **Hamamelis vernalis** 'Sandra'.

BERRYING SHRUBS

Cotoneaster horizontalis, **Cotoneaster** 'Hybridus Pendulus' (grown as a small weeping tree), and **Skimmia japonica reevesiana**.

Euonymus fortunei cultivars, especially those with variegated leaves, thrive in containers. They are grown for their attractive foliage and make a good foil for more brightly coloured plants (Help the Aged Garden, Chelsea Flower Show, 1990)

ROSES

Both shrub and climbing roses grow well in containers. However, do not go for the very vigorous roses but rather for the more restrained and smaller-growing kinds.

For example, among the species and their hybrids we can especially recommend **Rosa** 'Canary Bird', **R. moyesii** 'Geranium' and **R. glauca** (syn. **rubrifolia**). The comparatively modern hybrid musk roses are excellent for containers. Among the modern shrub roses, we recommend particularly the smaller English roses and 'Golden Wings'. The small polyantha roses are excellent, too, like 'The Fairy' and 'Yesterday'.

Smallish climbing and pillar roses include 'Golden Showers' and 'Parkdirektor Riggers'.

CONIFERS

Upright cone-shaped conifers in tubs can make superb focal points (see Creating pleasing effects, this chapter), while spreading ground-cover types help to provide a different shape in groups of plants. Always choose smallish or slow-growing types.

We especially recommend **Cephalotaxus harringtonia** 'Fastigiata' (narrowly conical), **Chamaecyparis obtusa** 'Tetragona Aurea' (conical), **Juniperus communis** 'Hornibrookii' (prostrate), **Juniperus communis** 'Repanda' (prostrate), **Juniperus horizontalis** 'Wiltonii' (prostrate), **Taxus baccata** 'Repens Aurea' (dwarf, spreading), and **Taxus baccata** 'Standishii' (columnar).

CLIMBERS AND WALL SHRUBS

Do not grow very vigorous or large climbers or wall shrubs in containers, as they will not appreciate the restricted root run. Instead, go for smallish and restrained kinds.

SPRING
Clematis alpina 'Frances Rivis' and **Clematis macropetala** cultivars. Container grown clematis still need cool and shaded roots.

SUMMER
Clematis (large-flowered garden cultivars), **Clematis viticella** cultivars, **Hedera colchica** 'Sulphur Heart' (syn. 'Paddy's Pride), **Hedera helix** cultivars, **Jasminum humile** 'Revolutum', and **Sollya heterophylla**.

AUTUMN
Clematis × jouiniana 'Cote d'Azure', **Clematis tibetana vernayi** (syn. **C. orientalis**) and **Clematis tangutica**.

WINTER
Clematis cirrhosa balearica and **Jasminum nudiflorum**.

HARDY PERENNIALS

We strongly suggest the use of some perennials in groups of plants as they contrast so well with woody kinds such as shrubs, and we find that many contrast superbly with paving and architecture. Most perennials, unless very small growing, are best planted in their own containers.

Not all hardy perennials are suited to container growing by any means. We have found that some do not attain their full height and refuse to flower well when their roots are restricted. However, the following are recommended.

SPRING
Bergenia cultivars, **Euphorbia characias**

Small roses are ideal for containers, especially miniatures like 'Pretty Polly' (*Garden for Roses, Chelsea Flower Show, 1990*)

wulfenii, **Helleborus atrorubens**, **Helleborus foetidus**, **Helleborus argutifolius** (syn. **H. lividus corsicus**), and **Helleborus orientalis**.

Alchemilla mollis or lady's mantle is a hardy perennial which produces clouds of green-yellow flowers in summer. It thrives in containers and associates well with many plants (*Gardener's Cottage, Sussex*)

SUMMER

Agapanthus Headbourne Hybrids, **Alchemilla mollis**, **Campanula persicifolia**, **Dianthus** 'Doris', **Echinops humilis** 'Taplow Blue' (must have a deep container), **Eryngium alpinum** and **Eryngium tripartitum** (must have deep containers), **Hemerocallis** cultivars, **Nepeta** cultivars, **Osteospermum barberiae**, **Osteospermum ecklonis**, **Penstemon** cultivars, **Sisyrinchium striatum**, and **Zantedeschia aethiopica** 'Crowborough'.

FOLIAGE

Acanthus mollis latifolius and **Acanthus spinosus** (provide deep containers), **Artemisia absinthium** 'Lambrook Silver', **Carex morrowii** 'Evergold', **Hosta** (any species and cultivars), **Iris pallida** 'Variegata', **Kniphofia** (any species and cultivars, and best in deep containers), **Ophiopogon planiscapus** 'Nigrescens', **Rodgersia** (any species), **Ruta graveolens** 'Jackman's Blue', **Stachys byzantina**, and **Tellima grandiflora** 'Purpurea'.

AUTUMN

Liriope muscari, **Schizostylis coccinea** and cultivars.

WINTER

Iris foetidissima and **Iris unguicularis** (syn. **I. stylosa**).

Hostas and ferns in containers would make a pleasing feature in a shady spot, but make sure the soil is kept moist (*Manor House, Chenies, Buckinghamshire*)

BULBS

Miniature and small spring-flowering bulbs are particularly useful for groups of container plants, because they contrast so well with other kinds. If you have sufficient containers a few could be devoted purely to spring bulbs, but you should remember that for about eleven months of the year these pots or tubs will contribute nothing in the way of colour and interest, and should be stored in a spare part of the garden.

The alternative, which is perhaps even more effective, is to plant the bulbs around larger items such as shrubs and trees, and among perennials.

SPRING

Chionodoxa sardensis, **Crocus chrysanthus** cultivars and other species, **Cyclamen coum**, **Cyclamen repandum**, **Galanthus nivalis** and cultivars, **Leucojum vernum**, **Muscari** species, **Narcissus bulbocodium**, **Narcissus cyclamineus**, **Ornithogalum balansae**, **Scilla** species, and **Tulipa** species.

SUMMER

Allium species (large kinds are best in their own containers), **Crinum × powellii** (best in their own deep container), and **Lilium** (any species and hybrids – best in their own deep containers).

AUTUMN

Crocus (species such as **goulimyi, medius** and **speciosus**), **Cyclamen hederifolium** (syn. **C. neapolitanum**), **Cyclamen purpurascens** (syn. **C. europaeum**), **Galanthus reginae-olgae** and **Nerine bowdenii** (best in own container as it makes large clumps).

WINTER

Eranthis hyemalis.

ORNAMENTAL GRASSES

The ornamental grasses contrast marvellously with broad-leaved plants, including many shrubs and hardy perennials, and they associate particularly well with paving and architecture and so are especially recommended for patios. Each kind is best grown in its own container, although very small grasses could, perhaps, be incorporated into tubs with shrubs or other perennials.

Cortaderia selloana 'Pumila', **Festuca glauca, Hakonechloa macra** 'Albo-aurea', **Helictotrichon sempervirens, Miscanthus sinensis** cultivars, **Molinia caerulea** 'Variegata', **Stipa calamagrostis**, and **Stipa pennata** are all candidates for your pots.

BAMBOOS

Like other grasses, bamboos also associate well with paving, architecture and broad-leaved plants. Grow them in their own containers. The smaller more restrained kinds are recommended for tubs, such as **Pleioblastus viridistriatus**.

ALPINES

Many alpines of restrained habit can be grown in mini rock gardens created in genuine old stone sinks or imitations, and in troughs, as mentioned earlier. Plant them in a well-drained, gritty, soil-based compost in which you have partially sunk a few small, well-shaped pieces of rock. Trailing and prostrate alpines can be

Any lily species and hybrids are suited to container cultivation but they are best in their own deep containers. Ideally the tubs should be shaded, with the lilies' heads in the sun (*Vale End, Surrey*)

Sempervivums or houseleeks will grow anywhere, even on roofs and in old walls, so it comes as no surprise to learn that they revel in the comparative luxury of containers. They are an ideal choice for shallow containers, such as this bowl, where the soil is likely to dry out rapidly in warm weather. There is a huge number of species and hybrids from which to choose and the succulent foliage may be green, purple or red (*Dale House, Sussex*)

planted at the edge of the container so that they can flow over the sides, while hummock-forming or bushy kinds are planted in the centre. One or two specimens of the tiny **Juniperus communis** 'Compressa'

(Noah's Ark juniper) can be included to give height. It is very slow-growing, but will eventually reach 75cm (30in). After planting, cover the compost surface with a layer of stone chippings.

Several small shrubs and perennials which we recommended for rock gardens are also suitable for growing in sinks and troughs, including **Armeria maritima** 'Vindictive', **Daphne cneorum, Dianthus deltoides, Euryops acraeus, Hypericum olympicum** and **Thymus** 'Porlock'. An alpine specialist's catalogue will reveal many more plants which are suitable for sink gardens.

266

SELECT LIST OF PLANTS

The plants in the following easy-reference lists, extracted from the main text, are in our opinion the creme de la creme.

TREES

GOOD FOCAL POINTS
Malus 'Royal Beauty'
Prunus 'Spire'
Pyrus salicifolia 'Pendula'

FOR WOODLAND GARDENS
Betula pendula 'Dalecarlica'
Davidia involucrata
Magnolia campbellii and cultivars
Stewartia koreana

BOLD FOLIAGE
Catalpa bignonioides
Paulownia tomentosa

COLOURED FOLIAGE
Gleditsia triacanthos 'Sunburst' (yellow)
Populus × candicans 'Aurora' (variegated)
Prunus cerasifera 'Rosea' (bronze-purple)
Robinia pseudoacacia 'Frisia' (golden-yellow)
Sorbus aria 'Lutescens' (cream-white)

AUTUMN LEAF COLOUR
Acer rubrum
Liquidambar styraciflua 'Lane Roberts'
Malus tschonoskii
Nyssa sylvatica
Prunus sargentii
Sorbus sargentiana

NOTABLE FLOWERS
Spring
Amelanchier lamarckii
Cornus nuttallii
Malus floribunda
Prunus Subhirtalla 'Pendula Rubra'
Summer
Eucryphia glutinosa
Koelreuteria paniculata
Autumn and winter
Prunus subhirtella 'Autumnalis Rosea'

FOR FRUITS
Arbutus unedo 'Rubra'
Crataegus prunifolia
Malus 'Golden Hornet'
Sorbus vilmorinii

ORNAMENTAL BARK
Acer davidii 'George Forrest'
Acer griseum
Eucalyptus niphophila
Prunus serrula
Salix alba 'Chermesina'

SHRUBS FOR FLOWERS

SPRING ARISTOCRATS
Magnolia × soulangeana and cultivars
Mahonia aquifolium 'Apollo'
Viburnum plicatum 'Mariesii'

SPRING-FLOWERING FOR WOODLAND
Embothrium coccineum lanceolatum
Kalmia latifolia
Pieris japonica 'Purity'

SELECT LISTS OF PLANTS

SPRING-FLOWERING FOR MIXED BORDERS
Berberis 'Goldilocks'
Cornus florida 'Cherokee Chief'
Fothergilla major
Paeonia lutea ludlowii
Stachyurus chinenensis

SUMMER ESSENTIALS
Hydrangea paniculata cultivars
Hydrangea serrata cultivars

SUMMER BORDER MISCELLANY
Abelia grandiflora
Caryopteris × clandonensis 'Heavenly Blue'
Cornus kousa chinensis
Fuchsia magellanica 'Versicolor'
Hebe 'Marjorie'
Hibiscus syriacus 'Bluebird'
Leycesteria formosa

SUMMER, HOT AND DRY POSITIONS
Cistus corbariensis
Genista aetnensis
Potentilla arbuscula 'Beesii'
Spartium junceum

WINTER
Viburnum tinus 'Eve Price'

FRAGRANT FLOWERING SHRUBS

SPRING
Choisya ternata
Daphne odora 'Aureomarginata'
Magnolia stellata 'Waterlily'
Osmanthus delavayi
Syringa meyeri 'Palibin' (syn. **S. velutina**)
Viburnum carlesii 'Diana'

SUMMER
Cytisus battandieri 'Yellow Tail'
Philadelphus 'Beauclerk'
Romneya coulteri

AUTUMN
Mahonia japonica
Osmanthus armatus

WINTER
Chimonanthus praecox 'Grandiflorus'
Hamamelis mollis 'Pallida'
Lonicera × purpusii 'Winter Beauty'
Viburnum farreri

CAMELLIAS

C. japonica 'Adolphe Audusson'
C. × williamsii 'Donation'

RHODODENDRONS

R. augustinii
R. luteum
R. mucronulatum
R. orbiculare
R. rex fictolacteum
R. yakushimanum

HYBRIDS
'Bow Bells'
'Britannia'
'Crest'
'Cynthia'
Lady Chamberlain 'Exbury'
'Loder's White'
'Mrs G. W. Leak'
'Pink Pearl'
'Sappho'
'Yellow Hammer'

DECIDUOUS HYBRID AZALEAS
'Berryrose'
'Gibraltar'
'Irene Koster'

'Narcissiflorum'
'Persil'

EVERGREEN HYBRID AZALEAS
'Addy Wery'
'Hinodegiri'
'Hinomayo'
'Palestrina'

HEATHERS

Calluna vulgaris cultivars 'Gold Haze',
'H. E. Beale', 'Peter Sparkes', 'Sister Anne'
Erica arborea 'Alpina'
Erica × darleyensis 'Silberschmelze'
Erica carnea (syn. **E. herbacea**)
cultivars 'Myretoun Ruby', 'Springwood
Pink', 'Springwood White', 'Vivellii'
Erica tetralix 'Con Underwood'
Erica vagans cultivars 'Lyonesse' and
'Mrs D. F. Maxwell'

SHRUBS WITH DISTINCTIVE FOLIAGE

Fatsia japonica
Ilex × altaclerensis 'Camelliifolia'
Phlomis 'Edward Bowles'
Phormium tenax 'Purpureum'
Phormium cookianum 'Tricolor'
Viburnum davidii
Yucca filamentosa 'Bright Edge'

SHRUBS WITH COLOURED FOLIAGE

RED/PURPLE
Acer palmatum 'Bloodgood'
Corylopsis willmottiae 'Spring Purple'
Corylus maxima 'Purpurea'
Cotinus coggygria 'Velvet Cloak'
Photinia × fraseri 'Red Robin'
Pieris formosa forrestii and forms
Pittosporum tenuifolium 'Purpureum'

YELLOW/GOLD
Acer shirasawanum 'Aureum' (syn. **A. japonicum** 'Aureum')
Aucuba japonica 'Crotonifolia'
Corylus avellana 'Aurea'
Elaeagnus × ebbingei 'Gilt Edge'
Ilex × altaclerensis 'Golden King'
Philadelphus coronarius 'Aureus'

GREY/SILVER
Artemisia 'Powis Castle'
Buddleia fallowiana
Helichrysum italicum serotinum
Ilex aquifolium 'Handsworth New Silver'
Perovskia atriplicifolia 'Blue Spire'
Salix lanata

WHITE VARIEGATED
Cornus alternifolia 'Argentea'
Griselinia littoralis 'Dixon's Cream'
Pittosporum tenuifolium 'Irene Paterson'
Prunus laurocerasus 'Marbled White'
Rhamnus alaterna 'Argenteovariegata'
Weigela praecox 'Variegata'

SHRUBS FOR AUTUMN LEAF COLOUR

Acer palmatum 'Osakazuki'
Cotinus 'Flame'
Euonymus alatus 'Compactus'
Hamamelis vernalis 'Sandra'
Rhus typhina 'Dissecta' (syn. **R. t.** 'Laciniata')

AUTUMN-BERRYING SHRUBS

Berberis wilsoniae
Callicarpa bodinieri 'Profusion'
Cotoneaster 'Cornubia'
Euonymus europaeus 'Red Cascade'
Ilex aquifolium 'J. C. van Tol'
Pernettya mucronata cultivars
Pyracantha 'Mohave'

269

Skimmia japonica reevesiana
Viburnum opulus 'Notcutt's Variety'

SHRUBS WITH COLOURED STEMS

Acer palmatum 'Senkaki'
Cornus alba 'Sibirica'
Rubus cockburnianus

ROSES

SPECIES AND THEIR HYBRIDS
Rosa 'Mermaid'
R. 'Canary Bird'
R. glauca (syn. **R. rubrifolia**)
R. moyesii 'Geranium'
R. sericea pteracantha (syn. **R. omeiensis pteracantha**)

OLD-FASHIONED ROSES
'Cardinal de Richelieu'
'Fantin-Latour'
'Madame Hardy'
'Maiden's Blush'

BOURBON ROSES
'Boule de Neige'
'Madame Isaac Pereire'
'Zephirine Drouhin'

HYBRID MUSK ROSES
'Ballerina'
'Felicia'
'Penelope'

MODERN SHRUB ROSES
'Golden Wings'
'Gertrude Jekyll'
'Graham Thomas'
'Mary Rose'
'William Shakespeare'

CLIMBING AND PILLAR ROSES
'Golden Showers'

'Madam Gregoire Staechelin'
'Parkdirektor Riggers'

RAMBLERS
'Albéric Barbier'

CONIFERS

LARGE
Abies koreana
Chamaecyparis lawsoniana 'Pembury Blue'
C. l. 'Stewartii'
Ginkgo biloba
Metasequoia glyptostroboides
Picea breweriana
Picea omorika
Picea pungens 'Hoopsii'
Pinus montezumae
Taxus baccata 'Dovastonii Aurea'
Thuja plicata 'Aurea'

DWARF
Abies balsamea 'Hudsonia'
Calocedrus decurrens 'Berrima Gold'
Chamaecyparis lawsoniana 'Aurea Densa'
Chamaecyparis thyoides 'Purple Heather'
Cryptomeria japonica 'Vilmoriniana'
Juniperus communis 'Compressa'
Juniperus squamata 'Blue Star'
Picea pungens 'Globosa'
Pinus strobus 'Nana'
Thuja orientalis 'Rosedalis'

GROUND-COVER
Juniperus horizontalis 'Wiltonii'
Taxus baccata 'Repens Aurea'

CLIMBERS AND WALL SHRUBS

SPRING
Clematis alpina 'Francis Rivis'
Clematis macropetala 'Maidwell Hall'

Wisteria sinensis

SUMMER
Abutilon × suntense 'Jermyns'
Actinidia kolomikta
Berberidopsis corallina
Campsis radicans
Clematis florida 'Sieboldii'
Clematis viticella 'Alba Luxuriens'.
Large-flowered clematis 'H. F. Young' and
'Niobe'
Fremontodendron 'California Glory'
Hedera algeriensis 'Margino-maculata'
Hedera helix 'Buttercup'
Jasminum officinale
Lonicera periclymen 'Graham Thomas'
Magnolia grandiflora
Passiflora caerulea
Solanum crispum 'Glasnevin'

AUTUMN
Clematis tibetana vernayi (syn. **C.
orientalis**)
Clematis tangutica
Parthenocissus henryana
Vitis coignetiae

WINTER
Clematis cirrhosa balearica
Garrya elliptica 'James Roof'
Jasminum nudiflorum

PERENNIALS TO ASSOCIATE
WITH SHRUBS

SPRING FLOWERS
Bergenia × schmidtii
Euphorbia characias wulfenii
Helleborus argutifolius (syn. **H. lividus
corsicus**)
Polygonatum × hybridum
Pulmonaria angustifolia 'Azurea'

SUMMER FLOWERS
Agapanthus Headbourne Hybrids

Hedera helix cultivars can be used to trail over
the edges of tubs. They are particularly effective
in old stone containers in classical styles, and they
thrive in shady places (*Coates Manor, Sussex*)

Alchemilla mollis
Astilbe × arendsii 'Fanal'
Campanula persicifolia 'Telham Beauty'
Crocosmia 'Emily McKenzie'
Delphinium elatum hybrids
Echinops humilis 'Taplow Blue'
Eryngium tripartitum
Hemerocallis 'Golden Chimes'
Iris sibirica 'Perry's Blue'
Macleaya microcarpa 'Coral Plume'
Meconopsis betonicifolia
Nepeta 'Six Hills Giant'
Oenothera tetragona 'Fireworks'
Paeonia 'Bowl of Beauty'
Persicaria bistorta 'Superba' (syn.
Polygonum bistorta 'Superbum')
Salvia nemorosa 'Lubeca'

SELECT LISTS OF PLANTS

FOLIAGE
Acanthus spinosus
Artemisia absinthium 'Lambrook Silver'
Hosta 'Halcyon'
Hosta sieboldiana elegans
Iris pallida 'Variegata'
Kniphofia caulescens
Rheum palmatum 'Bowles' Crimson'
Rodgersia pinnata 'Superba'
Ruta graveolens 'Jackman's Blue'
Stachys byzantina 'Silver Carpet'

AUTUMN FLOWERS
Anemone × hybrida 'Bressingham Glow'
Aster frikartii
Liriope muscari
Schizostylis coccinea 'Sunrise'
Sedum 'Autumn Joy'

WINTER FLOWERS
Iris unguicularis

BULBS TO ASSOCIATE WITH SHRUBS

SPRING
Chionodoxa sardensis
Crocus thomasinianus
Erythronium dens-canis
Fritillaria meleagris
Galanthus nivalis
Muscari azureum
Narcissus cyclamineus
Scilla siberica
Tulipa tarda

SUMMER
Allium sphaerocephalon
Lilium martagon

AUTUMN
Colchicum autumnale
Crocus speciosus
Cyclamen hederifolium
Nerine bowdenii

ORNAMENTAL GRASSES

Cortaderia selloana 'Sunningdale Silver'
Festuca glauca
Helictotrichon sempervirens
Milium effusum 'Aureum'
Miscanthus sinensis 'Zebrinus'
Molinia caerulea 'Variegata'
Phalaris arundinacea 'Picta'
Stipa calamagrostis

BAMBOOS

Pleioblastus viridistriatus
Sasa veitchii
Thamnocalamus spathaceus

FERNS

Athyrium filix-femina
Dryopteris filix-mas
Matteuccia struthiopteris
Osmunda regalis
Polystichum setiferum 'Plumoso-divisilobum'

The large evergreen shrub **Acacia dealbata**, or silver wattle, is one of the first of the spring shrubs to flower in the cool conservatory

SELECT LISTS OF PLANTS

ALPINES

SPRING
Convolvulus cneorum
Daphne cneorum
Genista lydia

SUMMER
Armeria maritima 'Vindictive'
Campanula cochlearifolia
Dianthus deltoides
Helianthemum 'Wisley' cultivars
Hypericum olympicum
Spiraea japonica 'Alpina'
Thymus drucei cultivars

PEAT-GARDEN PLANTS

SPRING
Andromeda polifolia 'Compacta'
Cassiope lycopodioides
Kalmia polifolia
Lithospermum diffusum 'Heavenly Blue'
Pieris japonica 'Little Heath'
Primula whitei
Ramonda myconi
Shortia uniflora 'Grandiflora'

Dwarf species rhododendrons
R. impeditum
R. polycladum 'Scintillans' (syn. R. scintillans)

Dwarf hybrid rhododendrons
'Blue Diamond'
'Cowslip'
'Elizabeth'
'Praecox'
'Temple Belle'

SUMMER
Arctostaphylos uva-ursi
Ourisia coccinea

AUTUMN
Gentiana sino-ornata

CONSERVATORY PLANTS

SPRING
Acacia dealbata
Leptospermum scoparium 'Keatleyi'

SUMMER
Abutilon 'Ashford Red'
Bougainvillea spectabilis
Brunfelsia pauciflora
Cestrum aurantiacum
Clianthus puniceus
Erythrina crista-galli
Hibiscus rosa-sinensis 'Cooperi'
Hoya carnosa
Jasminum polyanthum
Lantana camara
Lapageria rosea
Nerium oleander
Plumbago auriculata
Tibouchina urvilleana

The almost hardy scrambling climber, **Clianthus puniceus**, or parrot's bill, flowers during summer. There are numerous cultivars with red, pink or white flowers

GLOSSARY OF BOTANICAL TERMS

This brief glossary contains commonly used botanical and horticultural terms

Alternate
Leaves carried singly at each node
Anther
Part of the stamen which carries pollen
Axil
An angle formed by leaf stalk with stem and containing axillary bud.
Bipinnate
Doubly pinnate
Bract
A modified leaf, found around flowers.
Campanulate
Shaped like a bell (flowers).
Calyx
A ring of sepals around a flower, originally forming the outer part of the flower bud.
Catkin
A long thin collection of flowers.
Clone
A group of plants which are genetically identical and propagated vegetatively.
Compound
Refers to leaves formed of several parts.
Cone
Fruit produced by conifers and containing the seeds.
Corolla
An assemblage of petals.
Corona
Petal-like growth. May be part of the corolla.
Corymb
A flower-head, flat-topped or dome-shaped.

Crown
Part of a plant at soil level where buds are produced (eg with herbaceous perennials).
Cultivar
A variety which originated under cultivation.
Cyme
A flower head, flat-topped or dome-shaped.
Deciduous
A plant which drops its leaves each year.
Dentate
A leaf with toothed margins.
Dioecious
When male and female flowers are carried on separate plants.
Double
Flowers with more petals than usual.
Downy
Covered with soft hairs.
Elliptic
Refers to leaves of this shape, wide at the centre and narrower at each end.
Entire
Leaves with completely smooth edges (as opposed to toothed or dentate).
Evergreen
A plant which retains its leaves all the year round. Older foliage is, however, shed throughout the year. Semi-evergreen: a plant which is normally evergreen but may lose a portion or all of its leaves during a hard winter or in a cold area.
Filament
An anther's stalk.
Floret
An individual flower in a head of many flowers.

GLOSSARY OF BOTANICAL TERMS

Frond
The leaf of a fern.

Fruit
The organ that carries seeds.

Glabrous
Devoid of hairs.

Glaucous
Refers to a colour: blue-grey, blue-green or blue-white.

Globose
Globe-shaped, usually referring to flower heads.

Herbaceous
A plant that dies down to the ground in autumn each year.

Hermaphrodite
A flower which contains both male and female organs.

Hirsute
Covered with stiff or coarse hairs.

Hybrid
A plant derived from a cross between two species.

Indumentum
A dense covering of hairs.

Influorescence
The flowering part of plants.

Lanceolate
Leaves shaped like a lance or sword.

Lateral
Usually refers to side shoots.

Leaflet
Part of a compound leaf.

Linear
Shape of a leaf, long and very narrow, margins parallel.

Monoecious
Male and female flowers on same plant but carried separately.

Node
A joint on a stem, from which a leaf or leaves are produced.

Oblong
Refers to leaf shape, length greater than width, sides virtually parallel.

Orbicular
Refers to leaf shape, virtually circular.

Oval
Refers to leaf shape, broadest part in middle.

Ovary
Organ found in the female part of the flower, carrying embryonic seeds.

Ovate
Refers to leaf shape, like a hen's egg.

Palmate
Refers to lobed leaves which are somewhat hand-shaped.

Panicle
A raceme which branches.

Pea-like
Refers to flowers which resemble those of the pea in shape.

Pedicel
The stalk of a flower.

Peduncle
The stem of a cluster of flowers.

Perianth
A combination of the corolla and calyx in a flower.

Petal
A segment of the corolla.

Petiole
A leaf stalk.

Phyllode
A flat leaf stalk which looks like a leaf.

Pinnate
A compound leaf consisting of numerous leaflets.

Pistil
A combination of the stigma, style and ovary (female part of flower).

Plumose
Feathery in appearance.

Pubescent
Covered with soft short hairs.

Raceme
A tall unbranched cluster of stalked flowers.

Rhizome
A creeping underground stem.

GLOSSARY OF BOTANICAL TERMS

Rootstock
Roots and lower part of stem of a grafted plant.

Scale
A very much reduced leaf, as in many conifers.

Semi-evergreen
See Evergreen.

Sepal
A segment of the calyx.

Sessile
Stalkless.

Simple
Refers to leaves which are not divided into leaflets.

Spike
Rather like a raceme except that flowers are sessile (like a poker in shape).

Sport
A mutation.

Stamen
The combination of filament and anther.

Stigma
An organ in female part of flower, situated at the top of the style to receive pollen.

Stipule
Leaf or scale-like organ at base of petiole (in some plants).

Stolon
Stem which creeps above the ground, or sometimes just below soil surface.

Style
A stalk which carries the stigma.

Sub-shrub
Woody-based plant whose top may die back in winter.

Sucker
Shoot produced on root of plant.

Tendril
Thread-like appendage used by a plant for grasping support.

Tomentose
With tomentum.

Tomentum
A covering of short woolly hairs densely matted.

Trifoliate
Three-leaved.

Trifoliolate
A leaf consisting of three leaflets.

Tuber
Swollen underground storage organ.

Umbel
A cluster of flowers with (usually) a flat top, the stalks arising from a central point.

Undulate
Edges of leaves are wavy.

INDEX

INDEX

INDEX

279

INDEX

INDEX

INDEX

INDEX

INDEX

INDEX

INDEX

INDEX

INDEX

① Acer · small ✓

② Sorbus — medium

③ Sorbus — medium ✓

④ Juniper — 6 ft in 10yrs ✓

⑤ Yew - Taxus baccata — small ✓

⑥ Prunus Kursar — small ✓

⑦ Hazel — medium ✓

⑧ Sorbus (common) — quite tall

⑨ Wild Cherry — quite tall ✓

⑩ Holly x 3 ✓

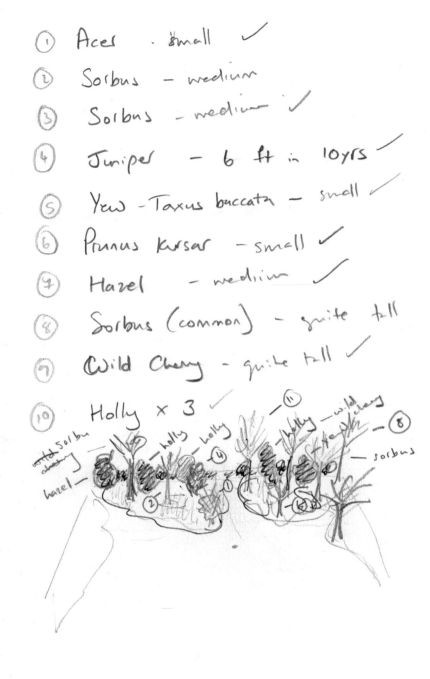

⑪ Silver Birch ✓